YIDDISHKEIT

◀◼▶◼▶◆◀◼▶

YIDDISHKEIT

❖◀❖◀❖◀❖▶❖▶❖▶❖

Jewish Vernacular & the New Land

❖◀❖◀❖▶❖▶❖▶❖

Edited by Harvey Pekar & Paul Buhle
with Hershl Hartman

Introduction by Neal Gabler

ABRAMS COMICARTS, NEW YORK

Editor: Charles Kochman
Assistant Editor: Sofia Gutiérrez
Designer: Misha Beletsky
Art Director: Michelle Ishay-Cohen
Design Manager: Neil Egan
Production Manager: Ankur Ghosh

Library of Congress Cataloging-in-Publication Data:

Yiddishkeit : Jewish vernacular and the new land /
edited by Harvey Pekar and Paul Buhle ; introduction
by Neal Gabler
    p. cm.
    Includes bibliographical references and index.
    ISBN 978-0-8109-9749-3 (alk. paper)
    1. Yiddish literature—United States—Comic books,
strips, etc. 2. Yiddishists—United States—Comic
books, strips, etc. 3. Theater, Yiddish—United
States—Comic books, strips, etc. 4. Jews in motion
pictures—Comic books, strips, etc. 5. Jews—United
States—Social life and customs—Comic books, strips,
etc. 6. Graphic novels. I. Pekar, Harvey. II. Buhle,
Paul, 1944-
    PJ5125.Y527 2011
    839'.109973—dc22
                                        010041873

DAN ARCHER: 18–27 (art), 41–85 (art); NATHANIEL
BUCHWALD: 88–90 (text); PAUL BUHLE: 29–38

(text), 189–94 (text), 217–19 (text); STEVE CHAPPELL:
Illustration of Paul Buhle (back jacket flap); BARRY
DEUTSCH: 175–78; GARY DUMM: 92–135 (art), 207–16
(art), 228–30 (art); DANNY FINGEROTH: 171–74 (text);
HARVEY FINK: 150–51 (translation); MARVIN
FRIEDMAN: 184, 186–88, 240; PETER GULLERUD: 39–
40 (art); HERSHL HARTMAN: 11, 88–90 (translation),
228–30 (text); SABRINA JONES: 224–27; NEIL KLEID:
171–74 (art); PETER KUPER: 86, 189–94, 202; AARON
LANSKY: 217–19 (text); DAVID LASKY: 14–15 (art); SAM
MARLOW: 217–19 (art); HARVEY PEKAR: 14–15 (text),
18–27 (text), 41–85 (text), 204–5 (text), 207–16 (text),
220–23 (text); ALLEN LEWIS RICKMAN: 92–135 (text);
ELLIS ROSEN: 217–19 (art); SARA I. ROSENBAUM:
14–15 (art); SHARON RUDAHL: 152, 154, 156–57, 159–70;
181–83 (art); 196–98; 204–05 (art), 220–23 (art); SPAIN
RODRIGUEZ: 142–51 (art), 199–200 (art), 231 (art);
GREG RUTH: Illustration of Harvey Pekar (back
jacket flap); JOEL SCHECHTER: 142–51 (text), 199–200
(text), 231 (text); STEVE STERN: 224–27 (text); NICK
THORKELSON: 29–38 (text and art); DAVE WAGNER:
189–94 (text); JOE ZABEL: 207–16 (art)

Allen Lewis Rickman wishes to thank Dr. Jeffrey
Veidlinger, Dr. Joel Rubin, YIVO and its excellent staff,
Motl Didner of the Folksbiene, the Dorot Collection at
the New York Public Library, Sheila Rubell, Shane Baker,
New Yiddish Repertory Theater for their assistance
throughout the development of this play, and Melanie
Mintz, Eva Beyder, Rukhl Schaechter, and Paula
Teitelbaum for permission to publish materials owned
by them.

ABRAMS
THE ART OF BOOKS SINCE 1949
115 West 18th Street
New York, NY 10011
www.abramsbooks.com

This book is dedicated to the memory of Harvey Pekar, one of the great creators of modern comics art by virtue of his scripts, his editing and publication initiatives, his public persona and frequent appearances, and, most especially, his personal generosity. Also to the Yiddish-language poets, fiction and nonfiction writers, critics, musicians, teachers, andw choral directors, for their dedication to the survival and health of the language and culture of *mamaloshen*, the "mother tongue."

ACKNOWLEDGMENTS

Thanks to the Joseph and Diane H. Steinberg Charitable Trust for assistance in the payment of artists, and to *Jewish Currents* editor Lawrence Bush, and Eddy Portnoy, for their dedication to Yiddishkeit and their encouragement for this project. Thanks to Allen Lewis Rickman, our part-time Yiddish *mashgiakh*. Special thanks to Abrams ComicArts editorial director Charles Kochman, whose vision for this book made it possible, and to assistant editor Sofia Gutiérrez: their hard work carried us through. And to the rest of the team at Abrams, especially designer Misha Beletsky.

CONTENTS

YIDDISHKEIT:
AN INTRODUCTION

☜ by NEAL GABLER

Perhaps the greatest difficulty in trying to describe "Yiddishkeit" to an English-speaking audience, as this book attempts to do, is that there is really no English equivalent for the word. "Yiddish culture" comes close, but Yiddishkeit is so large, expansive, and woolly a concept that *culture* may be too narrow to do it full justice. "Jewish sensibility" comes closer still because it internalizes the notion of Yiddish, places it in the head as well as on the stage and the page, but *sensibility* is itself a rather loose and elusive idea and within Yiddishkeit there are several sensibilities that, while closely connected, are still not congruent. In effect, Yiddishkeit isn't a thing or even a set of things, an idea or a set of ideas, which may explain why a book about Yiddishkeit is itself so sprawling, kaleidoscopic, disjointed, eclectic, and just plain messy. You really can't define Yiddishkeit neatly in words or pictures. You sort of have to *feel* it by wading into it.

The feeling, of course, is largely a function of language. Yiddish may be the most onomatopoeic language ever created. Everything sounds exactly the way it should: *macher* for a self-appointed big shot, *shlmiel* for the fellow who spills the soup and *shlmazel* for the poor guy who gets the soup spilled on him, *putz* for an active louse, *shmuck* for a hapless one (as in "poor shmuck"), *shnorer* for a freeloader, *nudnick* for a pest. The expressiveness is bound into the language, and so is a kind of ruthless honesty. Though, as this book points out, Yiddish has dozens of words for *imbecile*, a tribute to Jewish lucklessness, it also has an equal number of words to limn the many striations of being a jerk, a tribute to Jewish argumentiveness. These are words that flay the varnish off of language and lay it bare. There is no decorousness in Yiddish, nor much romance. It is raw, egalitarian, vernacular.

That is why, even though there was, as Harvey Pekar makes clear in these pages, a vibrant Yiddish literature, the whole idea of a *literature* may have been inimical to the very spirit of Yiddish. Sentiment, sensationalism, and formula—all of these were natural to a language that was focused on the here and now rather than on airy philosophical discourse, on the forcefulness of expression rather than on nuances, on brutal truthfulness rather than on fine emotions. Yiddish is a blunt instrument. That is its real charm, not the phony whimsy that Pekar so detests in the work of Isaac Bashevis Singer, perhaps the most famous Yiddish writer.

Indeed, the Yiddish litterateurs have largely been forgotten, in part because Yiddish is a language that lives more in the mouth than on the page. There is nothing highfalutin or literary about it. As an amalgamated language, borrowing freely from German and Polish and Hebrew with its own unique constructions and confabulations, it is, at its very core, a way to take high culture and reformulate it in a more democratic fashion. Instead of great works, its primary legacy is not only the Yiddishisms sprinkled into English for flavor or the subversive candor that impregnated American entertainment through Jewish comics but also the very democracy of Yiddish—its stubborn plebeian pride. Yiddishkeit seems to luxuriate in its own lack of elegance and its own marginalization, which is why a book of comics art, another outsider form, seems especially appropriate to describe it and why a wry *shlump* like the late Harvey Pekar seems an especially apt coauthor.

But if Yiddish is an outsider's means of expressing the world, it is also an outsider's way of experiencing it. Yiddishkeit may be thought of as an attitude—broad, even coarse, tough-minded, clear-sighted, unpretentious, and again, spitefully honest. Not incidentally, these were qualities that had helped Jews cope with a hostile world, and Yiddish became another weapon in that ongoing battle with gentile society. Jews would survive not by looking at the world through rose-colored glasses but by glaring over the tops of the frames. For a stateless people, as the Jews were before Israel, one might even say that Yiddishkeit became their state—not geographically, of course, but a state of mind. That is what Baruch Rivkin meant when he invented "Yiddishland," a sort of mental space, though his utopian peaceable kingdom bore little resemblance to the actual Yiddish state of mind, which was cantankerous rather than pacific, roiling rather than calm.

Yiddishkeit is abrasive. It is an attitude of challenge just as Yiddish is a language of challenge. As this book amply demonstrates, Yiddish artists were always attacking the status quo, and it is certainly no coincidence that many of these Yiddish artists, not to mention many grassroots Yiddishers, were political leftists. By the same token, the artistic and political Jewish establishments were afraid of Yiddish—afraid of the way it seemed to bulldoze right over politesse. Some were scandalized by the openness of sex in much of Yiddish literature. Others, like the German Jews who had emigrated to America, disdained the Yiddish theater here and tried to stop it because they felt it threatened their assimilation. Even the state of Israel reviled Yiddish, ostensibly for fear it would override Hebrew, and, as you will read, there were times when Israel outlawed the Yiddish theater. In effect, though, the real fear of Yiddishkeit was that it was too Jewish, too insular, too much an expression of the loud, wild, lively Jewish hoi polloi whom high-born Jews found so offensive. Who could imagine a state where the citizens spoke Yiddish?

Now that Jews have been largely assimilated into America, Yiddishkeit may seem both anachronistic and nostalgic here. Many Jews of my generation will no doubt remember, as I do, their grandparents speaking Yiddish when they didn't want the children to know what they were talking about. It became a kind of secret language. As the European-born and then the first American-born generations passed, they seemed to take Yiddish with them. And yet Yiddishkeit has managed to survive, if just barely, not because there are individuals dedicated to its survival, though there are, but because Yiddishkeit is an essential part of both the Jewish and the human experience.

We need Yiddish, with all its silly guttural power, to rip through the formalities, the prevarications, the pretensions, and the dishonesty. In a world that fetishizes money and status, Yiddishkeit shrugs at both. That was its function as the forces of so-called civilization bore down upon the Jews in Europe. And that is its function now.

NEAL GABLER, a senior fellow at the USC Annenberg School for Communication and Journalism, is an author, cultural historian, and film critic. His first book, *An Empire of Their Own: How the Jews Invented Hollywood* (1989), won the Los Angeles Times Book Prize and the Theatre Library Association Award. His second book, *Winchell: Gossip, Power, and the Culture of Celebrity* (1994), was named nonfiction book of the year by *Time* magazine. He is also the author of *Life the Movie: How Entertainment Conquered Reality* (1998) and *Walt Disney: The Triumph of the American Imagination* (2006), which was named the biography of the year by *USA Today* and won him his second Los Angles Times Book Prize. He is currently at work on a biography of the late senator Edward M. Kennedy. Gabler has held fellowships from the Freedom Forum Media Studies Center and the Guggenheim Foundation, and has served as a judge of the National Book Awards and the Los Angles Times Book Prizes. He was a panelist on *Fox News Watch* and *Today,* and has appeared on *The CBS Morning News, NewsHour, Entertainment Tonight, Charlie Rose,* and *Good Morning America.* He also hosted *Sneak Previews* for PBS. Gabler writes often for the *New York Times* and the *Los Angeles Times* and has contributed to numerous other publications, including *Esquire, Salon, New York, Vogue, American Heritage,* the *New York Republic, Us,* and *Playboy.*

VORTMAN'S GUIDE TO WRITING YIDDISH IN ENGLISH LETTERS

VOWELS

A as in *father*
E as in *lemon*
I as in *kid* or EE as in *heed*
O as in *not*
U as in *due* (not as in *but*)
EY as in *grey*
AY as in *aye*
OY as in *boy*

There's no need for an H when a word ends in a vowel.

CONSONANTS

KH as in *Bach*
DZH as in *judge* (take your pick)
G as in *give*
SH as in *shoot*
TS as in *fits*
TSH as in *pinch*
ZH as in *measure*

All other consonants and combinations are (usually) as in English. There are no doubled consonants in Yiddish (or in Hebrew, for that matter).

Yiddish is customarily printed in books, periodicals, signage, etc., using the Hebrew alphabet. However, for the purposes of accessibility, it was decided to use English transliteration for the Yiddish text in this book.

Readers will notice that individual sections of this book transliterate Yiddish words in varying ways (in fact, the title of this book, even, is sometimes spelled with the variant *Yiddishkayt*, a subject of much debate among some of our contributors. Ultimately, we went with the more common *Yiddishkeit*). While the editors accepted all variants of transliteration (out of deference to the individual writers), there is a Standard method, developed in the 1930s by the Yiddish Scientific Institute (YIVO), now known as the YIVO Institute for Jewish Research (www.yivoinstitute .org).

Above is an easy summary of the Standard. It was developed by Hershl Hartman, writing as the "Vortsman"—man of his word—for *YidBits*, the newsletter of Yiddishkayt (www.yiddishkayt.org).

EDITOR'S NOTE

This volume marks the final sustained script-work of Harvey Pekar, and that alone gives it a certain significance. It is also the last project he saw through to its near completion. In fact, Harvey selected, reviewed, and helped shape every strip in the book except one: Barry Deutsch's four-page biography of Zero Mostel, which was created after Harvey's death.

Harvey (who passed away on July 12, 2010) was not precisely a figure in the world of *Yiddishkeit*, but he was definitely a Yiddishist character, the ideal protagonist for a novel in that language, albeit a novel unlikely ever to be written. Harvey not only grew up in an immigrant, Yiddish-speaking milieu, he was also a self-educated, secular Jew who was a hipster and sentimentalist, a joke teller and moralist, at home more in conversation than in print or on film. His aesthetic judgments on every subject—from jazz to Yiddish literature—are often debatable and even idiosyncratic, but they are *his* views, with a degree of insight that few professors can marshal. The summation of the famed short story by I. L. Peretz, "If Not Higher," into a spare two panels [page 48, bottom] will likely make traditionalists wince, but Pekar had his own voice.

This *Yiddishkeit* anthology is an experiment several times over. The world of Yiddish (more accurately, secularist Yiddish) and *Yiddishkeit* (warm and earthy Jewishness growing out of the Eastern European experience) as language and culture in the United States has gained much sentimentalism, and perhaps even more satire, during the last century—but not a great deal of insight. Comics, apart from political cartoons, did not actually make much headway in Yiddish publications in their heyday. Yet the culture of Yiddish is so inherently vernacular that comics art provides a perfect venue for an exploration of issues and personalities. That we needed to present dialogue in English—in a few cases with Yiddish also intact—offered interesting challenges, likewise the use of reprinted images, mostly from the one hugely successful satirical Yiddish-language pictorial weekly, *Der Groyser Kundes* (*The Big Stick* or *The Big Prankster*), which was published during the immigrant years of 1909–27. Harvey and I are especially proud to include *The Essence*, a full-length play about the history of Yiddish theater, which also touches on various glimpses of social life, entertainment, Yiddish literature, and what we may describe as the culture of memories.

No single book, let alone a book of comics art, could capture the richness or, for that matter, the many contradictions of assimilation and cultural retention. *Yiddishkeit* is meant to bring personalities and at least some of the issues back to life in an accessible format especially suited to readers, Jewish or non-Jewish, but also suited to comics-art lovers of all ages throughout the world.

The list of contributors (not all of them Jewish, myself included) contains outstanding figures from the alternative world of comics art, but also a notable playwright, a distinguished magazine illustrator from the mid-twentieth century, a secular *vegvayzer*/leader who teaches and performs Jewish rituals, and, of course, alternative comics icon Harvey Pekar himself, who arguably did more than any other single figure to bring American comics into the twenty-first century. Collectively we comprise several generations, which seems to me a point in our favor: the eldest contributors can remember attending Yiddish summer camps of the 1930s; the youngest (notably, with Yiddish-speaking parents) are only a few years out of college and new to drawing Jewish faces and scenes. *Fun dor tsu dor*, which means "from generation to generation," might be as good a subtitle as any for this book, a collection whose appeal extends beyond the usual suspects who regularly traverse the worlds of comics and of *Yiddishkeit*. At any rate, that is, we hope so.

Paul Buhle
Madison, Wisconsin
January 2011

PAUL BUHLE has written, coauthored, and edited forty-two books, including the award-winning *The Art of Harvey Kurtzman: The Mad Genius of Comics*; *Jews and American Comics*; *Jews and American Popular Culture, Volumes 1–3*; and eight volumes of new comics art, five of them in collaboration with Harvey Pekar. Buhle is a Distinguished Lecturer for the Organization of American Historians and the American Studies Association. He lives in Madison, Wisconsin.

Mendele Moykher Sforim (Little Mendele the Bookseller)—the grandfather of both modern Yiddish and modern Hebrew literature—is shown (at right, his name emblazoned on the wagon) driving off the "Tired Old Stuff," i.e., simplistic early Yiddish stories and novels. This cartoon from 1911 also celebrates the publication of a deluxe edition of the twenty-volume collected works of Mendele (born Sholom Yankif Abramovitsh), who adopted his pen name to avoid the "shame" of writing in Yiddish.

ALL THE PEOPLE IN MY FAMILY FROM MY MOTHER'S GENERATION, and EVEN SOME OF MY COUSINS, WERE BORN IN EASTERN EUROPE, IN SHTETLS AROUND BIALYSTOK, POLAND.

Prologue

I WAS BORN IN THE U.S.A. (IN 1939), BUT MOST OF MY FAMILY SPOKE YIDDISH. IT WAS MY FIRST LANGUAGE.

GEY KAK IN YAM! *

*GO SHIT IN THE SEA.

I LEARNED ENGLISH and YIDDISH SIMUL-TANEOUSLY, AND SPOKE YIDDISH TO MY GRANDFATHER ESPECIALLY. MY GRANDFATHER HAD PROBABLY THE BEST SENSE OF HUMOR OF ANYONE LIVING IN MY TWO-FLAT HOME.

VOS MAKHSTU, ZEYDE? *

* HOW ARE YOU, GRANDFATHER?

MY AUNT and UNCLE and THEIR KIDS LIVED UPSTAIRS. BEFORE I WENT TO SCHOOL I USED TO TALK ENGLISH TO MY UPSTAIRS COUSINS. THEY SPOKE YIDDISH FLUENTLY, BUT THEY PREFERRED ENGLISH.

WHAT'S THAT SONG, MARTY?

"LAURA."

By Harvey Pekar, illustrated by Sara I. Rosenbaum and David Lasky

WHEN MY GRANDFATHER WAS SICK, HE USED TO CONTINUE TO KID AROUND WHEN HE WAS IN BED. I REMEMBER SO WELL, WHEN WE WERE PLAYING AROUND WITH HIS BELT, HE ASKED ME WHAT I WAS GOING TO DO WITH IT WHEN HE DIED.

I SAID:

IKH'L GEBN TSU MAYN TATN. *

* I'LL GIVE IT TO MY FATHER.

FOR SOME REASON THE PEOPLE IN THE ROOM THOUGHT THAT WAS CUTE.

HA HA HA HA HA HA HA HA HA HA HA

WHEN MY GRANDFATHER DIED, I DIDN'T SPEAK MUCH YIDDISH ANYMORE. MY PARENTS WERE WORKING ALL THE TIME IN THEIR SMALL GROCERY STORE.

ANYWAY, AFTER THAT I GRADUALLY LOST MY ABILITY TO SPEAK YIDDISH.

VOS IZ DAYN GESHEFT? *

* WHAT DO YOU DO FOR A LIVING?

THOUGH FOR SOME REASON I COULD STILL UNDERSTAND IT — MAYBE AS LONG AS THROUGH HIGH SCHOOL.

IKH BIN A YIDISHER SHRAYBER. *

* I'M A YIDDISH WRITER.

THE COLORFULNESS and THE RHYTHM OF YIDDISH MADE IT FUN TO LISTEN TO, EVEN THOUGH I WAS LOSING TOUCH WITH IT.

CHAPTER 1.

The Emergence of Yiddish Culture

◆•►◆►●◄◆►●◄◆►●◄◆•◄◆•●

Literature has been singularly important to Yiddish, no doubt because the once largely spoken language had to be justified, that is, legitimated, in order to continue to exist among an increasingly literate population. If this claim is too grand, Yiddish writers of every (secular) kind, from novelists to poets and critics, certainly played a central role across the Ashkenazic Jewish world from the 1860s until the Holocaust. Yiddish newspapers, along with Yiddish novels, plays, and poetry, had a global readership; Yiddish books and periodicals flourished from Kiev to Buenos Aires to Los Angeles (as well as the most important cultural center, New York City). But it is easy to forget, for instance, that some key Yiddish literature was meant to be sung, often by choruses increasingly made up of singers with Yiddish as their own second language. In a broader sense, Yiddish continues to exist as a vibrant part of popular culture, adding a twang to spoken language that can still be heard on the theater stage, in films, and on television, connoting "something Jewish" and often something humorous.

‭יודדיסהלאנד‬ (YIDDISHLAND)

PART ONE: YIDDISH CLASSICS

WRITTEN BY HARVEY PEKAR · ILLUSTRATED BY DAN ARCHER

No one knows for certain when Yiddish, the language of East European Jews, evolved, but certainly it was centuries ago.

So far the first written evidence of it is a couplet in a prayer book from Worms in 1272.

Yiddish, though written in the Hebrew alphabet, is basically derived from German, and is in fact considered a German language with some Hebrew additions.

SPRECHEN ZIE YIDDISH?

But as the Jews spread across Europe, they picked up some words from the French, Italians and Slavs.

chaud, lent, cholent!*

*'TSHOLNT' IN YIDDISH, MEANING 'HOT STEW'

Many Yiddish speakers lived in the Slavic countries and Romania.

THE EARLIEST PIECE OF YIDDISH LITERATURE, "VIRTUOUS JOSEPH," FOUND IN EGYPT, IS FROM 1382.

SINCE THAT DATE, VARIOUS POEMS AND FABLES IN YIDDISH HAVE BEEN FOUND. THE STORIES OF RABBI NACHMAN OF BRATSLAV WERE YIDDISH FABLES, BUT THE ORIGIN OF YIDDISH FINE ART LITERATURE IS RELATIVELY RECENT.

MANY SAY IT BEGAN IN THE SECOND HALF OF THE 19th CENTURY, WITH MENDELE MOCHER SFORIM (THE GRANDFATHER), I.L. PERETZ (THE FATHER) AND SHOLEM ALEICHEM (THE SON).

1836-1917   1851-1915   1859-1916

HOWEVER, JOSEPH PERL'S "REVEALER OF SECRETS" WAS PRODUCED EARLIER THAN THAT. INITIALLY WRITTEN IN HEBREW IN 1819, IT WAS TRANSLATED INTO YIDDISH FOR THE MASSES.

OTHERWISE FINE YIDDISH WRITERS SUCH AS AYZIK-MAYER DIK AND ITSIK-YOYL LINVETSKY WERE ACTIVE AS PROSE FICTION WRITERS BEFORE OR AT THE SAME TIME AS MENDELE.

TAP TAP

IT TOOK YIDDISH A WHILE TO GAIN LITERARY IMPORTANCE, AS SOME TRAGIC EVENTS SLOWED ITS ACCEPTANCE.

IN 1648 THE UKRANIAN **BOGDAN CHMIELNICKI** BEGAN A SERIES OF **POGROMS** THAT CLAIMED THE LIVES OF **HUNDREDS OF THOUSANDS OF JEWS** AND CONSIDERABLY LOWERED THEIR **STANDARD OF LIVING** AND **EDUCATION**.

THE ARRIVAL OF **FALSE MESSIAH SABBATAI ZEVI** AND **JACOB FRANK** IN THE **17th CENTURY** ALSO HAD A HORRIBLE EFFECT ON JEWISH LIFE IN EUROPE, AS THE COMMUNITY WAS **SPLIT**.

SABBATAI ZEVI WAS FORCED TO BECOME A MUSLIM BY THE TURKS, **FRANK** WOUND UP A ROMAN CATHOLIC.

WHEN THE **18th CENTURY** ARRIVED, EASTERN EUROPEAN JEWISH LIFE HAD BEEN **STAGGERED**.

THEN, TO THE RESCUE, SOME SAY, CAME **ISRAEL BAAL SHEM TOV**, "THE WONDER WORKER!"

A **MYSTIC** AND STUDENT OF THE **CABALA**, HE BEGAN THE **CHASSIDIC MOVEMENT**, STATING THAT:

EVEN **POOR, UNEDUCATED JEWS**

DESERVE **RESPECT!**

HE EMPHASIZED **JOY** AND ENCOURAGED **SINGING, DANCING** AND EVEN SOME **DRINKING** AMONG HIS FLOCK. HE ALSO EMPHASIZED **YIDDISH**, BECAUSE IT WAS THE DAY-TO-DAY LANGUAGE OF **POOR** AND **WORKING CLASS JEWS** —

MANY OF WHOM WERE **NOT** FLUENT IN **HEBREW**.

THE **BAAL SHEM TOV'S** FOLLOWERS **WORSHIPPED HIM** AND THOUGHT THAT **HE** AND SOME OF THE **CHASSIDIC RABBIS** COULD PERFORM **MIRACLES**.

SOME OF THESE **'MIRACLE RABBIS' SHAMELESSLY EXPLOITED** THEIR FOLLOWERS.

A GROUP OF **ANTI-CHASSIDIC** JEWS (CALLED THE **MISNAGDIM**) ACCUSED THE CHASSIDIM OF **ACCEPTING SUPERSTITION** AND **ATTACKED** THEM. SOME MISNAGID RABBIS **EXCOMMUNICATED** CHASSIDIM.

MOST NOTABLY, **ELIJAH THE VILNA GAON** (GENIUS), ONE OF THE MOST **LEARNED** AND **RESPECTED** JEWISH CLERGYMEN.

AS THIS WAS GOING ON, SOME **CHASSIDIC RABBIS** WERE REGARDED AS HAVING **SUPERHUMAN POWERS** AND A **SPECIAL RELATIONSHIP** WITH GOD, THEY WERE CALLED **TSADIKS.**

THE POSITION OF **TSADIK** BECAME DYNASTIC AND TSADIKS WERE SEEN BY THE CONGREGATIONS AS **MIRACLE MAKERS.**

IN THE EARLY **18TH CENTURY** THE **HASKALA** (JEWISH ENLIGHTENMENT) AROSE IN **EASTERN EUROPE.**

HASKALA FOLLOWERS (OR **MASKILIM**) EMPHASIZED THE ROLE OF **SECULAR LEARNING** AND **DENOUNCED SUPERSTITION** AND **CORRUPTION** AMONG THE CHASSIDIM.

ONE OF THE MASKILIM, **JOSEPH PERL** (1773-1839), A MAJOR FIGURE IN THE ANTI CHASSIDIC MOVEMENT IN **GALICIA** – THEN PART OF THE **AUSTRIAN EMPIRE** –

HAD BEEN A **CHASSID** AS A YOUNGER MAN, AND WROTE A BOOK **EXPOSING** CHASSIDIC PRACTICES AND BELIEFS CALLED **ON THE NATURE OF THE CHASSIDIC SECT.**

IT WAS WRITTEN IN **GERMAN** AND SUBMITTED FOR PUBLICATION TO THE AUSTRIAN AUTHORITIES

PERL CONDEMNED THE CHASSIDIM, MAINLY BY QUOTING FROM THEIR WORKS.

HOWEVER, THE AUSTRIANS WOULDN'T LET IT BE PUBLISHED BECAUSE THEY THOUGHT IT WOULD SET ONE POPULATION AGAINST ANOTHER, AND WOULD CAUSE A **RISE OF ANTI-SEMITISM** AMONG NON-JEWS.

FRANZ I
OF AUSTRIA ←

PERL WAS A **WELL-READ** AND **TRAVELLED** PERSON. HE TRANSLATED **HENRY FIELDING'S TOM JONES** INTO HEBREW, THUS SHOWING THAT HE WAS A VERY MODERN THINKER FOR HIS TIME

WHAT'S MORE, PERL WAS **NOT DISCOURAGED BY** AUSTRIAN AUTHORITIES AND IN 1819 PUBLISHED THE NOVEL **"THE REVEALER OF SECRETS"** IN HEBREW, WHICH HE **TRANSLATED INTO YIDDISH** SO IT COULD BE READ BY THE MASSES.

THE BOOK WAS A **SAVAGE ATTACK** ON CHASSIDISM.

BUT IT WAS MORE A **GREAT SATIRE** THAT WAS WRITTEN IN A STYLE **FAR AHEAD** OF ITS TIME, IT COULD BE VIEWED AS FORECASTING TODAY'S **POST-MODERNISM.**

REVEALER OF SECRETS WAS THE **FIRST HEBREW** AND **FIRST YIDDISH** NOVEL. IT WAS PUBLISHED **FAR BEFORE** YIDDISH FINE LITERATURE, WHICH BEGAN **MID 1860s**

IT IS AN **EPISTOLARY NOVEL** WHICH BEGINS WITH ONE CHASSID WRITING TO ANOTHER ABOUT A BOOK THAT **RIPS** CHASSIDISM.

THE **COMMON FATE** OF BOOKS **CRITICIZING** CHASSIDISM WAS FOR THEM TO BE **BOUGHT UP** COMPLETELY AND **BURNED**.

HOWEVER, THE FIRST CORRESPONDENTS IN THIS NOVEL **CANNOT** GET HOLD OF A **SINGLE COPY** OF THIS BOOK,

WHICH IS REALLY *ON THE NATURE OF THE CHASSIDIM SECT.*

THIS DRIVES THEM **CRAZY** AND THEY ENLIST THEIR FRIENDS IN **GALICIA** AND **RUSSIAN-HELD POLAND** TO FIND IT. IT'S A **NEVER ENDING** QUEST.

IN *REVEALER OF SECRETS* THERE IS AN **ENLIGHTENING** PORTRAIT OF LIFE IN **POLAND** AND **GALICIA** AS WELL. JEWS THERE DID NOT EXACTLY LIVE IN THE **LAP OF LUXURY**.

IN FACT, READING ABOUT THE JEWS' **POVERTY** AND HOW GENTILES FREQUENTLY **MURDERED** THEM IN **POGROMS**, IT IS HARD TO BELIEVE WHY EASTERN EUROPEAN **CHRISTIANS** THOUGHT THEY WERE BEING **EXPLOITED** BY JEWS.

THERE WERE INDEED **SEVERAL** SIGNIFICANT YIDDISH PROSE WORKS PUBLISHED **DURING THE 1860s**, INCLUDING WORKS BY AUTHORS WHO HAVE NOT RECEIVED THE **PRAISE OF MENDELE MOCHER SFORIM**, BUT CERTAINLY **DESERVE IT.**

ONE OF THE **FINEST** EARLY YIDDISH WRITERS, HE'S CALLED 'PROBABLY THE **FIRST PROFESSIONAL YIDDISH WRITER'** WAS **AYZIK-MAYER DIK** (**1814 - 1893**). DIK WAS KNOWN FOR AUTHORING SENTIMENTAL WORKS FOR WOMEN.

HIS WORK IS **DIFFICULT TO LOCATE** TODAY.

HOWEVER, HIS EXCELLENT STORY "THE PANIC" OR "THE **LITTLE TOWN OF HERRES"** (**1868**) CAN BE FOUND IN ISACHIM NEVGRI'S ANTHOLOGY OF YIDDISH LITERATURE, **NO STAR TOO BEAUTIFUL.**

THIS VERY **FUNNY** STORY DEALS WITH A **UKAZ** * RUMORED TO **RAISE THE MINIMUM MARRIAGE AGE** FROM 16 TO 18 FOR MEN AND FROM 14 TO 16 FOR WOMEN.

YOU MUST BE AT LEAST **16 OR 18** TO GO ON THIS RIDE

*DECREE OR EDICT

THIS IS A **NOVELTY** IN THE TOWN OF HERRES, WHERE PEOPLE SOMETIMES MARRIED **MUCH YOUNGER** AND CONSIDERED 16 AND 18 **RATHER OLD** TO BE GETTING HITCHED

THERE IS INDEED AN **ENSUING PANIC** IN HERRES—A RUSH TO GET THOSE UNDER 16 AND 18 MARRIED **BEFORE** THE UKAZE IS ISSUED. THEY FEEL **TIME IS RUNNING OUT** ON THEM.

SOON IT'S ALMOST TO THE POINT WHERE **BABIES** ARE **SNATCHED** OUT OF THEIR CRIB TO BE **MARRIED.**

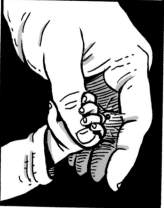

DIK DOES POINT OUT THAT THE **MARRIAGE PANIC** IN HERRES EVENTUALLY **STOPS**, BUT IT WAS FOLLOWED BY **ANOTHER** PANIC OVER **TORAH SCROLLS** COMMISSIONED BY **CRAFT BROTHERHOODS**.

"EVERY MONTH BRINGS **NEW GANGS** WHO BUILD **NEW ALTARS**... IF A MAN **TRULY** WANTS TO WORSHIP GOD HE CAN FIND A PLACE IN OUR **EMPTY GREAT SYNAGOGUE** OR IN THE **PRAYER ROOMS**."

ANOTHER **ANTI-CHASSIDIC** BOOK WAS **ITSIK-YOYL UNYETSKY'S** *THE CHASSIDIC BOY* (1867).

LIKE **PERL, LINYETSKY** (1839-1915) **RIPPED** THE CHASSIDIM. HIS **FATHER** WAS A **RABBI** AND **MARRIED HIM OFF** TO A **12-YEAR-OLD** GIRL WHEN HE WAS **14**.

THE MATCH **DID NOT WORK**, SO THE FATHER MADE HIS SON **DIVORCE HER** AND GOT HIM MARRIED **AGAIN** TO A DEAF, MENTALLY HANDICAPPED GIRL.

FINALLY HE WAS ABLE TO **DIVORCE HER** AND MARRIED A **WOMAN OF HIS CHOICE** IN **1863**.

WINK

THE CHASSIDIC BOY, AN AUTOBIOGRAPHICAL BOOK, WAS SERIALIZED AND BECAME QUITE POPULAR. IT'S QUITE AMUSING - HE ZEROES IN ON THE BLIND FAITH OF CHASSIDS IN THEIR RABBIS WITH GUSTO.

A PREGNANT WOMAN ASKS HER CHASSIDIC HUSBAND IF HE THINKS THE CHILD WILL BE A BOY. HE RESPONDS:

WHAT ARE YOU BLABBERING ABOUT?

THE RABBI CLEARLY SAID A GIRL—

SO HOW CAN YOU ASK?

HE FOLLOWS THIS UP WITH :

DON'T WORRY!

IF IT'S REALLY A BOY,

THE TSADIK CAN CHANGE IT INTO A GIRL!

HE CONTINUES TO BERATE HIS WIFE ABOUT THE TSADIK:

AND WHAT MIRACLES- OH WOW!

JUST IMAGINE, YOU DUMMY—

"HE TURNED THE DUKE OF PARISELIVKEI INTO A WEREWOLF,

AND WITH JUST A WAVE OF HIS STICK HE DROVE AWAY THE DARK CLOUDS IN A PITCH BLACK NIGHT SO HE COULD BLESS THE NEW MOON!"

THE CHASSIDIC BOY WAS AN IMPORTANT YIDDISH WORK, BUT LINNETSKY DIDN'T FOLLOW UP WITH MANY MORE SIMILAR WORKS AND TODAY IS UNFORTUNATELY FORGOTTEN.

THE YIDDISH PRESS

D aily Yiddish newspapers began to emerge during the mid-1880s with the East European Jewish migration westward. Although these papers appeared in many parts of the world, they were most successful in New York, with local editions available in scattered cities. The *Forverts* (*Forward*), published daily from 1897, was by far the most successful, reaching more than half a million readers by 1920 and slowly declining until a daily schedule was abandoned in the 1990s (the *Forverts* appears now as a weekly, and sponsors the English-language *Forward*). In its heyday, the Yiddish press had at least four dailies in New York alone, and nearly all of them, including the socialist and anticommunist *Forverts*, survived beyond the mid-twentieth century. Other dailies include *Der Tog* (*The Day*), a middle-of-the road pro-Zionist paper considered upscale in a mostly blue-collar world; *Morgn Zhurnal* (*Morning Journal*), Orthodox and politically conservative; and *Morgn Frayhayt* (*Morning Freedom*), which was pro-communist. Other political factions published weeklies, including *Fraye Arbeter Shtime* (*Labor's Free Voice*), which, until its 1976 demise, was the oldest anarchist publication in the United States. Originally styled in *daytshmerish*, a heavily German-inflected language, more literary Yiddish usage evolved with the daily press, arguably reaching its apex with the *Morgn Frayhayt*. Several ultra-Orthodox newspapers survive, such as *Di Tsaytung* (*The Newspaper*) and *Der Algemeyner Zhurnal* (*The General Journal*), neither of which adheres to the rules of spelling and grammar of modern Yiddish, preferring the *heymish* (homey, common) language of their readers.

BARUCH RIVKIN'S SHRAYBER UN ARBETER*

WRITTEN BY PAUL BUHLE & NICK THORKELSON • DRAWINGS BY NICK THORKELSON

*WRITERS & WORKERS

THE YIDDISH DAILY: A COMMON SIGHT ON NEW YORK'S SUBWAYS & STREETS IN THE EARLY 20th CENTURY

BUT FEW OUTSIDERS REALIZED THE TREASURES THAT LAY WITHIN.

WHILE THE OUTSIDE PAGES OF A TYPICAL YIDDISH PAPER WERE FILLED WITH POLITICAL NEWS—NOT THAT DIFFERENT FROM WHAT YOU COULD FIND ELSEWHERE...

...IT WAS THE INSIDE PAGES THAT OFFERED NEWS & IDEAS ABOUT YIDDISH CULTURE—

—AND IT WAS HERE THAT READERS LOOKED TO FIND WHAT WAS UNIQUE & BRILLIANT!

WRITING IN THE PAGES OF YIDDISH PAPERS LIKE *ARBETER FRAYND*, *FRAYE ARBETER SHTIME*, *DOS NAYE LAND* AND *DER TOG*, THE CRITIC **BARUCH RIVKIN** CAME UP WITH THE IDEA THAT YIDDISH, FOR A PEOPLE WITHOUT A GEOGRAPHICAL PLACE, WAS ITS OWN IMAGINED COUNTRY.

CAFE

RIVKIN'S YIDDISHLAND WAS AN EGALITARIAN, EVEN ANARCHISTIC "PEACEABLE KINGDOM" —

—A PLACE WHERE THE DREAMS OF YIDDISH WRITERS, TEMPERED BY THE POGROM & SWEATSHOP, COULD LEAD THE WAY TO DIGNITY & FREEDOM.

WHERE DID THESE IDEAS COME FROM?

RIVKIN WAS BORN IN THE HALF-JEWISH MARKET TOWN OF YAKOBSHTAT, IN THE BALTIC REGION ONCE KNOWN AS COURLAND WHICH WAS THEN PART OF THE RUSSIAN EMPIRE. HIS FATHER WAS A TEAMSTER.

FORMERLY GERMAN-DOMINATED, YAKOBSHTAT WAS GOING RUSSIAN UNDER COMPULSION, BUT HIGH CULTURE REMAINED GERMAN WHILE POOR JEWS SPOKE YIDDISH.

RIVKIN WOULD LATER WRITE OF THE "BARONIAL FANTASIES" OF YAKOBSHTAT'S UPWARDLY MOBILE JEWS, INSPIRED BY THE PRESENCE OF BONA FIDE GERMAN BARONS IN THE TOWN.

ONCE MY FATHER & HIS HORSES DROVE AROUND JUST SUCH A DRUNKEN BARON FOR HOURS! FINALLY:

YOU DIRTY JEW, I'M NOT PAYING YOU NOTHING!

BOP!

ON THE OTHER HAND, WOULD YOU ACCEPT THIS WATCH?

WHAT ARE YOU DOING IN THERE, SON?

WHAT ARE YOU DOING OUT THERE, POP?

WHILE SOME LOOKED BACK TO AN IDEALIZED BARONIAL PAST, MORE & MORE OF YAKOBSHTAT'S YOUNGEST & POOREST WERE STIRRED BY THE DREAM OF A REVOLUTIONARY FUTURE.

RIVKIN HIMSELF, AFTER DOING JAIL TIME FOR ACTIVITIES ON BEHALF OF THE BUND (JEWISH SOCIALIST PARTY), HAD TO FIND HIS WAY TO LONDON VIA SWITZERLAND, JUST IN TIME TO MISS THE **1905 REVOLUTION.**

1905, SOMETIMES CALLED THE DRESS REHEARSAL FOR THE DECISIVE 1917 RUSSIAN REVOLUTION, SEEMED AT FIRST TO VINDICATE THE JEWISH SOCIALIST DREAM OF WORKER SOLIDARITY OVERCOMING TYRANNY & EXPLOITATION—

—BUT AS THE REBELLION FALTERED, THE CZARIST GOVERNMENT INCITED GENTILES TO SCAPEGOAT JEWS FOR THE UNREST. DREADFUL POGROMS THROUGHOUT 1905–1906 KILLED FROM 1500 TO 3000 JEWS. FOR MANY JEWISH WRITERS & ACTIVISTS, ANY HOPE FOR A UNITED WORKERS' MOVEMENT ENDED HERE.

RIVKIN IN LONDON WENT THE OTHER WAY, EMBRACING THE STATELESS IDEAL OF ANARCHISM. WHILE WRITING IN YIDDISH FOR THE ANARCHIST NEWSPAPER ARBETER FRAYND, HE CAME UPON HIS LIFE'S WORK: PROMOTING & INTERPRETING URBAN YIDDISH LITERATURE.

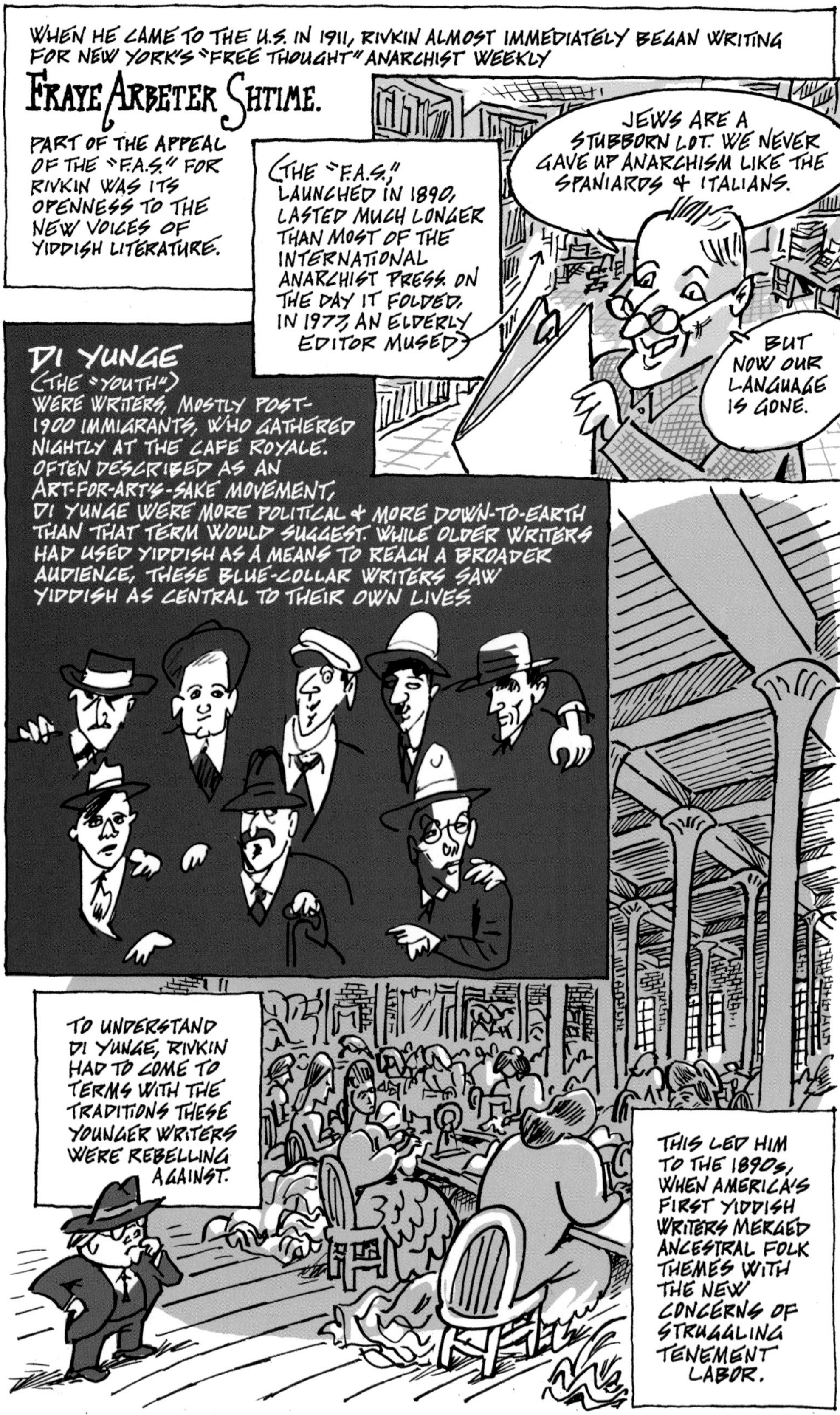
WHEN HE CAME TO THE U.S. IN 1911, RIVKIN ALMOST IMMEDIATELY BEGAN WRITING FOR NEW YORK'S "FREE THOUGHT" ANARCHIST WEEKLY
FRAYE ARBETER SHTIME.
PART OF THE APPEAL OF THE "F.A.S." FOR RIVKIN WAS ITS OPENNESS TO THE NEW VOICES OF YIDDISH LITERATURE.
(THE "F.A.S." LAUNCHED IN 1890, LASTED MUCH LONGER THAN MOST OF THE INTERNATIONAL ANARCHIST PRESS. ON THE DAY IT FOLDED, IN 1977, AN ELDERLY EDITOR MUSED)
JEWS ARE A STUBBORN LOT. WE NEVER GAVE UP ANARCHISM LIKE THE SPANIARDS & ITALIANS.
BUT NOW OUR LANGUAGE IS GONE.
DI YUNGE (THE "YOUTH") WERE WRITERS, MOSTLY POST-1900 IMMIGRANTS, WHO GATHERED NIGHTLY AT THE CAFE ROYALE. OFTEN DESCRIBED AS AN ART-FOR-ART'S-SAKE MOVEMENT, DI YUNGE WERE MORE POLITICAL & MORE DOWN-TO-EARTH THAN THAT TERM WOULD SUGGEST. WHILE OLDER WRITERS HAD USED YIDDISH AS A MEANS TO REACH A BROADER AUDIENCE, THESE BLUE-COLLAR WRITERS SAW YIDDISH AS CENTRAL TO THEIR OWN LIVES.
TO UNDERSTAND DI YUNGE, RIVKIN HAD TO COME TO TERMS WITH THE TRADITIONS THESE YOUNGER WRITERS WERE REBELLING AGAINST.
THIS LED HIM TO THE 1890s, WHEN AMERICA'S FIRST YIDDISH WRITERS MERGED ANCESTRAL FOLK THEMES WITH THE NEW CONCERNS OF STRUGGLING TENEMENT LABOR.

TWO OF RIVKIN'S FAVORITE POETS FROM THE 1890s, YOSEF BOVSHOVER & MORRIS ROSENFELD, WROTE OF THE SWEATSHOPS, AND THEY KNEW WHEREOF THEY SPOKE.

LOOK!

UP!

THE WEALTH YOU CREATE

THE HAPPINESS YOU DESERVE

THE COFFIN WHERE YOU LIVE

BOVSHOVER WAS THE WILD ANARCHIST DREAMER, WHOSE POEMS RAGED ALMOST AS MUCH AT HIS FELLOW TOILERS ENDURING OPPRESSION AS AT THE RULERS/EMPLOYERS OPPRESSING THEM.

BOVSHOVER'S POVERTY DROVE HIM MAD, OR SO THE PEOPLE AROUND HIM THOUGHT.

WORKERS! JOIN YOUR REASON WITH YOUR MIGHT!

HE SPENT THE LAST 15 YEARS OF HIS LIFE IN A POUGHKEEPSIE ASYLUM.

RIVKIN

BOVSHOVER'S ROUGH CONDITIONS— THE SLUM & THE SWEATSHOP—MADE HIM PROCLAMATORY & DIDACTIC.

ROSENFELD WAS CALLED THE "TEARDROP POET," AFTER HIS "TEARDROP MILLIONAIRE" POEM IN WHICH THE WORKERS' POET, LACKING WEALTHY PATRONS, IS PAID IN TEARS FOR HIS TROUBLE.

NEVERTHELESS, COMPARED TO BOVSHOVER, ROSENFELD WAS SUCCESSFUL, AT LEAST FOR A TIME— ESPECIALLY AFTER A HARVARD PROF TRANSLATED & PUBLISHED HIS POEMS TO GREAT ACCLAIM UNDER THE TITLE SONGS OF THE GHETTO.

GETCHER JUDEO-GERMAN POETRY RIGHT HERE!

HE WAS ALSO SUCCESSFUL POLITICALLY, AT LEAST IN THE SENSE THAT HIS WORDS BECAME PART OF THE LABOR MOVEMENT'S CULTURAL LEGACY.

VU LEBNS VELKN BAY MASHINEN, DORTN IZ MAYN RUE PLATS *

IN ROSENFELD, THE WORKPLACE BRINGS CONTENT TO FORM. THE POOR BECOME HEROES IN THEIR OWN WORKING CLASS LIVES AS JEWS.

RIVKIN

* WHERE LIVES ARE WITHERING AT MACHINES, THERE IS MY HOME.

RIVKIN HAD 2 OTHER GREAT FAVORITES FROM THE YEARS BEFORE DI YUNGE, ABRAHAM LIESSEN & ABRAHAM REISEN.

ABRAHAM LIESSEN, MELANCHOLY POET OF NATIONALIST THEMES, DECIDED WHILE STILL IN VILNA THAT MARXISM ALONE COULD NOT DESCRIBE JEWISH LIFE:

IN OUR TOWNS A WORKER BECAME A PETIT BOURGEOIS AS SOON AS HE MARRIED!

IN NEW YORK, LIESSEN'S AMBIVALENT POSITION HELPED HIM TO GRASP THE MIXED EMOTIONS OF JEWISH AMERICANS FEELING AT HOME & NOT AT HOME IN THE NEW WORLD.

I HAVE NONE FOR WHOM TO DIE & NONE FOR WHOM TO LIVE.

IN HIS POEM "THE SPIDER WEBS," LIESSEN TEASES AMERICAN GENTILES WITH THE METAPHOR OF A CONCEITED SPIDER

HERE COME DA SUCKERS.

WHO BELIEVES THE LIGHTS OF THE STATUE OF LIBERTY SHINE FOR HIM ALONE.

A FEELING BURNED IN HIM WITH AN UNQUENCHABLE FIRE: HIS ETERNAL-JEWISH EMOTION!

I COME TO SING THROUGH GENTILES AND DOGS.

ABRAHAM REISEN WROTE IRONIC STORIES THAT CAPTURED PERFECTLY THE YIDDISHE GASN, THE JEWISH STREETS OF NEW YORK.

MY FIRST EDITOR IN NEW YORK!

IN ONE TYPICAL STORY, "THE BATTLE OF THE SEXES," HARRY (A "SPORT") PANICS WHEN HIS FIANCÉE FANTASIZES ABOUT MAKING AS MUCH MONEY AS HE DOES.

GET THAT NONSENSE OUT OF YOUR HEAD, IDA!

VERY DIFFERENT IN TONE, REISEN'S FURIOUS POEMS POSE THE UNANSWERABLE DILEMMAS OF THE UPROOTED:

IN "THE LAST STREET," THE EMIGRANT REJECTS THE BACKWARDNESS OF THE SHTETL.

HERE ENDS THE VILLAGE.

THE WORLD BEGINS HERE.

BUT IN "THE PAIR," THE EMIGRANT'S DESTINATION IS REVEALED TO BE A TRAP.

LOOK, MY DEAR, A CITY!

THERE'LL BE WORK FOR US INDEED!

DEATH

HUNGER

IN ONE OF HIS MOST FAMOUS POEMS, "A FAMILY OF EIGHT" SHARES TWO SMALL BEDS.

I KNOW THE GRAVE IS NARROW TOO—

LET ME DIE.

BUT AT LEAST THERE WE COULD LIE SEPARATELY

BUT IT WAS DI YUNGE THAT FASCINATED RIVKIN. AMONG THE WRITERS HE MOST ADMIRED, **JOSEPH OPATOSHU** WONDERFULLY SHOCKED THE YIDDISH READING COMMUNITY WITH UNVARNISHED PORTRAITS OF THE UNSEEMLY UNDERSIDE OF JEWISH LIFE.

PHILIP ROTH'S GOT NOTHING ON ME.

IN OPATOSHU'S SHORT STORY "MAY THE TEMPLE BE RESTORED," A ROUGH MERCHANT CONFLATES HIS FINANCIAL TROUBLES WITH THE TRAGEDIES OF JEWISH HISTORY.

BLAM! BLAM!

MAY THE TEMPLE BE RESTORED! WHERE'S MY BONUS?

GEE, TAKE IT EASY.

IN OPATOSHU'S BEST-KNOWN NOVEL, ROMANCE OF A HORSE THIEF, THE TOUGH & IMPULSIVE YOUNG THIEF ZANVL RESPONDS TO SETBACKS WITH VIOLENT FANTASIES.

I'LL STEAL THE GOLD MADONNA FROM THE POLISH CHURCH.

THAT WILL BUY ME HORSES & WEAPONS & MEN.

WE'LL HOLE UP IN THE FOREST & LOOT ALL THE ESTATES AROUND.

THE WHOLE REGION WILL FEAR US.

THEN RACHEL WILL HAVE TO MARRY ME!

BUT SHLOYME, ZANVL'S FATHER & MENTOR IN THIEVERY, REVEALS THE ENDGAME OF A WORLD-BEATING OUTLAW.

MY BEARD IS GOING GREY!

I CAN'T GO BACK TO JAIL!

WHY COULDN'T I BE RICH & RESPECTABLE LIKE THE GUYS I USED TO ROB WITH?

A LARGER FIGURE IN THE MILIEU, **DAVID IGNATOV** WAS A LEADER OF DI YUNGE.

HIS EARLY WORK ON THE HASSIDIC TRADITION LED TO HIS BEST NOVELS THAT FUSED MYSTICISM WITH SOCIAL CRITICISM.

HIS 1918 NOVEL IN KESLGRUB (IN THE CAULDRON) EVOKES THE CITY AS A LIVING BODY. HE PRESENTS A VISION OF NEW YORK CITY EMERGING FROM SLEEP, WITH LIGHTS LIKE FLAMES OF THE RISING SUN GREETING THE HALF-ASLEEP PEOPLE ON THEIR WAY TO WORK.

WHAT DO WE NEED THE ARMORY SHOW FOR?

WE GOT CUBISM ALL AROUND US, EVERY MORNING.

THE EMERGENCE OF YIDDISH CULTURE

RIVKIN'S FAVORITE YUNGE POET BY FAR WAS **MOYSHE LEYB HALPERN.** A REBEL AMONG REBELS, GALICIAN-BORN HALPERN SPENT 10 YEARS IN VIENNA STUDYING MODERN LITERATURE BEFORE COMING TO NEW YORK IN 1908.

LONG FOR HOME AND HATE YOUR HOMELAND.

EUROPE

BE A FLECK OF ASH FROM A BURNING TOWER.

FROM THE POEM "HOMESICK"

HALPERN WORKED AT PAPER HANGING & OTHER TAXING BLUE-COLLAR JOBS, PRODUCING SOME OF HIS BEST WORK THROUGH SUFFERING & SADNESS.

PTUI!

IN THE POEM "FROM MY VISIONS" HALPERN AVERTS HIS EYES FROM SUFFERING, BUT IMAGINES THAT IF GOD WERE PRESENT HE WOULD TAKE ACTION—BY DESTROYING EVERYTHING!

IN THE 1920s HE THREW HIMSELF INTO THE YIDDISH LEFT & THE COMMUNIST-AFFILIATED *MORGN FRAYHAYT,* LECTURING & AGITATING WHILE CONTINUING TO WRITE.

GRANDMOTHER & MARX, WRAPPED IN COBWEBS

WHAT DID THE FORTUNE-TELLER SAY.?

TAILOR JAKE IS THE ONE FOR ME.

HIS POEM "TUESDAY" PLAYS WITH THE TRADITIONAL LABOR POEM. THESE WORKING GIRLS LOOK TO ROMANCE, NOT STRIKE OR REVOLUTION, FOR THEIR DELIVERANCE.

HE DIED EXHAUSTED IN 1932, A FEW YEARS AFTER LEAVING POLITICS BEHIND.

I AM NOT WHAT I WANT

I AM NOT WHAT I THINK

I AM THE MAGICIAN

AND I AM THE MAGIC TRICK

FROM THE POEM "MY RESTLESSNESS IS LIKE A WOLF'S"

MOYSHE-LEYB WAS STARVED PHYSICALLY & SPIRITUALLY & THUS WE LOST HIM.

ANOTHER IMPORTANT FIGURE ASSOCIATED WITH DI YUNGE WAS **MOYSHE NADIR**. LIKE OPATOSHU, NADIR WAS A GADFLY WHO ENJOYED SHOCKING THE YIDDISH ESTABLISHMENT. A FREQUENT COLLABORATOR WITH THE SATIRICAL CARTOONIST/PUPPETEERS OF MODICUT THEATRE, NADIR COMES ACROSS AS A SUBVERSIVE HIPSTER FANTASIST.

IN ONE PROPHETIC & VERY SHORT STORY, "THE MAN WHO SLEPT THROUGH THE END OF THE WORLD," NADIR'S PROTAGONIST KVETCHES IN THE FACE OF AN INCOMPREHENSIBLE OBLITERATION.

IF THE WORLD WENT UNDER, IT WENT UNDER. IT WAS NEVER MY WORLD!

BUT MY WATCH! A TWO DOLLAR WATCH! IT WASN'T EVEN WOUND!

WHAT PROMPTED NADIR TO IMAGINE THE END OF EVERYTHING? PERHAPS HE WAS A LATTER-DAY BOVCHOVER, ANGRY AT HIS FELLOW JEWS FOR HANGING ON TO THE TOKENS OF A DYING PAST.

OR WAS HE HAVING A PREMONITION OF THE CATACLYSM TO COME?

INEVITABLY A NEW GROUP OF YIDDISH WRITERS SOUGHT TO OVERTHROW THE PRINCIPLES OF DI YUNGE. THAT GROUP, **IN ZIKH** (THE INTROSPECTIVISTS) EMBRACED FREE VERSE, ABSTRACT LANGUAGE AND, AT LEAST IN THEIR MANIFESTO, SOLIPSISM. **CELIA DROPKIN**, IN POEMS OFTEN COMPARED TO SYLVIA PLATH'S, FOUND IN THESE PRINCIPLES THE MEANS TO VIOLATE TABOOS AGAINST FEMALE SENSUALITY.

NOW, OUT OF ME, SPURTS MY MOTHER'S HOLY, DEEPLY HIDDEN LUST!

IN "YOU PLOWED MY FERTILE SOIL" HER LOVER RENOUNCES THE GIFTS HE GIVES THROUGH PROCREATION. LIKE NADIR'S KVETCHER, HE CLAIMS TO BE A DISINTERESTED BYSTANDER.

WHO SOWED THIS POPPY?

PAPA!

AS "THE CIRCUS LADY," DROPKIN REVEALS A SECRET: SHE WANTS TO FALL UPON, NOT DANCE AMONG, THE DAGGERS.

I WANT MY BLOOD TO HEAT YOU, THROUGH & THROUGH!

MOST MALE YIDDISH CRITICS (INCLUDING, UNFORTUNATELY, RIVKIN) FOUND DROPKIN'S SEXUAL FRANKNESS EMBARRASSING.

THE EMERGENCE OF YIDDISH CULTURE

RIVKIN, WHO DIED BEFORE THE FULL FACTS OF NAZI CRIMES BECAME KNOWN, & BEFORE THE COLD WAR DASHED POSTWAR OPTIMISM, REMAINED HOPEFUL TO THE END. HE NEVER STOPPED LOOKING FOR AN EGALITARIAN REDEMPTION, A WORLD COMMUNITY IN WHICH YIDDISH TOOK ITS PROPER PLACE.

A RELATED THEME EMERGES FROM YIDDISHE YONTOYVIM, A COLLECTION OF HIS ESSAYS PUBLISHED AFTER HE DIED. HERE HE ARGUES THAT JEWISH HOLIDAYS, LIKE ROMAN CATHOLIC CARNIVAL WITH ITS "WORLD TURNED UPSIDE DOWN," OFFERED A LIBERATED SPACE WHERE THE CENTURIES SINCE TORAH DAYS DISSOLVED, & JEWS COULD BREATHE FREE.

YVETTE 'n' PAUL

PAUL BUHLE ONCE INTERVIEWED RIVKIN'S DAUGHTER, YVETTE WEST, HERSELF A LIFELONG ANARCHIST, AS PART OF AN ORAL HISTORY PROJECT.

MY FATHER'S 2nd WIFE & I DID NOT GET ALONG, BUT I GIVE HER CREDIT FOR GETTING HIS BOOKS PUBLISHED.

IN FACT SHE GAVE ME THESE BOOKS OF HIS. YOU SHOULD HAVE THEM.

MY REAL MOTHER COULDN'T KEEP HOUSE BUT SHE HAD A HUGE PERSONALITY.

MY FATHER WOULD COME HOME & FIND ALL HER WOMAN FRIENDS THERE & HE WOULD YELL, "IF YOU DON'T LEAVE AT ONCE I WILL DROP MY PANTS!"

THAT WAS THE ATTITUDE. WOMEN WERE NOT RESPECTED.

HE ONCE VISITED ME IN LAKE PLACID, IN THE ADIRONDACKS, AND SAID, "THIS REMINDS ME OF MY CHILDHOOD."

I WAS SHOCKED! I ALWAYS THOUGHT OF HIM AS A COSMOPOLITAN!

I UNDERSTAND YOUR FATHER WAS INTERESTED IN MYSTICISM?

SURE. CONAN-DOYLE, ANNIE BESANT, ALL THAT SPIRITUALISM STUFF. WHEN MY YOUNGER SON WAS BORN, MY FATHER SAID, "HE WILL BE ME!"

NO WAY!

MY SON IS A WARM PERSON! A LABORATORY TECHNICIAN!

THANX & A TIP O' THE KAPELUSH TO TAMIMENT LIBRARY, NYU, FOR THE YVETTE WEST INTERVIEW!

THE YIDDISH POETS &
THE CHORUS

The two drawings that follow illuminate the Yiddish labor chorus. One of the sturdiest forms of progressive popular culture, the chorus is now more than a century old and still vibrant in scattered North American cities. David Edelstadt, an anarchist Yiddish poet born in Kaluga, Russia, who wrote about suffering

David Edelstadt. Illustration by Peter Gullerud

and redemption, provided the lyrics to some of the most moving labor songs before succumbing to tuberculosis at age twenty-six in 1892. Jewish neighborhoods in New York, Chicago, and Los Angeles had their own choruses, often a mixture of men and women, groups peaking in size from the 1920s to the '40s.

Brighton Beach Yiddish Chorus, 1939. Illustration by Peter Gullerud

ﬠﬦﬥﬤﬦﬥﬠﬡ YIDDISHLAND

PART TWO : YIDDISH MODERNISTS

WRITTEN BY HARVEY PEKAR · ILLUSTRATED BY DAN ARCHER

THERE WAS **SOME** PRAISEWORTHY YIDDISH LITERATURE WRITTEN **BEFORE 1860**, INCLUDING TALES BY **RABBI NACHMAN OF BRATSLAV**, WHOSE **ORAL TALES** WERE TRANSCRIBED AND PRINTED.

BUT THE **GENERAL CONSENSUS** SEEMS TO BE THAT **YIDDISH FINE ART LITERATURE** BEGAN IN **1864** WITH THE PUBLICATION OF **MENDELE MOCHER SFORIM'S** *THE LITTLE MAN*, SUPPOSEDLY THE AUTOBIOGRAPHY OF A **SWINDLER**, WHO NEAR **DEATH** REPENTS HIS **SINS**.

THIS WAS A PORTRAIT OF THE KIND OF **SWINDLER** ONE OCCASIONALLY RAN ACROSS IN JEWISH COMMUNITIES **LARGE** AND **SMALL**, ie. **SHTETLS** (VILLAGES).

MENDELE WAS HIMSELF THE INVENTION OF WRITER SHOLOM ABRAMOVITSH (1836-1917).

MENDELE PAINTS A CLEAR PICTURE OF THE ORG-ANIZATION OF JEWISH SOCIETY. THE WORK CERTAINLY CONTAINS MANY HUMOROUS PORTIONS—

INTELLECTUALS

TRADESMEN

THE POOR

BUT SOME CRITICS HAVE DESCRIBED THEM AS BITTER AS WELL.

A MORE BRUTAL NOVEL IS *FISHKE THE LAME*, DEALING WITH A GROUP OF PEOPLE WHO GO FROM TOWN TO TOWN BEGGING FOR A LIVING.

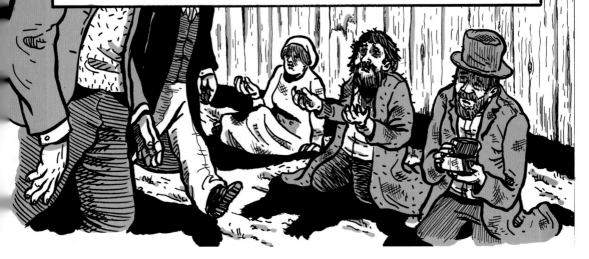

THE OLD HORSE (1873) STARS A JEWISH HORSE WHO COMPARES HIS SUFFERING TO THAT OF THE JEWISH PEOPLE.

YOU FOOL!

YOU YOURSELF ARE A HORSE HARNESSED IN THE SERVICE OF A MASTER

WHO IS ABUSING YOU CURSING YOU LASHING YOU

AND YOU YOURSELF ARE TREMBLING AT HIS EVERY GLANCE!

BENJAMIN THE THIRD IS MODELLED ON DON QUIXOTE. MENDELE'S HERO, BENJAMIN, TAKES A TRIP IN HIS OWN GEOGRAPHICAL REGION BUT IS SO NAIVE HE THINKS HE'S TRAVELLED THE WORLD.

WE ARE ON A QUEST

TO FIND THE RED JEWS BEYOND THE KINGDOM OF PRESTER JOHN!

ONE OF MENDELE'S MOST AMUSING WORKS, IT IS ALSO SYMPATHETIC TO HIS CHARACTERS, BENJAMIN AND SENDERL, THE EQUIVALENT OF SANCHO PANZA.

THE WISHING RING, MENDELE'S PERSONAL **FAVORITE** WORK, TAKES PLACE IN **RUSSIAN-CONTROLLED** TERRITORY...

...AND IS KIND OF A **SURVEY** OF THE **INEQUITIES** JEWS HAVE TO **PUT UP WITH.**

ALTHOUGH **MELODRAMATIC** AT TIMES, IT IS OFTEN **VERY MOVING. MENDELE** MAKES CLEAR HOW JEWS **SUFFER** AT THE HANDS OF **CHRISTIANS**...

...THEY ARE **DISCRIMINATED** AGAINST AT **EVERY TURN.**

MENDELE ALSO DEMON-STRATES JEWS GROWING **HARDENED**...

...AND **EXPLOITING** OTHER JEWS.

MENDELE WORKED ON THIS BOOK FOR YEARS, FINISHING IT IN THE LATE 1880s, AFTER JEWS HAD SUFFERED A WAVE OF POGROMS EARLIER IN THE DECADE.

HE DOES NOT MAKE MUCH OF AN ATTEMPT AT SOLVING THE PROBLEM, WHICH INDEED PERSISTED TO 1945.

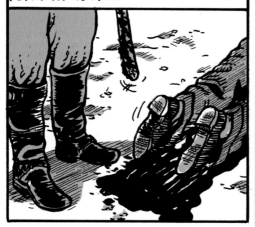

BUT HIS PERCEPTIVE AND OFTEN HUMOROUS PROSE DOES GIVE US A CLEAR PICTURE OF WHAT JEWS HAD TO PUT UP WITH OVER THE CENTURIES.

IN ITSELF, THE WISHING RING MAY BE MENDELE'S GREATEST ACHIEVEMENT IN A DISTINGUISHED CAREER. HE DESERVES HIS HIGH POSITION AMONG YIDDISH NOVELISTS.

BUT I'M **NOT SO SURE** ABOUT THE **ACCOLADES** GIVEN TO THE **CELEBRATED** I.L. PERETZ, **MENDELE'S** SUPPOSED SON.

PERETZ MAY BE THE **MOST PUBLICLY RESPECTED** YIDDISH WRITER. HE DOES **SOME** THINGS **VERY WELL**: HE **CONSTRUCTS** AND **PACES** HIS SHORT STORIES ADMIRABLY; HIS **PROSE** IS **VERY CLEAR**; HE MAKES HIS POINTS **FIRMLY** AND WITHOUT **WASTING** WORDS; HIS **DIALOGUE** IS OFTEN **AMUSING**.

YET **SOME** OF HIS **STORIES** (HE WROTE **NO NOVELS**) SEEM BASED ON **FOLK TALES** AND ARE **EXCESSIVELY SENTIMENTAL**.

I REFER TO SUCH PIECES AS **"BUNTCHEH THE SILENT"** AND **"IF NOT HIGHER"**. BUNTCHEH, A PORTER, WAS SUBJECT TO **DEPRIVATION** IN HIS LIFE BUT WAS SO **HUMBLE** HE NEVER COMPLAINED.

HUFF

WHEN HE GETS TO **HEAVEN** EVERYONE THERE IS **DELIGHTED**. HE IS OFFERED **EVERYTHING** HE SEES. IS HE **GREEDY**? **NO**! HE ONLY WANTS A **ROLL WITH BUTTER** FOR BREAKFAST DAILY.

VELL, IF I COULD HAVE...

THERE'S **IRONY** HERE, BUT IT'S **OVERWHELMED** BY **SCHMALTZ**.

"IF NOT HIGHER" IS ABOUT A **RABBI** WHO DISAPPEARS EVERY FEW DAYS FOR A WHILE. SOMEONE **FOLLOWS HIM** AND FINDS HE'S CHANGED TO **WORKER'S CLOTHES** AND GOES AROUND DOING **GOOD DEEDS** FOR THE POOR.

WHEN NEWS GETS OUT HIS **FOLLOWERS** BELIEVE ONE DAY HE'LL **"ASCEND** RIGHT TO **HEAVEN."** SOMEONE **HEARS** THIS AND **REMARKS**:

IF NOT HIGHER!

SHOLEM ALEICHEM, THE GRANDSON, WAS AND IS THE MOST BELOVED YIDDISH WRITER. HE WAS A FINE HUMORIST WITH A SEEMINGLY ENDLESS SUPPLY OF JOKES AND CLEVER REMARKS.

BUT THERE ARE **TRAGIC MOMENTS** IN HIS STORIES AS WELL, SUCH AS THE TROUBLE **TEVYE THE DAIRY MAN** HAS WITH HIS **DAUGHTERS**, AND THE **SPIRITING AWAY** OF EUROPEAN JEWISH WOMEN TO **ARGENTINA** (BY **JEWS**) TO BECOME **PROSTITUTES**.

SHOLEM ALEICHEM CAME TO **AMERICA** IN 1913 AND LATER **DIED** IN THE **BRONX**. OTHER **YIDDISH WRITERS** CHOSE TO **STAY BEHIND** IN EUROPE.

MOST YIDDISH WRITERS GREETED THE **NEW SOVIET UNION** WITH **JOY**: THE **RED ARMY** DEFEATED THE **ANTI-SEMITIC 'WHITES'**, ANTI-SEMITISM WAS **DISCOURAGED** (EVEN IN A PHONOGRAPH RECORDING BY **LENIN**) AND FOR **SOME YEARS**, YIDDISH INSTITUTIONS WERE OFFICIALLY **SUPPORTED**, YIDDISH **CELEBRATED** AS A **JEWISH LANGUAGE**

BY THE **1930s**, ALL THIS SEEMED **OVER** IN RUSSIA, BUT THE **POPULAR FRONT** AGAINST FASCISM PARTLY **REVERSED** THE TREND. THE CAMPAIGN FOR **YIDDISH** LEGITIMACY WAS ALSO **BUOYED** BY JEWISH SUPPORTERS OF RUSSIA IN U.S. + **ELSEWHERE**

DURING WW2, SOME JEWISH WRITERS BECAME GREAT **NATIONAL HEROES**

EVERYTHING **ENDED** WITH THE **ACCELERATED** ANTI-SEMITISM OF THE **LATE 1940s**. STARTING IN 1948, **STALIN** HAD LEADING YIDDISH WRITERS AND ACTORS, AS WELL AS JEWISH SOCIAL ACTIVISTS, **ARRESTED** AND MURDERED.

THE **VICTIMS** INCLUDED **SEVERAL** GREAT WRITERS: NOVELISTS **DAVID BERGELSON** AND **DER NISTER (PINCHUS KAGANOVICH)**, POETS **PERETZ MARKISH, ITZIK FEFFER, DOVID HOFSHTEYN, LEYB KVITKO**...

... AND **MANY OTHERS** WHO **WEREN'T TRIED** BUT WHO SIMPLY **DISAPPEARED** INTO THE **GULAG**.

BERGELSON (1884-1952) LIVED IN GERMANY DURING THE 1920s AND HIS WORK HAD SOME THINGS IN COMMON WITH FRANZ KAFKA.

ONE OF HIS MOST STRIKING PIECES IS "AMONG REFUGEES" (1923), WHICH DEALS WITH A YOUNG JEWISH REFUGEE WHO WANTS TO ASSASSINATE THE VICIOUS UKRANIAN POGROM LEADER, SYMON PETURA, WHO'S IN BERLIN.

THE REFUGEE DOES NOT ACCOMPLISH HIS OBJECTIVE, BUT, IN A CASE OF LIFE IMITATING ART, PETURA WAS MURDERED IN PARIS BY A YOUNG JEW IN 1926.

I HAVE KILLED A GREAT ASSASSIN!

WHO WAS FOUND INNOCENT BY THE FRENCH JUDICIARY

BERGELSON WAS AN EXCELLENT TECHNICIAN WITH A FINE EYE AND EAR. HIS NOTICE OF LITTLE THINGS ENRICHES HIS WORK, MAKES IT MORE PERSONAL.

A BRILLIANT ACHIEVEMENT OF BERGELSON'S IS THE NOVELLA JOSEPH SCHUR, DEALING WITH A YOUNG, PROSPEROUS AND UNSUCCESSFUL SUITOR WHO THINKS HIS DREAM MARRIAGE MAY HAVE BEEN BROKERED IN KIEV.

UNLIKE PINSKI, WHO ALSO WRITES ABOUT ANOTHER PROSPEROUS JEW (ARNOLD LEVENBERG), JOSEPH SCHUR IS VERY AWARE OF HIS JEWISH BACKGROUND AND RELIGION.

THE DETAILS OF THIS NOVELLA ARE SO INTELLIGENTLY CHOSEN AND PLACED THAT ONE FEELS, WHILE READING IT, LIKE HE IS IN THE MIDDLE OF A MOVIE.

DER NISTER, THE HIDDEN ONE, WAS BORN IN 1884 AND DIED IN 1950 IN THE GULAG, ALSO A VICTIM OF STALIN.

AN EARLY **SYMBOLIST**, HIS WORK INITIALLY **CONFUSED** SOME **CRITICS** BUT EVENTUALLY HE CAME TO BE HIGHLY **RESPECTED**.

RUSSIAN **AUTHORITIES** HAD **NO** USE FOR **HIM** AND HE HAD TO RESORT TO WRITING **TECHNICAL ARTICLES** TO MAKE A LIVING.

BUT IN 1935 DER NISTER BEGAN WORK ON A "**REALISTIC NOVEL**", *THE FAMILY MASHBER*.

IT TAKES PLACE IN THE CITY OF **BERDICHEV** ("**N**" IN THE NOVEL), **DER NISTER**'S BIRTHPLACE, LOCATED IN **WESTERN UKRAINE**, WHICH WAS **RULED BY RUSSIANS** BUT WITH A **LARGE POLISH POPULATION**.

POLISH **PLOTS** AND ATTEMPTS TO **OVERTHROW THE RUSSIANS** PLAY A ROLE IN THIS **TWO-VOLUME NOVEL**

A **THIRD** VOLUME WAS WRITTEN, BUT **LOST**

HOW **REALISTIC** THE BOOK IS IS **DEBATABLE**. A COUPLE OF THE KEY CHARACTERS ARE **IDEALIZED**, THEY HAVE THE **RIGHT ANSWER** FOR EVERYTHING

THERE ARE ALSO MANY **GROTESQUES** IN **MASHBER**, BUT THIS IS TO BE **EXPECTED** IN A CITY IN WHICH A **NUMBER** OF **INHABITANTS** LIVE ON A DAY TO DAY BASIS.

ORDINARY LIFE IN **N.** (OR **BERDICHEV**) IS DESCRIBED WITH **RICH DETAIL** BY **DER NISTER**. IT WAS **NONSENSE** FOR **GENTILES** TO DESCRIBE THE **JEWS** AS **WEALTHY EXPLOITERS**, WHEN ONLY A **SMALL CLASS** OF THEM WERE **RICH** AND **POWERFUL**, WHILE **MOST** LIVED IN **NEAR POVERTY**.

IN **FACT**, JEWS LIVED ON THE **EDGE OF STARVATION**, USING THEIR **WITS** TO STAY A **STEP AHEAD** OF THE **GRIM REAPER**.

THE FAMILY MASHBER DESCRIBES THE **TRAGIC FALL** OF THE HOUSE OF **MASHBER**, A **DECENT** AND **HONEST** BANKER WHO, WHEN HE RUNS INTO **BAD LUCK**, IS **ABANDONED** BY **N.'S JEWS** AND WINDS UP IN **PRISON**.

THERE ARE **THREE** MASHBER BROTHERS: **MOSHE**, THE **BANKER**; THE OLDER · **LUZI**, A BRATI- SLAVER **SECT LEADER** AND A MAN WITH AN **INFALLIBLE MORAL COMPASS**; THE YOUNGEST BROTHER, **ALTER**, IS DISPLAYED AS **MENTALLY ILL**, BUT HE HAS **LUCID PERIODS** AFTER HE'S **LITERALLY** TAKEN A **FALL**.

THE **TROUBLE** IS, THE **NEXT** TIME HE TAKES A **FALL**, HE BECOMES **ILL AGAIN**.

THE REPORTEDLY **BRIGHT** BUT **ACCIDENT-PRONE** ALTER IS PERHAPS THE MOST **POORLY-DEVELOPED** CHARACTER IN THE BOOK.

OVERALL *THE FAMILY MASHBER* IS ONE OF THE **FINEST** YIDDISH NOVELS

BUT I **DON'T AGREE** WITH THOSE WHO **PRAISE IT EVEN MORE**

AS A "**MASTERPIECE**" OF WORLD WRITING.

HARVEY

INCIDENTALLY, **DER NISTER** DOES NOT ABANDON **SYMBOLISM** AND **MYSTICISM** HERE, HE JUST PRESENTS THEM IN A **DIFFERENT CONTEXT.**

FORTUNATELY, A **NUMBER** OF EUROPEAN YIDDISH AUTHORS **EMIGRATED** TO THE **U.S., CANADA** AND **ENGLAND**; SOME OF THE **BEST**, IN FACT.

ABRAHAM REISEN (1876-1953) WAS ONE OF THE FINEST YIDDISH SHORT STORY WRITERS. HIS WORK WAS SUBTLE, SOMETIMES NOT MUCH MORE THAN AN ANECDOTE, BUT INSIGHTFUL AS WELL.

LIKE IN HIS STORY, "**THE JEW WHO DESTROYED THE TEMPLE**", WHICH TAKES PLACE IN THE **CATSKILLS**, WHERE HE MEETS A PERMANENT RESIDENT OF THE AREA NAMED **HENRY ROSEN**, A YIDDISH-SPEAKING JEW WHO IS **PROUD** OF BEING AN **AMERICAN CITIZEN**.

HE IS **EMBARRASSED** BY MORE OLD-FASHIONED JEWS WHO CAN'T STOP THEIR **OLD COUNTRY** BEHAVIOUR,

MUMBLE ~~~
MUMBLE ~~

HE WRITES ABOUT THIS **RECENT ARRIVAL** WHO HAS THE **NERVE** TO **PRAY OUT LOUD** ...

BARUCH ATAH ADONAI ...

THE **CANTOR** STARTED OFF,

AND THE **GREENHORN** BEGAN **CHANTING ALONG** — AS THOUGH HE WERE BACK IN **POLAND** SOMEWHERE!

SO I WENT UP TO HIM AFTER THE SERVICE AND REMARKED **GENTEELY** IN YIDDISH:

THIS IS A **TEMPLE**, NOT A BES MEDRESH·

IT'S **NOT** CUSTOMARY TO PRAY **OUT LOUD** HERE.

* STUDY-HOUSE

SO HE **SMIRKS** AND ANSWERS:

WELL THIS IS **AMERICA**, AND IF YOU CAN TURN A **SHUL*** INTO A **CHURCH**

THEN YOU CAN **CERTAINLY** TURN A TEMPLE INTO A **STUDY-HOUSE**!

* SYNAGOGUE

PROBABLY THE **MOST POPULAR** OF ALL YIDDISH AUTHORS WAS SHOLEM ASCH (1880–1957), WHOSE WORK WAS **TRANSLATED** INTO A NUMBER OF LANGUAGES AND APPEALED TO GENTILES AS WELL AS JEWS.

ASCH, ORIGINALLY INFLUENCED BY PERETZ, LIKED TO WRITE ABOUT TOUGH, VIOLENT JEWS, AS IS CLEARLY ILLUSTRATED BY "MOTKE THE THIEF". ASCH DID NOT LIKE SEEING JEWS TAKING CRAP FROM ANYONE.

MOTKE IS A CORNY, IF RATHER ENTERTAINING BOOK TO READ, BUT ITS HARD TO BELIEVE A YOUNG BOY TOOK SO MANY BRUTAL BEATINGS AND STILL WENT ON TO BE A TOP-NOTCH CRIMINAL.

HIS WHOLE SHTETL WAS INVOLVED IN THE WALLOPING.

ASCH BECAME VERY CONTROVERSIAL WHEN HE TRIED TO RECONCILE JUDAISM AND CHRISTIANITY IN LATER NOVELS, SUCH AS THE NAZARENE.

ANOTHER THING YOU SHOULD KNOW ABOUT ASCH - HE WAS ONE OF THE FIRST YIDDISH AUTHORS TO WRITE EXPLICITLY ABOUT SEX.

A **WRITER** ALSO ASSOCIATED WITH THE **HASKALAH** BUT WHO CAME TO THE FORE AFTER **DIK** AND **LINYETSKY** WAS **YANKEV DINESON** (1866 - 1919).

KNOWN TO SOME **CRITICS** AS THE **FATHER** OF **SCHMALTZY** YIDDISH ROMANCE, DINESON GOT A **SLOW START** IN HIS CAREER AS HE WAS **CRITICIZED** BY SOME **HEBRAISTS** FOR WRITING IN YIDDISH AND TOOK IT TO HEART.

AFTER **SOME YEARS** HE SAW THROUGH THEIR **PREJUDICE** AND WROTE IN YIDDISH **AGAIN.** HIS NOVEL, **THE CRISIS** (1905), DEMONSTRATES THAT HE WAS A **TECHNICALLY FINE** AND **OBSERVANT** CHRONICLER OF EVERYDAY JEWISH LIFE.

WHAT A **BUNCH** OF **KVETCHERS!***

*COMPLAINERS

TOP NOTCH YIDDISH WRITERS WERE BORN IN **RUSSIA** BEFORE THE **REVOLUTION. UNFORTUNATELY,** SOME STAYED THERE, THINKING THE **SOVIET GOVERNMENT** WOULD BE RELATIVELY **TOLERANT.**

ACTUALLY A GREAT DEAL OF EXCELLENT **RUSSIAN EXPERIMENTAL WRITING** WAS DONE IN THE **1920s,** BUT WHEN **STALIN** TOOK CONTROL — **FORGET IT.**

HE WAS A **HUGE ANTI-SEMITE,** AND ONE OF HIS GOALS WAS TO **CRUSH** JEWISH WRITERS.

FORTUNATELY DAVID PINSKI (1872-1959) WAS ABLE TO GET OUT OF RUSSIA IN TIME, SETTLING IN NEW YORK IN 1899. HE LATER MOVED TO ISRAEL.

PINSKI HAS BEEN CITED AS ONE OF THE FIRST YIDDISH WRITERS TO CHAMPION SOCIALISM/THE LABOR MOVEMENT.

ACTUALLY PINSKI GOT MORE ACCLAIM FOR HIS PLAYS THAN ANYTHING ELSE, BUT HE WAS ALSO A FINE PROSE FICTION AUTHOR.

THE MISERABLE LOT OF JEWISH WORKERS IS PORTRAYED IN "AND THEN HE WEPT," IN WHICH A LABOURER WHO HAS MAINTAINED A CHEERFUL DEMEANOR GETS INVOLVED IN A FIGHT WITH HIS FAMILY AND BREAKS DOWN, CRYING.

"IN THE MADHOUSE", ORIGINALLY WRITTEN IN 1893, DEMONSTRATES PINSKI'S SYMPATHY FOR THE MENTALLY ILL DURING A MONOLOGUE BY AN ASYLUM'S INMATE.

MORE TYPICAL IS PINSKI'S "ARNOLD LEVENBERG": A NON-YIDDISH-SPEAKING AMERICAN UPPER CLASS BACHELOR BUSINESSMAN IN HIS THIRTIES, LIVING IN NEW YORK JUST BEFORE THE STOCK MARKET CRASH.

LEVENBERG AWAKENS ONE DAY AFTER A **DREAM** AND REALIZES THAT IT'S **ABOUT TIME** HE GOT **MARRIED.**

HE MAKES A **LIST** OF HIS **TOP PROSPECTS,** BUT **EVERYTHING** SEEMS TO **FALL THROUGH** FOR HIM!

HEY, WHERE ARE YOU GOING?

TAXI!

FINALLY HE MEETS A **GOOD-LOOKING** BUT **NOT STUN-NINGLY BEAUTIFUL** YOUNG WOMAN, AND, AFTER A PERIOD OF **IRRESOLUTION, MARRIES** HER.

PRESUMABLY **EVERYONE** LIVES **HAPPILY** EVER AFTER.

THIS SOUNDS LIKE A TRITE PLOT,

AND IT IS —

— BUT FOR A **COUPLE** OF **REASONS,** THE NOVEL HAS **SOME** INTEREST.

SELDOM HAVE YIDDISH WRITERS DEALT WITH **RICH AMERICANS.** LEVENBERG HAS PRACTICALLY **NO KNOWLEDGE** OF HIS JEWISH **BACKGROUND,** AND DOESN'T SEEM TO CARE. (HE'S NOT **DENOUNCED** FOR IT THOUGH).

ROSH HASHANAH — WHAT'S **THAT?**

EVIDENTLY **PINSKI** DIDN'T STAY IN THE GHETTO ALL DAY LONG — HE GOT OUT AND SAW THE TOWN.

THERE'S ALSO SOME **NICE,** FAIRLY EARLY (1928) **STREAM** OF **CONSCIOUSNESS** AND INTERIOR MONOLOGUE WRITING HERE.

LEON KOBRIN, WHO CAME TO THE US IN 1892, SAW A DIFFERENT SIDE OF AMERICAN LIFE BEFORE BECOMING A POPULAR SHORT STORY... WRITER AND DRAMATIST.

HE WORKED IN **SWEATSHOPS**, LIVING A **LOWER CLASS LIFE** AND **WRITING** ABOUT IT.

IN **FACT**, HE TALKS ABOUT **BRAWLS** HE GOT INTO IN THE **STATES**, AND **PROSTITUTION**.

KOBRIN WAS **POPULAR** IN HIS DAY, BUT THERE'S **NOT MUCH INTEREST** IN HIS WORK **NOW**, EVEN THOUGH SOME OF THE STUFF HE WROTE MUST HAVE BEEN **SHOCKING** TO SOME **READERS**.

WHAT IS THIS?

HE WRITES ABOUT **WHORE HOUSES!**

JOSEPH OPATOSHU, AN **ADMIRABLE** NOVELIST, CAME TO THE U.S. IN 1907 AND RECEIVED AN ENGINEERING DEGREE, BUT NEVERTHELESS STUCK TO WRITING.

HE'S WRITTEN ABOUT A **VARIETY** OF SUBJECTS, INCLUDING *"A DAY AT REGENSBERG"*, SET IN THE **MIDDLE AGES**, AND **ISRAEL** UNDER THE **ROMANS**.

HIS **MOST FAMOUS** WORK IS *"IN POLISH WOODS"*, WHICH AGAIN DEALS WITH **CHASSIDS**. HE GIVES A **RICH**, SWEEPING ACCOUNT OF THE LIFE OF **POLISH JEWS**.

ARGUABLY THE **FINEST ALL ROUND** YIDDISH WRITER IS JACOB GLATSTEIN, PERHAPS BEST KNOWN AS A **POET**, BUT ALSO A SUPERBLY INTELLIGENT **PROSE WRITER**.

MY FAVORITE WORKS BY HIM ARE "VEN YASH IZ GEFOREM" (HOMEWARD BOUND) AND "VEN YASH IZ GEKUMEN" (HOMECOMING AT TWILIGHT).

THESE DEAL WITH GLATSTEIN'S RETURN TO POLAND, AFTER TWENTY YEARS, TO VISIT HIS SICK MOTHER.

THE BOOKS DESCRIBE GLATSTEIN'S JOURNEY AND THE VARIETY OF PEOPLE HE MEETS. HE'S A VERY INSIGHTFUL WRITER WHO NOTED THE ANTI-SEMITISM DURING THE 1930s. HE DEMONSTRATES A SHREWD SENSE OF HUMOR TO GO WITH HIS VIVID PROSE, INCLUDING INTELLIGENT USE OF STREAM-OF-CONSCIOUSNESS TECHNIQUE.

PERHAPS THE HIGH POINT OF THE TWO BOOKS IS GLATSTEIN'S MEETING WITH A SIXTEEN-YEAR-OLD CHASSID, WHO'S BOTH BRIGHT AND NAIVE.

ANOTHER GLATSTEIN WORK IS "EMIL UN KARL," AN ACCOUNT OF TWO VIENNESE BOYS, ONE JEWISH, ONE GENTILE, JUST AT THE TIME THE NAZIS HAVE TAKEN OVER AUSTRIA.

YOU CAN ALMOST CRY WHEN YOU START THINKING ABOUT WHAT THE FUTURE HOLDS FOR HIM.

PERHAPS THE MAJOR JEWISH AVANT-GARDE LITERARY FIGURE WAS MOISHE NADIR (1885-1943), BORN ISAAC REISS IN NARAYEV, GALICIA, EMIGRATED TO NEW YORK IN 1898.

NADIR WENT TO ENGLISH SCHOOLS FOR A COUPLE OF YEARS, THEN WORKED AT FLUNKY JOBS.

HE BEGAN WRITING FOR NEWSPAPERS IN 1902, THEN WENT BACK TO GALICIA, THINKING TO RESETTLE, BUT MISSED NEW YORK AND RETURNED.

HE WORKED FOR JEWISH HUMOR PUBLICATIONS AND ASSOCIATED WITH A GROUP OF NEW JEWISH WRITERS LABELLED "DI YUNGE."

HIS FIRST BOOK, *VILDE ROYZN* (1915), WAS QUITE CONTROVERSIAL, OWING TO THE SEXUAL REFERENCES IN HIS FREE VERSE POEMS.

NADIR WAS A BOHEMIAN, WEARING A CAPE AND SCARF. NOT MANY EASTERN EUROPEAN JEWS WERE IN THOSE DAYS.

HE EVEN HAD A GENTILE GIRLFRIEND (SHIKSA).

IN 1916 HIS PROSE-POETRY WAS PUBLISHED BY THE NEWSPAPER "TAG", AND COLLECTED IN A VOLUME.

From Man to Man

Moishe Nadir

HE WROTE FOR A COMMUNIST PAPER FOR YEARS, BEGINNING IN THE MID-1920s.

HE EVEN WENT TO THE USSR IN 1926, AND STATED THAT COMMUNISM WOULD WIPE OUT HUMAN MISERY.

THE STALIN-HITLER AGREEMENT IN 1939 HOWEVER SOURED HIM ON COMMUNISM, AND HE BEGAN RIPPING IT IN HIS ARTICLES.

AFTER NADIR'S WRITING CAREER GOT GOING, HE USED A VARIETY OF FORMS: PROSE, POETRY, PROSE-POETRY, PLAYS, FEUILLETONS.

NADIR WAS AN EXCEPTIONALLY ADMITTED MODERNIST - A RARITY AMONG JEWISH WRITERS IN THE EARLY 20TH CENTURY.

BUT HE WOULD BE FOLLOWED BY MANY MORE.

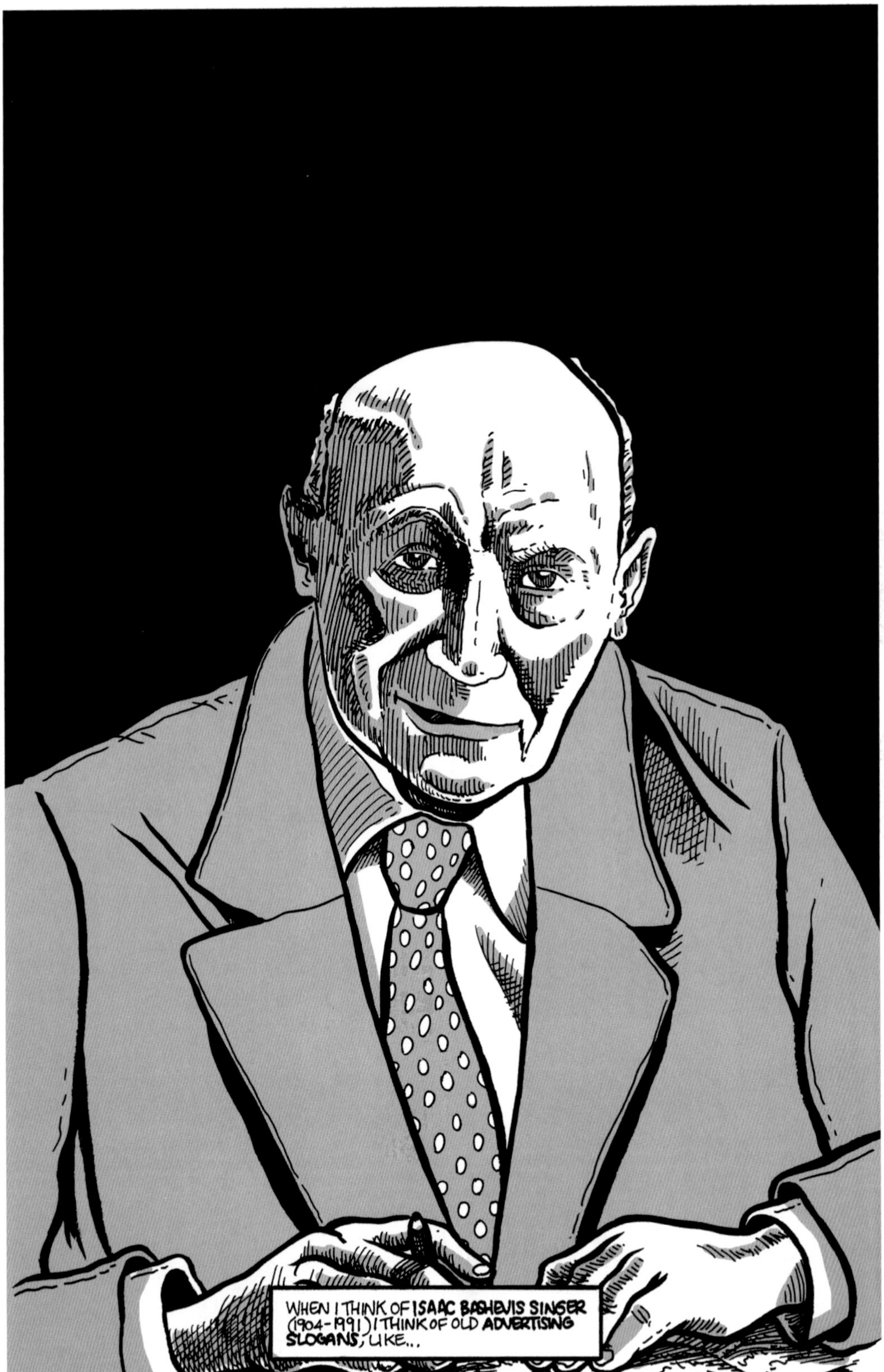
WHEN I THINK OF ISAAC BASHEVIS SINGER (1904-1991) I THINK OF OLD ADVERTISING SLOGANS, LIKE...

THE WIT
THE WARMTH
THE WISDOM

I.B. SINGER

SIGH

BLEAH

SINGER CONNED THE PUBLIC FOR YEARS WITH HIS WISE OLD MAN ROUTINE, WHICH IS REFLECTED IN HIS BOOKS.

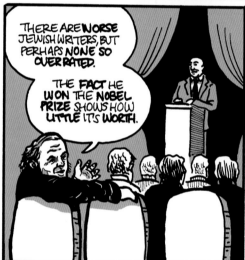

THERE ARE WORSE JEWISH WRITERS, BUT PERHAPS NONE SO OVERRATED.

THE **FACT** HE **WON THE NOBEL PRIZE** SHOWS HOW LITTLE IT'S **WORTH**.

HIS **FATHER** WAS A **CHASSIDIC RABBI** AND THIS CAN BE SEEN IN HIS WORK, FULL OF **COLORFUL CHARACTERS** AND **MYSTERY.**

HE WAS A **CLEVER** AND VERY **SUCCESSFUL POPULAR WRITER** AND CERTAINLY KNEW HOW TO PLAY HIS **JEWISH CARD** (CORNY SENTIMENTALITY).

YENTL

I.B.

I.J

HE **CAN'T HOLD A CANDLE** TO MEN LIKE **BERGELSON, GLATSTEIN,** OR EVEN HIS OWN **BROTHER, ISRAEL JOSHUA SINGER,** WHOSE *THE BROTHERS ASHKENAZI* IS ESPECIALLY **IMPRESSIVE.**

BUT IT WAS **IB "BASHEVIS" SINGER** WHO **WON OVER THE PUBLIC,** NOT TO MENTION **RONALD REAGAN** —

WHO PRESENTED HIM WITH THE **PRESIDENTIAL MEDAL OF MERIT.**

NOT EVERY JEWISH WRITER WHO TRAVELED WEST FROM EASTERN EUROPE WOUND UP IN THE USA. ESTHER SINGER KREITMAN (1891 – 1954), THE SINGER BROTHERS' SISTER, LIVED IN BELGIUM AND ENGLAND.

SHE WAS **NOT A PROLIFIC WRITER**, BUT HER NOVEL, *DEBORAH*, IS **SOLID** AND **THOUGHT-PROVOKING**. IT'S AN **AUTOBIOGRAPHICAL** WORK, AND EMPHASIZED IN PART THE **DIFFICULTY** SHE HAD ACQUIRING A **SECULAR EDUCATION**.

JEWISH WOMEN, UNTIL RECENTLY, HAVE BEEN **TERRIBLY DISCRIMINATED AGAINST** BY JEWISH MEN. THE MEN DIDN'T, AS A RULE, **BEAT THEM**, BUT **CLOSED OFF** MANY OPPORTUNITIES.

OFTEN WHEN JEWISH WOMEN **HAD** TO **WORK** IT WAS TO **SUPPORT** THEIR **TORAH** AND **TALMUDIC SCHOLAR HUSBANDS**, WHO **SAT AT HOME**, STUDYING.

CHAVA ROSENFARB (1923-), A SURVIVOR OF THE HOLOCAUST WHO SETTLED IN CANADA, HAS WRITTEN SEVERAL BOOKS, OF WHICH *BOCIANY* AND ITS SEQUEL, *LOVE AND LODZ*, PARTICULARLY STAND OUT.

HERE SHE HAS SET HER WORKS BOTH IN A SMALL TOWN, **BOCIANY**, AND A LARGE CITY, **LODZ**, IN THE **FIRST QUARTER** OF THE TWENTIETH CENTURY.

THE PEOPLE WHO ARE FINALLY THE **FOCUS** OF ATTENTION ARE A YOUNG MAN, **YACOV**, AND A YOUNG WOMAN, **BINELE**, WHO ARE BROUGHT UP IN **BOCIANY** AND **MIGRATE** TO **LODZ**.

WHERE, IN **FITS** AND **STARTS**, THEY ARE **DRAWN TOGETHER**.

IN **BOCIANY** WE MEET **YACOV** + **BINELE** AS CHILDREN OF **SHOPKEEPERS** (YACOV'S MOTHER, BINELE'S FATHER) WHO ARE **DESPERATELY** TRYING TO **PROVIDE** FOR THEIR CHILDREN. OF THE MANY **PROBLEMS** FACING THEM, **ONE** IS THAT THE **JEWISH COMMUNITY** LIVES UNDER THE **THREAT** OF A **POGROM**.

AND THE **JEWS** OF **BOCIANY** ARE **POOR**, ALMOST **TOO POOR** TO SUPPORT **RETAIL** ESTABLISHMENTS.

ALSO **DIFFICULT** FOR THEIR **ELDERS** TO DEAL WITH IS THAT THEIR **KIDS** ARE **NO LONGER** **UNQUESTIONINGLY RELIGIOUS**. SOME DRIFT TO THE **JEWISH BUND**,* OTHERS TO THE **COMMUNIST PARTY**.

*LABOR ORGANIZATION

THE **DEVOUTLY RELIGIOUS** CAN'T UNDERSTAND THE **"UNBELIEVERS,"** THE DAYS OF **ORTHODOX SUPREMACY** ARE OVER.

BOCIANY HAS A LOVELY **RURAL** SETTING, WHICH **ROSENFARB** CAPTURES WITH HER **LYRICAL** WRITING.

LODZ, ON THE OTHER HAND, IS A **BIG**, **CROWDED**, **INDUSTRIAL** CITY.

IT TAKES **TIME** FOR **BINELE** AND **YACOV** TO GET TO KNOW AND DEAL WITH **LODZ**. **BINELE**, THOUGH **STREETWISE**, IS **ILLITERATE**.

WHAT DOES THIS **SAY**?

SUBJECT TO INFLUENCES BY **SOCIALISTS** AND **COMMUNISTS**, **YACOV** IS WON OVER TO **SECULARISM** SLOWLY.

BINELE, HOWEVER, HAS BEEN SECRETLY **HANGING OUT** WITH A POLISH **CATHOLIC FAMILY** SINCE SHE WAS A **CHILD**

AND DOES **NOT** HAVE AS DIFFICULT A TIME **ADJUSTING** TO THINGS.

ROSENFARB'S PLOTS ARE SOMETIMES **PREDICTABLE**, BUT SHE BRINGS HER CHARACTERS **TO LIFE**.

THE **ROUTINE** OF EASTERN EUROPEAN COMMUNITY LIFE HAS BEEN PORTRAYED **CONVINCINGLY** BY A NUMBER OF **YIDDISH AUTHORS**.

THE **JEWS** SUFFERED SO MUCH INTO THE TWENTIETH!

WHAT WERE THE **GENTILES** SO **AFRAID** OF—

THAT A **ROTHSCHILD** WOULD **BUY POLAND** AND **RUSSIA** AND TURN IT OVER TO **JEWISH RULE**?

AMONG THE **BEST** JEWISH **PROSE ARTISTS** IS **KADYA MOLODOWSKY** (1894-1975) FROM **BELARUS**, WHO LATER BECAME A FEATURE ON THE **KIEV, WARSAW** AND **NEW YORK** LITERARY SCENES.

MOLODOWSKY IS KNOWN MAINLY AS A **POET**, BUT CHECK OUT HER BOOK OF SHORT STORIES **A HOUSE WITH SEVEN WINDOWS**. TALK ABOUT **FUNNY**!

MOST OF THE STORIES TAKE PLACE IN EITHER **EUROPE** OR **NEW YORK**.

MOLODOWSKY HAS A GREAT **EAR**, A GREAT **MEMORY** AND A GREAT **SENSE OF TIMING**.

SO, LISTEN

THE WIND-UP WAS...

YOU WANT AN **EXAMPLE**?

OK, HERE'S ONE FROM "**A FUR COAT**."

JACK MANDEL, A.K.A. YANKEL MANDEL-BAUM, WAS AT A **LANDSLEIT*** BALL. HE'D BEEN **MARRIED** ONCE BEFORE BUT WAS **SO CHEAP** HE **DIVORCED** HIS WIFE TO **KEEP** EXPENSES DOWN.

*FELLOW JEWS (LIT. "LANDSMEN")

AT THE BALL WAS **TSILIE BELKIN**, THIRTYISH, NEVER MARRIED AND A **SHARP DRESSER**. JACK LIKED HER RIGHT AWAY.

HOWEVER, HE KEPT ASKING HER STUFF LIKE:

HOW MUCH DID THAT COAT COST YOU?

WHEN HE DID THIS, TSILIE THOUGHT HE WAS **JOKING**.

WHAT A LIVE WIRE!

SO THEY GOT **MARRIED** AND ONE DAY **TSILIE**, WHO HAD A **NICE JOB** HERSELF, ORDERED A **FUR COAT**.

YES TUESDAY WOULD BE FINE

JACK FOUND OUT ABOUT IT,

AND **CANCELLED** THE ORDER.

HE TOLD TSILIE:

IT'S TOO MUCH MONEY ALL AT ONCE.

TOO MUCH ALL AT ONCE.

IT WAS A MISUNDERSTANDING.

EVERYTHING STAYS JUST AS I ARRANGED IT WITH YOU.

JACK RAN OVER AND SAID:

I'M WARNING YOU

I'M WARNING YOU

TSILIE LEPT.

SLAM

WELL, THAT'S WHAT HAPPENS WHEN YOU MARRY AN OLD MAID

ALL OF A SUDDEN, A COAT!

Illustration by Peter Kuper

CONEY ISLAND SUMMER

Yiddish-speaking left-wingers, and not only left-wingers among Jewish immigrants, felt themselves strangers in the United States until at least the New Deal era of the thirties. Anti-Semitism was common, peaking with the return of the Ku Klux Klan during the 1920s. For Yiddish radicals, the hope was for a socialism that would sweep away all the bad things, replacing them with brotherhood and cooperation. The national prosperity of the 1920s and the success of Jewish immigrants, from show business (and other businesses) to trade unionism, crystallized a changing response. By this time Jews had begun to interact more widely with American popular culture and to discover for themselves the economic opportunities as well as the delights of big cities and mass populations. Thus, the stylish Yiddish magazine *Der Hamer* (*The Hammer*), a left-wing but artistically experimental publication of the 1920s–30s, discovered America on its own terms. The writer Nathaniel Buchwald, soon to become a most distinguished critic of Yiddish theater in the United States, recorded his own response to visiting the grandest of American amusement parks, Coney Island. The crowds there were not "political," but they were so full of life that the scene itself suggested hope and even optimism for the human condition and civilization's prospects. Artist Peter Kuper adds his own visual interpretation of the *Hamer* essay, translated by Hershl Hartman.

CONEY ISLAND

———— ◆►◄◆ ————

☞ written by Nathaniel Buchwald, translated by Hershl Hartman

Originally published in *Der Hamer* (*The Hammer*), August 1926

A thin whistle tears through the air: "Peanuts. R-r-r-ed hot dogs!" Surf Avenue. Seething. Automobiles. A drive, a honk, a step on the gas. Stopped. Tensed hands on the steering wheel. Pedestrians mill before the wheels. Across the way: "R-r-r-ed hot!" Here, here, here for baths. Fifty cents. Cold and warm. A restaurant on the boardwalk. Waiting in line. Faster, already. Hot. Ocean breeze through sweaty shirts. A tin number badge on a rubber string.

On the sand—people. On the people—sand. People mixed with sand. Wet sand, damp sand, dry. Many people, very many, and probably still more. In the city, many people means many heads, many seats in a hall, hands on subway straps, feet and hats in a parade, spines bent over machines. Mouths in a cafeteria. One for each. A head—a person, a hat—a person. Here it's all thrown together. Feet and hands. Hands next to feet. Heads on chests. Heads near breasts. Hands and hips. Bare heads on bare knees. Eyes and breasts, eyes and hips. All together, one to the other. Limbs, limbs.

SO many people but there is no mass. So much in common but there is no communality. Separately, separately. Couples, groups, families, lovers, acquaintances. All nearby and all foreign: foreign castes, origins, richer and poorer, educated and common, immigrants and natives, Brooklynese Brownsville accents and Broadway jazz. Hatred and envy. Kikes and Yankees, loose women and busybodies, attractive bathing suits, decorated, seeded with colorful ribbons. Red, green, blue parasols. Finery and tease, coquettishness and competition. Neglected, raggedy bathrobes, dresses, rubber caps: one's stomach turns at the sight.

People revealed. Shame covered, as the police demand—wrapped in cloth but the person is undressed. Attractive bodies, thick legs, slender backs, hunched backs, pendulous breasts, men—woe to them; women—meat-cases full. Maidenly bodies, modest hips, compact breasts illuminate the bathing suit's cloth, pale faces, far-off gazes, and yet the bodies know very little. Missing is the discipline of clothing that would enclose, conceal, encorsetize. Missing is the uniform that would command respect even for the twisted, malformed men. There is no defense for ungainly, bellied, sag-breasted, wide-hipped women. Hatefulness goes naked here. And beautiful bodies too. Bodies beautiful, freed of clothes that conceal.

From the sand into the water. Swimming, splashing, screaming. Clouded water, sand and water. Ropes—for protection; strong arms—protection and trembling. Swimming out. O, how joyful to surrender to the sea! Like a lover, like caressing a woman. Caressing, and clowning and laughing. Oh-ha-ha!

Swim over here! Rhythmically, rhythmically one's arms stroke and one's legs propel forward. Water, water, all is water, and all is rhythm, the precise enforced rhythm of required movement. Farther, farther. Tired arms, tired legs. Prone. Slowly, toward the shore, breathing heavily. At the sand. On the sand. People and sand. People and water. Water and sand. People and water, and sand.

On the boardwalk. Clothes. Such a wide thoroughfare and no cars in sight. And one can walk wherever one wishes. Walking, just walking. Smooth boards, an easy walk. The boardwalk—a rendezvous for half a million. At this street, at the other one, a few blocks down, or closer, that's where we'll meet on the boardwalk. On one side— railing, sand, sea, light towers, shores, distance. On the other—swimming, guessing, drinking, riding, swinging, twisting, pushing. Entrance to Steeplechase Park, to

Child's Restaurant, to Feltman's. Thousands of people eating sausages, all—sausages. Dusk comes on. Lanterns are lit. A long, wavy line of lanterns. A whistle from behind. A rolling pushchair. And they're not embarrassed. They've paid, they'll be tipping. And the black man is not embarrassed, either. Hired. So much per day. Wages. A job.

Clothed, all clothed. Manners, politeness. Literati stroll, discussing literature. Housewives stroll, discussing lemon pie. Stores, restaurants, games, guessing, shooting. Everything one needs. But it's the boardwalk, and the magic of an easy smooth path conquers the carnival attractions. This is for strolling. The stroll of civilization, among electric lamps, among machinery, among stalls and barkers. And nature— waiting at hand. The stroll of New York, of the store, the factory, the office, the tenement. The expanse of New York's congestion. The air of New York's closeness. The languidness of New York's speed.

Back to Surf Avenue. Neither an avenue nor a street, but a whirlwind in space. To the highest heights, to rooftops left and right, not quite, there roars a din, masculine, whistling, hoarse: "Here, here, I can shout louder!" Here, there, up, down, now shaking, now trembling, now flying down. Now it rises up. "R-r-red hot dogs!" Light, light, lamps, spotlights, red, green, dots, rays streaming, stains of light. Traffic signals seem lost. A world of wax, of hunchbacks, freaks, giants, dwarfs, a boy with a calf's eye. "Popcorn, Cracker Jacks, here, here!"

Hot and sweaty. Ice cream melts in one's hand, asphalt melts under one's foot, dollars melt in one's fist. A dollar—gone, dimes, nickels, another dollar, more dimes, cheap. Three balls for a dime. If you hit it, you get this Kewpie doll. Who needs a Kewpie doll? What for? You need it. And if you don't? It's just cheap. One dime, three balls. You hit—you win. Winning—one must win. I'll show them. I—the expert. Devil take it! Didn't hit. Almost. Three more balls. Thank you. Almost came close. Change for five dollars. Yes, sir. "R-r-red hots, popcorn, Cracker Jacks, here, here!"

Luna Park. It's royal, they won't fool you. The people are dressed in uniforms with brass buttons, with caps. A responsible institution. Not just a carnival at the seashore. Overheard, an orchestra, through the covered towers and scaffolding. The music swells and spreads, and it's bright and crowded. One stands in line. One waits. It's worth it. A powered car pulls upward, barely moving. Electric? Who knows how it works? Downhill, in a boat. Like an arrow shot from a bow. Crash into the water. Will it turn over? Never. It's Luna Park, after all, so many people who've paid money. Uniforms won't allow an overturn. Reliable machinery. The devil knows how it works. Probably on electricity. On the airplane. Maybe it's dangerous? Don't be foolish, it's Luna Park, where anything goes. One's head grows dizzy. No matter. Hooray! Higher, higher! The higher, the better. It's good that it's dangerous. A scream and another scream. One scream chases the other. Screaming in rhythm. A crash, screaming and laughter. Slowly, lower, the speed decreases. Again for another dime. Devil take it, another care. "Hot dogs, here, here!"

In the midst of the towers and the machinery, the twisting, thrusting, rising, shaking to the minute, to the second, to the dot in the midst of it all that possessed jubilation of mechanical accuracy—a little stream, a little boat, an idyll, a place to sit and pine. One dime. Boating in the Tunnel of Love. In the tunnel—darkness. People sit in pairs, in pairs. No screaming, what for? Love. Closer, bolder, one may. It's a Tunnel of Love. Tomorrow she will be proper. In the city; "How do you do?" And no more than a smile, a touch of her hand. Here it's carnival. Deliberately came here, to the Tunnel of Love. Rearrange one's clothes before coming out into the light. Again? How does one suggest it? Eh, heh, why don't we go—? Alight! Change for ten dollars. Yes, sir, thank you. "R-r-red hot dogs! Cracker Jacks, popcorn, here, here!"

Bent and crazy, bent and crazy. One mirror—a giant of a man presses up to the sky, his nose measurable by a yardstick. Another mirror—a belly like a bass drum, a watermelon of a nose, a face like a kneading trough. A third mirror—a barrel-like body, swaying on two spears. Farther, farther. Well, try going farther. The stairs trick you in and there's no exit. A step ahead, a push back. On all fours. Laughter with a thin note of fear. Perhaps there really is no exit? Foolishness, Luna Park, supposed to be this way. Uniforms, money, paid. Finally out, a platform. Ha-ha-ha! Ha-ha-ha! Skirts blown upward. From a hole in the ground, a blast of pressurized air. In front of everyone, men's grazes are electrified toward the legs, toward the silk underpants. On to a slide, who knows how many stories high. Arms together! Legs together! "Let 'er go!" Sliding downward, as if toward death. No danger. Carefully arranged. No more than a thrill. Loop-the-Loop. Slowly upward, slowly downward, faster, wilder, up and down. Toward the heavens, to the abyss. On rails. With electricity. Pay as you leave. Again. A drink. "Ice cold soda, lemonade, ginger ale, here, here! R-r-red hots!"

Late. Exhausted. No more taste for tumult. Home. The city beckons. To the subway. Open doors, all seats taken. Better to wait. An empty train will come. Well, hurry up, why are they waiting? Lean on me, just so. Embraced. Caressed. Tired. Next station. Next station—what does it matter? We're riding home. Today was carnival. Tomorrow—New York. "Red hot dogs!" "Steeplechase!" "Luna Park." Next station. Dream or reality?

CHAPTER 2.

Yiddish Theater & Film

W̶ho would have expected, during the early 1880s, when Jewish Americans were few and mostly of German background, that a dozen or so years later, Second Avenue Broadway would rival the original in vivacity, art, and popular following (not to mention pay scales for unionized actors)? Then came the flood of Yiddish-speaking immigrants from Eastern Europe.

The concentration of that population within or not too distant from Greater New York made a huge difference. But there were other factors. One of the favorite quips of the age ran like this: A Jew on the street looks at the choices of cultural expression, a synagogue and a brothel, and he chooses the combination of both, that is, Yiddish theater. Since Jewish women were avid theatergoers (and filmgoers) by the 1920s, this adage definitely leaves something to be desired. Still, Yiddish theater was entertainment that could be and often was soulful, but also funny, romantic, and tragic. Some actors were well known for hurling insults at an indifferent audience, while others played Shakespearean roles—in Yiddish.

Yiddish film followed theater, using many of the same actors, musicians, even sets. Of all the forms, this one had the least time for development before the end came. Music, including the one major pop-culture influence that was not secular, the cantorial repertoire heard on Yiddish-language radio, on phonograph records, and in endless performances, was its own world. And remains so now, in revival.

The play that follows, *The Essence: A Yiddish Theatre Dim Sum* by Allen Lewis Rickman, was first performed by Rickman, Yelena Shmulenson, and Steve Sterner in 2007. Designed to be "99⁴⁴⁄₁₀₀% nostalgia-free," *The Essence* introduces Yiddish language and Yiddish theater to new audiences via scenes from plays, songs, anecdotal material, episodes from Jewish history, and "irrelevant interludes." It has played to sold-out houses at New York's New Yiddish Rep and has toured throughout the Northeast and Europe.

THE ESSENCE
A YIDDISH THEATRE
DIM SUM

STEVE STERNER

YELENA SHMULENSON-RICKMAN

ALLEN LEWIS RICKMAN

THE ESSENCE
A YIDDISH THEATRE DIM SUM

☞ written by Allen Lewis Rickman

☞ illustrated by Gary Dumm

FEATURING THE WORK OF AN AWFUL LOT OF GREAT YIDDISH PLAYWRIGHTS, LYRICISTS, AND COMPOSERS

I will tell you, ladies and gentlemen, how much better you understand Yiddish than you imagine.
—Franz Kafka, after attending a Yiddish play

The Yiddish theater lives on miracles.
—Joseph Buloff

This is an entertainment designed to be performed by three people:

STEVE,

YELENA,

& ALLEN.

The stage is bare, except for a piano, which is played by Steve and Yelena; and a piano bench, a chair, and a high stool, which are rearranged to form the various 'sets.' Upstage left is a coatrack full of costumes, hats, and hand props; upstage center and overhead is a screen on which supertitles are projected.

In the sections of the play where Yiddish is spoken, English translations appear in supertitles. Those translations are printed here on the left side of the page; the Yiddish spoken (or sung) onstage is printed in italics on the right, transliterated into appropriate dialects.

We begin in black with Yelena singing and Steve on piano. The lights come up gradually on her during the song.

In a corner of the Great Temple
sits a widow, Bas Tsion.

In a cradle nearby is Yidele, her only child.
She rocks him gently and sings this song.

In dem Beys Hamikdesh, in a vinkl kheyder *zitst di almune Bas Tsien aleyn*	
Ir ben-yukhidl, Yidele, vigt zi keseyder *in zingt im tsim shlufn a lidele sheyn*	

 Lights slowly up full. Allen speaks as Yelena continues the song.

 A lot of you may have heard this song, it's the most famous Jewish lullaby. But listen closely—it's more than that. Avrom Goldfadn, who wrote it, was a poet, and every word and image means something. The mother's name, Bas Tsion, is Hebrew; but her child's name, Yidele—"Little Jew"—isn't Hebrew, it's Yiddish. The mother is Ancient Israel; the child is everything since.

Under Yidele's cradle is a little
white goat. The goat has gone traveling.
Selling.

That will be your calling, too.
Selling raisins and almonds.
Sleep, Yidele.

Inter Yidele'z vigele *shteyt a klor-vays tsigele* *Dus tsigele iz gefurn handlen*
Dus vet zayn dayn beruf *Rozhinkes mit mandlen* *Shluf-zhe, Yidele, shluf*

 Here's the second verse.

This song, my child, is full of prophecy.
You shall be scattered all over the world.

You will be a merchant of all kinds of grain,
and you will be very successful.

And when that happens, Yidele, remember
this song, "Raisins and almonds."

That will be your calling—
Yidele will be in trade.

Sleep, Yidele.

In dem lidl, mayn kind, ligt fil neviyes *Az di vest amul zayn tzezeyt af der velt*
A soykher vesti zayn fin ale tvies *In vest in dem oykh fardinen fil gelt* *Ay-lu-lu…*
Az di vest vern raykh, Yidele, *Zolst zikh dermonen in dem lidele,* *"Rozhinkes mit mandlen"*
Dus vet zayn dayn baruf *Yidele vet alts handlen*
Shluf-zhe, Yidele, shluf

 Yidele was in trade because in the Diaspora the Jews were not allowed to own land. The goat comes from Jewish folklore; it's an image of loss. What Bas Tsion and Yidele have lost is Israel.

 That song is from the Yiddish theatre.

 Yiddish theatre. (pause) So what.

 You know, a lot of people don't understand Yiddish.

 A lot of people don't understand French, but they go to French movies.

But is theatre better when it's in Yiddish?

 All three look out, strike a contemplative pose, and say, "Hmmm."

 (thoughtfully) *Du ligt der hint bagrubn.* (thoughtfully) "That's where the dog is buried."

 You know, old people don't even say "Yiddish," they say "Jewish."

 Because the essence of 'Jewish'—the soul of 'Jewish'—is wrapped up in the Yiddish language.

 Joseph Papp said it was the *perfect* language for theatre. Its expressiveness is theatrical.

 That's because in Yiddish you can't just say things simply, you have to juggle the words and do tricks.

 Allow us to illustrate. In this scene three friends are out fishing. First, in English.

 They sit as on a boat and use dowels for fishing poles.

 Anything doing over there?

 Not a nibble.

 Nothing.

 This is just terrible.

 It's a total waste of time.

 Let's get out of here. Let's go get some sandwiches.

 I could go for a sandwich.

 Okay.

 …Boring, right? Okay, now here's the exact same scene in Yiddish. If you don't know the language, read the supertitles.

Anything doing over there? | *Vus tit zikh dortn?*

The plague of the firstborn. | *Makes bekhoyres.*

Fevers and kosher thread.

Kadukhes mit kusherer fudem.

 This is a hole in a fur sombrero.

Dus iz gor a lokh in spodek.

 It's useful during a ritual of penitence which entails waving a live chicken around your head.

Es toyg af kapures.

 Let's be rabbits. Let's go buy sandwiches.

Nu, lomir vern hozn. Mir'n geyn koyfn shnitkes.

 By me they wouldn't go barefoot.

Es vet nisht geyen bay mir borves.

 Agreed.

Opgemakht.

 You get the idea. They say that drama is life with the boring parts taken out. Translate life into Yiddish and it becomes theatrical.

 Yiddish theatre had enormous influence on the rest of American theatre. Acting styles. Directing. The most exciting, the most innovative set designers came from Yiddish theatre.

 Critics of all the major papers followed Yiddish theatre, even though there were no headsets, no supertitles, no translations. All those uptown writers—Percy Hammond, Brooks Atkinson, George Jean Nathan—the biggest *goyim* in the world, thought that Yiddish theatre was important.

 You know who else went to Yiddish theatre?

 Bing Crosby.

 Paul Robeson.

 Isadora Duncan.

 The King of Romania.

 The Queen of Holland.

 The Queen of Belgium.

 Not a one of them spoke Yiddish.

 In Paris even anti-Semites went to Yiddish theatre.

Molly Picon was sometimes called "The Jewish Helen Hayes." Helen Hayes went to one of Molly's shows, and afterward went to Molly's dressing room and said, "How do you do. I'm the *shiksa* Molly Picon."

 You know who else loved Molly Picon? Al Capone, the World's Greatest Gangster.

 Jacob P. Adler did THE MERCHANT OF VENICE on Broadway. The rest of the cast performed in Shakespeare's English; Adler played 'Shylock' in Yiddish. And the reviews were incredible.

 You know what else is incredible? The story of Yiddish theatre.

It starts like this:

 & &

Your dearest friends have gathered here to celebrate your birthday	*Tsu dayn gebortstog, tsu dayn yontif haynt* *Hobn zikh farzamelt dayne gute fraynt*
Everyone wishes you joy and happiness	*Yeder vinsht dir tsi getraye reyd* *fil nakhes un fil freyd*
You lovely child! We wish you health! Hurrah! Hurrah!	*Vivat, vivat, du libes kind!* *Vivat, mir vinshen dir gezint!* *Vivat, vivat, vivat!*

 That's the Jewish birthday song, and it also comes from a show by Goldfadn, who gave birth to the Yiddish theatre. Well, he was its father, anyway.

 Its mother was the Purim plays that Jews had put on for centuries, and sometimes still do. But its father was the failed newspaper publisher, failed medical student, failed teacher, failed ladies' hat shop manager, and successful poet, Avrom Goldfadn.

 Many of Goldfadn's poems had become popular songs. And one day in Jassy, Romania, in 1876, he was invited to perform at a wine garden.

 He went onstage dressed in a frock coat and cravat and recited a very long and very boring poem. The audience response? Absolute silence. Goldfadn understood: they were stupefied by his genius. So he recited them another poem. More silence. He started a third. By this time some people in the audience were ready to kill him. They had paid for entertainment, not to be bored into a coma by this windbag. A friend of Goldfadn's, a singer, yanked him offstage just as it was about to turn ugly; then the friend threw on a beard, jumped back onstage, and sang Goldfadn's song "The Happy Hassid."

 (plays and sings) Thank you, God, for your miracles and wonders— I married off my kids!

A dank dir, gotenyu, libhartsiger,
 getrayer, far ale dayne vinder!
 Kh'ob khasene gemakht, mit mayn vayb,
 ale mayne kinder!

 This the crowd loved.

Goldfadn got the point. The very next day he sat down and started writing theatre pieces in Yiddish, which is what he did for the rest of his life.

 He wrote the book, the music, the lyrics; he designed the sets, the costumes; he directed the shows, he produced them, he cast them—and there were no Yiddish actors yet, so he had to develop Yiddish actors too. And he and his various troupes toured his shows all over Eastern Europe.

 Some of the plots of Goldfadn's shows were original, some came from Jewish history, some from the Torah, and some from writers like George Eliot or Molière; sometimes his sources were absolutely ancient, 'bits' and scenes that you find in Italian *commedia*, in French clowning, in American burlesque. But when Goldfadn was done with them, they all seemed very Jewish.

☞ Allen comes DC as Hotsmakh, carrying a peddler's pack.

DI KISHUFMAKHERIN
The Witch

———◆◆◆———

by Avrom Goldfadn

☞ In a marketplace.

HOTSMAKH (chanting) Knicknacks and notions, priced to sell! You want expensive? Go to hell!

Tselnik! Tselnik! Koyft volvl benemunes, ikh zug aykh un leytsunes, ver s'vet veln tayer, der zol brenen in fayer! Tselnik! Tsel—

A MAN (Steve, at piano) What brings Hotsmakh here?

Vus tit ir du, Hotsmakh?

HOTSMAKH What brings Hotsmakh here?! "Take me, Satan!" What kind of question is that?!

A kashe vus Hotsmakh tit du, der rikh zol mikh nemen! Hotsmakh, in kik mikh un in kokh vetshere! Vus heyst?

I'm going around like I always do, to the coffeehouses, to the bars, to the sewers of hell—Take me, Satan!—looking to make a buck, brother! I got a wife and a crowd of kids! Take me, Satan!

Ikh gey mir vi mayn shteyger iz, fin di kave hayzelekh, fin di bir hayzelekh, fin al di shvartse yur, der rikh zol mikh nemen! Tomer vel ikh epes leyzn far skhoyre, parnuse, brider! A vayb mit a sakh kinderlakh, der rikh zol mikh nemen!

(chanting) Knicknacks and notions, priced to sell—

Koyft volvl benemunes, ikh zug aykh un leytsunes, ver s'vet veln—

A MEYDL (Yelena as an irritating adolescent) Do you have English needles?

Hotsmakh, Englishe nodlen hot ir?

HOTSMAKH Sure. They're so English they don't know one word of French. How many you need?

Nokh vus far Englishe, zey redn afile nisht eyn vort Frantsoyzish. Nor vifil darfste es, meydele?

MEYDL A gross, but—

A gros nodlen, ober—

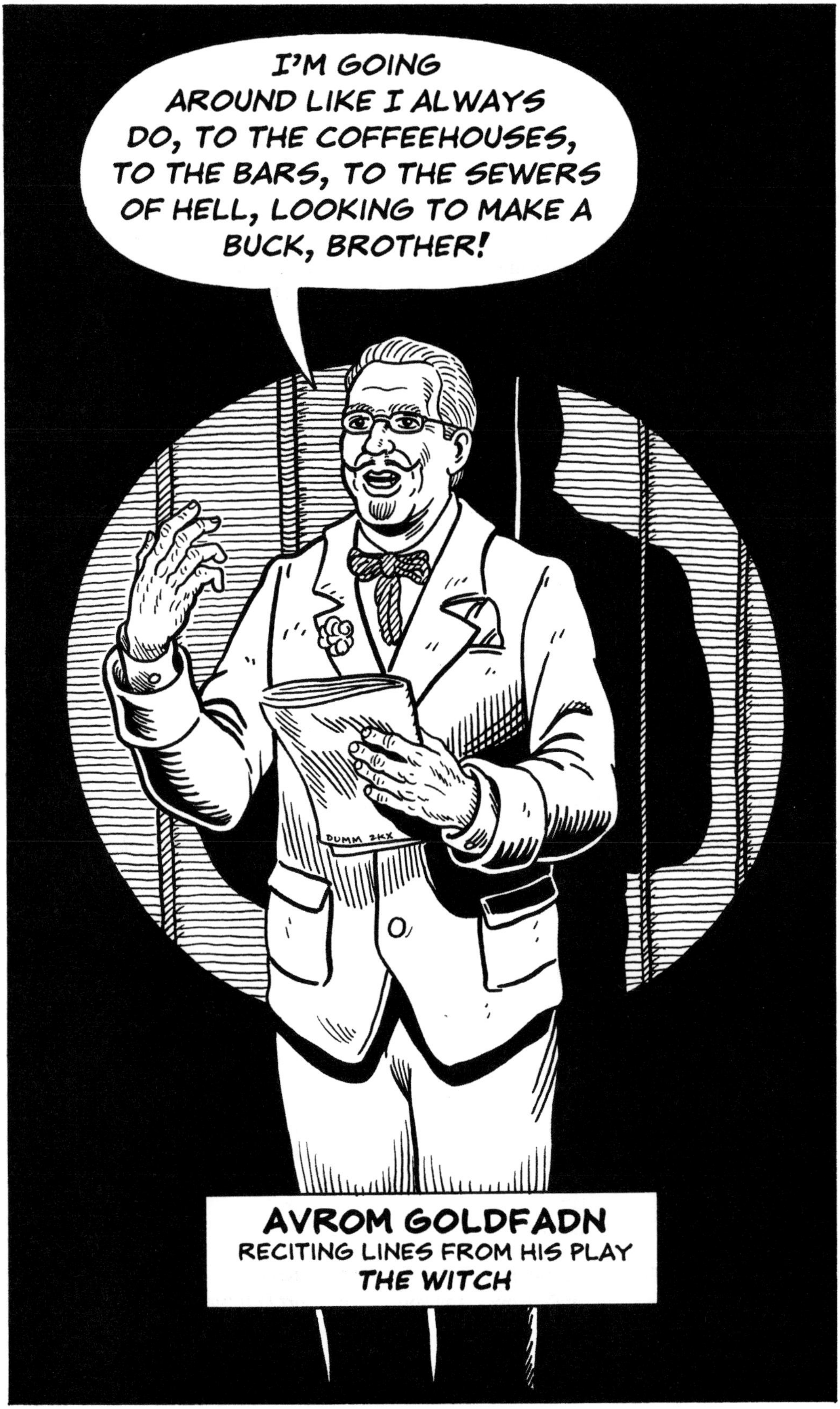
I'M GOING AROUND LIKE I ALWAYS DO, TO THE COFFEEHOUSES, TO THE BARS, TO THE SEWERS OF HELL, LOOKING TO MAKE A BUCK, BROTHER!
DUMM 2KX
AVROM GOLDFADN
RECITING LINES FROM HIS PLAY
THE WITCH

HOTSMAKH (opening his pack) A gross I sell very cheap.

MEYDL How much would it be?

HOTSMAKH Cheap! Thirty kopeks.

MEYDL That much?

HOTSMAKH If that's not less than I paid myself, may I not live to see my crowd of kids. But it's almost Sabbath, so let it go.

MEYDL It's too much. I'll give you twenty.

HOTSMAKH So young and already so sharp! All right, I'll take twenty-five. Hold out your hand and I'll count 'em out.

(counting them out into her hand) 1, 2, 3, 4, 5, 6—How old are you, that you can bargain like that already?

MEYDL I'm thirteen years old.

HOTSMAKH No kidding.

(counting)—13, 14, 15, 16, 17, 18, 19, 20—

And your father—you think I don't know him? That cheap crook!—how old is he?

MEYDL My father is thirty-five.

HOTSMAKH How do you like this kid, she lied about her own age, and now she's lying about her father's! She says he's thirty—?!! (she tries to correct him)

You can't fool me, your father's at least forty! You hear me? Forty!

(counting)—41, 42, 43, 44, 45, 46, 47, 48, 49, 50—

Look at her staring at me. Well, how old do you think I might be?

MEYDL Forty, I guess.

HOTSMAKH Forty—?!! I'm practically sixty!

A gros? A gros vel likh dir farkoyfn far velveler.

Vi tayer kost bay aykh a gros nodlen?

Nisht tayer. Draysik kopikes.

Draysik kopikes? Azoy tayer?

Ikh zol azoy derleybn aheym tsi kimen tsi mayn vayb mit a sakh kinderlakh vi es kost mikh aleyn tayerer. Nor vayl lekuved shabes gib ikh zey dir avek far velveler.

S'iz tsi tayer. Ikh vel aykh nor gebn tsvontsik kopikes.

Aza kleyn meydele, in hot shoyn azoy groys seykhl tsi dingen zikh. Nor derfar vel ikh dir lozn far finef-in-tsvontsik kopikes in shtrek oys dayn sheyn hentele in lomikh dir uptseyln.

Eyns, tsvey, dray, fir, finef, zeks—Zug mir nor, meydele, vifl biste es azoy ingantsn alt vus di kenst shoyn azoy git dingen?

Ikh bin alt draytsn yur.

Azoy? Draytsn? Her a mayse.

Draytsn, fertsn, fiftsn [. . .], nayntsn, tsvontsik—

In vifl ken alt zayn dayn tate zol leybn, meynst ikh ken im nit, dem roytn ganef, vifl iz er shoyn alt?

Mayn tate iz alt a yur finef-in-draysik.

Vi gefelt zi aykh, ikh beyt aykh, ire yurn hot zi farleyknt in dem tatn'z yurn vil zi oykh farleykenen, der tate irer zugt zi iz alt a yur draysik—

Nishkushe, vest mikh nisht upnarn, ikh veys az dayn tate iz shoyn altavade a yur fertsik. Herst? Fertsik!

Eyn-in-fertsik, tsvey-in-fertsik, dray-in-fertsik [. . .], fiftsik.

Ot kikste mikh un, meydele, vifl meynste ashteyger zol ikh alt zayn azoy vi di zeyst mikh mitn kleynem berdele, ah?

Ikh veys? Efsher fertsik yur.

Fertsik zugt zi. Ikh bin azoy pavolye korev tsi zekhtsik, yo-yo—

—61, 62, 63, 64, 65, 66, 67, 68, 69, 70, 71, 72, 73—

Eyn-in-zekhtsik, tsvey-in-zekhtsik, dray-in-zekhtsik [. . .], dray-in-zibetsik

(sighs) May we both live to my grandfather's age, he should rest in peace. Oh, my grandfather—he lived to 125! Yes, indeedy!

Oy, oy, oy, halevay voltn mir beyde geleybt azoy fil vifl mayn zeyde hot geleybt, ikh hob gehat a zeydn, olev hashulem, hot er geleybt hindert-finef-in-tsvontsik yur! Yo, yo—

...126, 127, 128
(*You get the idea.*)
...142, 143, 144.

Hindert-finef-in-tsvontsik, hindert-zeks-in-tsvontsik [. . .], Hindert-fir-in-fertsik.

There's five left, take 'em, no charge, okay? Now give me the money and don't drop any needles. Your mother might say I cheated you.

O, zeyste meydele, ot iz nokh ibergeblibn finef nodlen, na dir zey avek, ikh vel dir far zey kayn gelt nit rekhenen, erlekh? Na gib aher gelt, in gey gikh aheym in zey di zolst zey nit farlirn, varim dayn mame ken nokh zugn az ikh hob dir nit erlekh upgetseylt.

(exiting) Knicknacks and notions, priced to sell...

Tselnik! Tselnik! Koyft volvl benemunes, ikh zug aykh un leytsunes, ver s'vet veln tayer...

Meanwhile across the ocean, New York was just starting to fill up with Jews, and the immigrants who had seen the Goldfadn shows back home sang the songs constantly.

In 1882, six years after The Night in the Romanian Wine Garden, a punk kid named Boris Thomashefsky learned those songs from his friends in the sweatshop. Then one of them, a man named Golubok, showed him a poster of his brothers' Yiddish theatre troupe—which was at that moment in London, where they were busy starving.

So this thirteen-year-old hondler somehow convinced a local bar owner, a man named Frank Wolf, to put up money to bring the Golubok troupe over and to hire a theatre. The troupe came over, Wolf rented a theatre on East Fourth Street, and they started rehearsals for Goldfadn's DI KISHUFMAKHERIN. Hundreds of Jews stood outside the rehearsal hall hoping to hear a snatch of a song or a piece of a scene.

But not everybody was so happy about Yiddish theatre's coming to New York. The already established Jewish community—the *yekes*, the German Jews, who had gotten here first—they didn't like the idea at all.

The *yekes* were both educated and pretentious, and they wanted to blend in with the Gentiles like crazy. You know, in the early days of Reform Judaism—which was a German Jewish movement—there was even a campaign to move the Jewish Sabbath to Sunday, so they could be more like Christians.

The *yekes* were horrified by their Eastern European cousins.

(German accent) Zese people just didn't fit in! Lieber Gott, zey were so...Jewish!

And their language! It was—

It was not a language! It was a "jargon," a low corruption of the beautiful language of Goethe und Schiller und Heine.

Whatever.

 The *yekes* really hated Yiddish. And one day a big, tough-looking guy stopped in at the KISHUFMAKHERIN rehearsals and flashed some kind of badge. He asked who was in charge, and somebody pointed out the kid—Thomashefsky. The man with the badge told Thomashefsky that he had better show up the next morning before "The Official Immigration Committee." Young Boris and the Goluboks showed up.

☞ Allen puts on a monocle, climbs onto a stool, and becomes a maniacal *yeke* "judge," screaming in German at the cowering Yelena and Steve as Thomashefsky and Golubok.

JUDGE You intend to perform "Yiddish theater"? (they nod)	*Ir zayt das di artistn vas heybn an tsi shpiln "idish teater"?*
Who brought you to America?	*Ver hot aykh gebrakht kayn America?*
THOM. I came with my parents, and Mr. Frank Wolf brought the others.	*Ikh bin gekumen mit mayn tate-mame, un zey un di iberike fun der trupe hot aribergebrakht Mr. Frenk Volf.*
JUDGE Frank Wolf?!! The merchant of beer?!!	*Frenk Volf, der vas hat a salon auf Essex Street und verkauft bir?*
THOM. He—	*Er—*
JUDGE SILENCE!	*Shvayg, yunge!*
Is it true that in your play there's a peddler called "Hotsmakh" who swindles a poor young girl buying pins from him?	*Iz das vor az in dem shtik vas ir shpilt, kumt for ein pedler vas ruft zish "Hotsmakh," un az der Hotsmakh bashvindlt eine oremes maedchen velshe kauft bay im shpilkes?*
GOLUBOK No, English needl—	*Nisht shpilkes, Englishe nodl—*
JUDGE SHAME ON YOU!	*Shemen zolstu zikh!*
You shall not dare to perform your "Yiddish theatre"! And if you defy us, stand warned that within twenty-four hours you shall be deported from America on a cattle-boat!	*Ir zolt nit vagn tsi shpiln ir "idish teater"! Und oyb ir vet unz nit folgn un ir vet dokh vagn tsi shpiln, zolt ir visn az in fir-un-tsvansik shtundn tsayt veln mir aykh mit an oksn-shif rausshikn fon America.*
We'll send you back where you belong!	*Mir veln aykh shikn ahin vuhin ir balangt!*

 But rehearsals continued anyhow. Came the opening night, you couldn't even walk down East Fourth Street, it was so packed with people trying to buy tickets. At eight o'clock the cast and the twenty-member chorus were ready behind the curtain; the twenty-four-piece orchestra played the overture. The audience applauded and the curtain was about to go up. Then somebody realized that the lead actress, Madame Krantsfeld, wasn't onstage. They searched the theatre. She wasn't there. The orchestra was told to play the overture again and Thomashefsky, who had been cast in a small role, ran to Madame Krantsfeld's apartment. She was lying on the couch with a towel on her forehead.

THOM. What happened? They're playing the whole overture again! We have to start the show! Come on, get moving! | *Krantsfeld! Vus iz gesheyn? Men darf dokh shoyn onheybn shpiln, der orkester shpilt dokh shoyn dus tsveyte mul di overtura! Vus zitst ir du? Kimt!*

 She answered languidly.

KRANTSFELD (Yelena again) Oh! My head... Oh! My teeth... Oh! My throat... Et cetera... I can't perform tonight... Perhaps some other time. | *Der kop tit mir vey... Di tseyn raysn mir ... Ikh bin heyzerik oykh... Hakitser, haynt ken ikh nisht shpiln. Men miz opleygn di forshtelung biz ikh vel zikh filn beser.*

☞ A single cough.

 Young Boris begged. Young Boris pleaded. It didn't help.

THOM. It helped like 'cupping' would help a corpse. | *Es hot mikh geholfn azoy vi a toytn bankes.*

 Young Boris went back to the theatre alone, by which time the orchestra had left. The chorus had left. Most of the audience had left. Those that remained entertained themselves by tearing the building to pieces. That was Day One of Yiddish theatre in America.

 Soon enough the truth came out: the *yekes* had paid Madame Krantsfeld three hundred dollars—which was a hell of a lot of money in 1882—and promised to set up her husband with a soda fountain on the Bowery, all in exchange for her agreeing not to appear that night.

 But needless to say, Yiddish theatre took off in America anyhow; also needless to say, Madame Krantsfeld was not to be a part of it. How successful Mr. Krantsfeld's soda fountain was is a fact that is lost to history.

 By the mid-1880s the Lower East Side was *ungeshtupt mit yidn*—'stuffed with Jews.' You couldn't swing a cat without knocking over six Jews. (Which was a very popular pastime in certain neighborhoods.) They came from all over Eastern Europe. Hundreds of thousands of them.

 Imagine yourself as one of those people. You pack a few bags, climb onto a wagon, and leave your home forever. There are no telephones, no video, no airplanes—you will never see or speak to your family, your friends again. You go to a place you know almost nothing about and start your whole life over. Is anyone that brave today?

 But America had no pogroms, no cossacks, no real anti-Semitism; it was nothing like Europe. Even better, it was the land of the Free Market, and there was no limit to what you could achieve. The Jews loved it, and the Yiddish theatre was filled with songs like this.

Zay Gebentsht, Du Fraye Land
Bless You, Land of Freedom

 & words by A. Shmerlewitz, music by Joseph Rumshinsky

Every Jew should express his loyalty to this Land of Freedom!	*Oysdrikn trayhayt tsi dize land fin frayhayt tin darf der Yid mit zayn yedes glid!*
When he comes here, he treasures this country—It gives him rights!	*Kimt er du zikh bazetsn, vet er visn tsi shetsn dus land vus git im fule rekht—Yo, yo!*
He doesn't miss the whip He remembers what life used to be like	*Nokh dem knut mer nit benken, eybik vet er gedenken az im iz ven gevezn shlekht*
Oy, become a citizen and live forever!	*Oy, oy, ver a birger, krig papirn, vesti eybik ekzistirn*
You'll be Uncle Sam's cousin—Vote!	*Oy, oy, ver nor Onkl Sem's mekhuten, zey du zolst nor kenen vutin*
Vote and be powerful! No one can harm you!	*Shtim up, vesti mekhtig zayn! Keyner vet kenen dir shlekhtes tin!*
And the world will again respect the Jewish nation, which honors the American flag	*In di velt vet vider shetsn fayn di yidishe natsyon Es bashitst di Amerikaner fon*
A blessing on this free land It's a marvel, especially to the Jews	*Geloybt un gebentsht zol zayn dus fraye land. S'iz a glik in iberhoypt far inz Yidn*
She reaches out the hand of friendship She gives us rights and joy and peace	*Frayndlekht raykht zi inz di hant, git inz rekhte, freyd, in fridn*
Become a citizen and have a voice Work hard and you'll do well	*Verst nor a birger, host a glaykhe deye Arbet nor flaysig, makhste di matbeye*
Give your children a happy life Bless you, Land of Freedom!	*Brengst dayne kinder tsi a gitn shtand Zay gebensht, di fraye land*
Jews are bankers, doctors, engineers, businessmen…	*Yidn bankirn, doktoyrim, inzhenirn Der miskher blit vi es kimt der Yid*
Just look at the stores on Broadway! At the stock market on Wall Street!	*In Brodvey zey gesheftn, internemen mit kreftn Vol Strit, a berze spekulant, yo, yo*
Sculpture, music, journalism, theatre—Jews can do everything here!	*Skulptur, muzik, nigine, zhurnalizm, in bine, dus ligt du in dem Yidn's land*
You can fill up the valleys with rocks and make roads!	*Oy, oy, berg mit shteyner trugst di iber in di tife toln griber*
Put the masses into mansions!	*Oy, oy, in di makhst dort glaykhe gasn, shtelst in raykhe hayzer masn*
No one can stop you, do what you want Here you're as good as anybody else	*Du versti keynmul nisht geshtert. Vus di vilst, kensti tin. In vi ale host du a glaykher vert*
The Jewish nation honors the American flag	*Di Yidishe natsyon es bashitst di Amerikaner fon*

 And now for:

AN IRRELEVANT INTERLUDE

 You know, you can tell a lot about a language—and about what's important to its speakers—by picking apart the vocabulary. For example, the Eskimos have dozens of words for snow.

 French is full of words for romance.

 And Yiddish has literally hundreds of ways to say—

☛ All three turn to the screen; it says, "Imbecile."

 I will now recite some modest examples.

 &   We will translate them for you.

     &

Nar.	Imbecile.
Tam.	Imbecile.
Ivan.	Imbecile.
Bulvan.	Imbecile.
Vayzusu.	Imbecile.
Beheyme betsuras odom.	Imbecile.
Pore adume.	Imbecile.
Idyot gomur.	Complete Imbecile.
Oks.	Imbecile.
Eyzl.	Imbecile.
Yankl Dondik. Avreymele Melamed.	John Q. Imbecile and his cousin.
Yold.	Imbecile.
Yolopatron.	Imbecile.
Teyrekh.	Imbecile.
Tipesh shebitipshim.	Imbecile.
Krimer kop.	Imbecile.
Kelbl.	Imbecile.
Kuni-leml.	Imbecile.
Moyshe Yoyne, Moyshe Yokl, Yokl ben Flekl.	Imbecile, Imbecile, Imbecile.
Shoyte, shmoyger, she'eynu yoydeye lishoyl.	Three More Imbeciles.
Shmendrik.	Imbecile.
Shmegde mit eysik.	Marinated Imbecile.
A kop vi an eysev.	A head like an Imbecile.
A goylem af redlekh.	Imbecile on Skates.
Loksh.	Imbecile.
Lekish.	Imbecile.
Loshik.	Imbecile.
Poyer. Khamoyer.	Imbecile. Imbecile.

Shtik holts, shtik ferd, shtik fleysh mit tsvey oygn.

 ...Well, that's poetry.

 &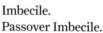

Imbecile.
Imbecile.

Muzhik.
Zhlob.

Khelmer khazn's indik.

The pet turkey of the idiot cantor in the town full of Imbeciles; in other words—

 & & Imbecile.

Khoyzek.
Khukhem fin der ma nishtane.
And, of course,
Shmuel Mordkhe Kalmen. (pause)

Imbecile.
Passover Imbecile.

 Sh-*shmuel*.

 M-*mordkhe*.

 K-*kalmen*. (pause) Put the initials together.

 And now back to our story.

 Remember the immigrants? Well, in a very short time they would all be Americanized. Some of them, maybe, too Americanized. In this scene Menakhem-Yoysef and Jack, two shady vaudeville producers, are looking for a new attraction.

Moshiakh In Amerike
The Messiah in America

by Moshe Nadir

☞ In Menakhem-Yoysef's midtown office.

MENAKHEM (Allen) There's nothing going on here! We need to get cooking, capeesh?	*M' darf epes nayes! Es zol zikh ton! S'hot shoyn lang nisht geton. Farshteystu mikh?*
JACK (Steve) Sure I 'capeesh,' my head ain't skinny.	*Avade farshtey ikh, mayn kop iz nisht oysgedart.*
MENAKHEM What about that Swedish Ballet?	*Vos iz gevorn mitn Shvedishn balet, Dzhekele?*
JACK They want too much money.	*S'iz gurnisht gevorn. Zey farlangen tsifil gelt.*
MENAKHEM There ain't no 'too much'—the more they get, the more they're worth. How much do they want?	*In teater-gesheft iz nishto kayn tsufil. Vos mer gelt an artist krigt, alts mer an artist iz er. Vifil viln zey, di Shvedishe tentser?*
JACK $3,200 a week.	*Tsvey-un-draysik hunderter a vokh.*
MENAKHEM That's too much. Besides, they dance too good, people won't like 'em.	*Dos iz tsufil! Akhuts dem zenen zey tsi-gute tentser. Dem Amerikanem oylem veln zey nisht gefeln.*
How about a cute tootsie that shot a few guys? Or some dame that jumped off a building and lived?	*Vos redt zikh vegn epes a tsatskele vos hot geshosn etlekhe mener? Oder epes a sheyn meydl vos iz aropgeshpringen fin eyn-un-tsvansikstn etazh un nisht derharget gevorn?*
JACK Well, there's one girl...	*S'du eyner aza froy...*
MENAKHEM What'd she do?	*Vos hot zi geton?*
JACK Swallowed her own teeth three times. She's in all the papers.	*Zi hot shoyn dray mul arayngeshlingen di eygene tseyn. Di bleter zenen fil mit ir.*
MENAKHEM Great, bring her in, we'll put her name up in lights! Can she sing?	*Gut, breng zi aher, mirn aroysshteln ir nomen in droysn farn teater in elektrishe oysies. Ken zi zingen?*
JACK No.	*Neyn.*
MENAKHEM Dance?	*Ken zi tantsn?*
JACK No.	*Oykh nisht.*
MENAKHEM Play an instrument?	*Ken zi shpiln af an instrument?*
JACK No.	*Oykh nisht.*
MENAKHEM Walk the high wire? Juggle?	*Ken si geyn af a shtrik? Ken zi heklen a zak mit di fis?*
JACK No.	*Oykh nisht.*
MENAKHEM She pretty?	*Iz zi a sheyne?*

JACK No. All she does is swallow her teeth.	*Oykh nisht. Zi ken gurnisht, akhits shlingen di eygene tseyn.*
MENAKHEM Maybe later in the season. Right now we need something bigger, something that 'cooks,' capeesh?	*Efsher shpeter in sezon. Ober itst darf men epes a gresere zakh, s'zol a nem ton, s'zol zikh epes tu-en, farshteyst?*
JACK I got it!	*Ikh hob es!*
MENAKHEM What?	*Vos?*
JACK A spitter!	*A . . . shpayer!*
MENAKHEM Come again?	*A shpayer? Vos heyst a shpayer?*
JACK It's the latest thing. It's this kid who spits farther than anybody. His record's six yards.	*S'iz a nayer zakh. S'do a bokher vus er ken shpayen vayter fin ale menshn. Zayn rekord iz zeks meter.*
MENAKHEM That's all? He's probably been outspat already.	*Zeks meter iz gornisht aza metsie. Mir dukht zikh az m'hot im shoyn aribergeshpign.*
JACK What are you talking about? Nobody spat six yards except "The Philadelphia Spitter," and he's dead!	*Vus red ir, mister Menakhem-Yoysef? Zeks meter hot bay inz nokh keyner nisht geshpign, akhits dem Philadelphia Shpayer. In yener iz shoyn geshtorbn!*
MENAKHEM *Sic transit gloria mundi . . .* How much does he want?	*Ot azoy shtarbn op di beste mener fun land. Vifl vet er nemen?*
JACK The spitter? Four hundred and fifty berries a show. Look, the kid earns it.	*Der shpayer? Er't nemen fir hindert in fiftsik tuler a forshtelung. Kh'meyn az er fardint dus erlekh.*
MENAKHEM Okay, but it's too much. What am I, some dreamer, I'm trying to bring on the Messiah or something?	*Fardinen fardint er dos avade, nor far mir iz dos tsufil. Arbetn lesheym ideal bin ikh nisht mekhuyev, ikh vil nisht aropbrengen moshiakhn.*
JACK Wait a minute—Why not bring on the Messiah? Ain't that as good as a spitter?	*Moshiakhn! . . . Shat, farvus take nisht arupbrengen moshiakhn? Az m'ken makhn a tuler, farvus nisht? Mit vus iz moshiakh erger fin dem shpayer?*
MENAKHEM This just 'yack-yack,' or you mean business?	*Du redst glat azoy, tsi du meynst 'business'?*
JACK I mean business. Look, America has so-and-so-many Jews. Am I right or am I right?	*Ikh meyn 'business.' Ir farshteyt, s'iz azoy: In Amerike hobn mir hekher azoy-fil-un-azoy-fil yidn. Bin ikh gerekht, tsi neyn?*
MENAKHEM Okay.	*Gerekht.*
JACK Okay. And every one of 'em is waiting for the Messiah, and they can each buy a ticket for, say, $1.75. Am I right or am I right?	*Ni, git, in yeder yid vart az moshiakh zol kimen. In yeder yid vus vart az moshiakh zol kimen ken koyfn, zugn mir, a bilet far* (beat) *a tuler mit finef-un-zibetsik-tsent. Bin ikh gerekht, tsi neyn?*
MENAKHEM Okay.	*Gerekht.*

JACK	Okay. Now, two thousand tickets a night…at \$1.75 apiece…is \$3,500 a night. Am I right or am I right?	*Iz rekhenen mir azoy: a tsvey toyznt menshn a nakht tsi a tuler mit finef-in-zibetsik-sent, hobn mir azoy groys vi dray toyznt finef hindert tuler a nakht. Bin ikh gerekht, tsi neyn?*
MENAKHEM	O-kay!…But where do you dig up a Messiah?	*Gerekht. Nor vu nemt men a moshiakhn?*
JACK	Don't interrupt, I'm calculating. Hey, we can do private salvations too. We'll make a 'Salvation Society' with the Messiah's name…What's the name of the Jewish Messiah?	*Vart oys, dervayl rekhenen mir. Akhits di dray-toyznt-finef-hindert tuler a forshtelung, kenen mir nokh hobn private oysleyzingen oykh. Mir'n makhn an aktsien-oysleyz-gezelshaft, af moshiakh's numen take. Vi heyst er dortn, der yidisher moshiakh?*
MENAKHEM	Hell if I know.	*Der ruekh veyst im.*
JACK	Never mind, we'll call it "The First Messiah Salvation Society." We'll charge five bucks a share—fifteen shares and you're saved.	*Ni, git, s'makht nisht oys. Mir rifn di gezelshaft aynfakh—"Di Ershte Moshiakh Oysleyz-Gezelshaft," tsi a finef tuler an aktsie, in az m'hot fiftsn aktsies, vert men oysgeleyzt.*
MENAKHEM	From what?	*Fun vos?*
JACK	Who cares? We'll be cookin' with gas. It's a nice idea, right?	*Vus iz der khilek? Der iker iz s'vet zikh a bisl tien. Ayo, s'iz an aynfal?*
MENAKHEM	It's a nice idea. Best of all, it's democratic. No more rich and poor—you pay five bucks a week, and you're saved.	*An aynfal iz dos. Iberhoypt gefelt mir di idey vayl zi iz a demokratishe. Nishto bay unz kayn orem un kayn raykhver s'git finef dolar, der vert oysgeleyzt.*
JACK	Like a layaway plan.	*M'ken oysleyzn af rates.*
MENAKHEM	The more I think about it, the more I like it. It's better than the spitter.	*Haklal, Jack, vos mer ikh batrakht di zakh, alts mer gefelt zi mir. Dos gefelt mir nokh beser funem shpayer.*
	Nothing against the spitter, you understand; hell, we turn dollars on the Messiah, we'll bring out the spitter too…The question is, where do you find a Messiah?	*Dos heyst, der shpayer iz oykh nisht shlekht, zolst nisht meynen, nor er vil tsufil gelt. Az mir'n makhn gelt bay moshiakhn, veln mir dernokh kenen aropbrengen dem shpayer oykh. Di gantse zakh iz, vu nemt men a…moshiakhn?*

☞ They pace back and forth, racking their brains.

| JACK | I got it! I have a greenhorn uncle, he's only in the country two weeks. *Peyes*, black coat, the whole shebang. Lemme call him. (into phone) Hello, Jackson 4031…Yes. | *Vi nemt men a moshiakhn? Shat, ikh hob es—Ikh hob a grinem feter. Er iz ersht tsvey vokhn fun Galitsye. Er trugt nokh a sametenem kapelyush in peyesshat, ikh vel im bald unklingen.* |
| | (to Menakhem) If we can get— | *Ven m'ken im aynredn—* |

JACK (into phone) Uncle Simcha? It's Jack. Listen, come over here, I have a job for you. Take the trolley car up to Forty-third Street and—What?...Of course for money!...Okay.	*Helo, feter! Feter Simkhe! Dus redt Jack...Yankl...Yo, Yankl. Hert, feter, ikh hob far aykh a gesheftl. Khapt zikh ariber aher. Nemt di troli-kar in geyt arup af der dray-in-fertsikster gas...Vus?...Yo, avade! Vuden, imzist?...Ni, git.* Good-bye.

 Hangs up.

If that baby ain't an A-Number-One Messiah, then I'm a Dutchman. And we'll get him cheap too, 'cause he needs work. See, he can't stand on his feet too long, he got a hernia.	*Er kimt shoyn. Oyb dus iz nisht der emeser moshiakh, veys ikh nisht vus. Der iker, m'ken im krign volvl, vayl er geyt arim un arbet. In datsu iz er nokh a kranker oykh, tsi lang af di fis ken er nisht shteyn, er hot nebekh a kilye.*
MENAKHEM Who cares? A Jewish Messiah oughtta have a hernia.	*S'makht nisht, farkert, s'iz nokh shener! A yidisher moshiakh darf hobn a kilye.*
(realizes) We'll need something for the papers. When's he coming?	*Mir'n darfn hobn epes far di bleter. Ven kumt er, der moshiakh?*
JACK Any minute.	*Er kimt bald.*
MENAKHEM Take this down: "Jews Rejoice! The Messiah Is Coming Any Minute!"	*Nu, gut, shrayb tsi: "Yidn Derfreyen Zikh Moshiakh Kumt Bald!"*

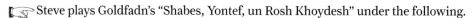

 Steve plays Goldfadn's "Shabes, Yontef, un Rosh Khoydesh" under the following.

 Even Goldfadn eventually came to America. But for him it was too late. He was an old man, and his folksy style of playwriting was passé—heavy drama by Jacob Gordin was the 'in' thing. The only source of income he had was a small stipend from Jacob P. Adler and Boris Thomashefsky. Charity.

He did have one play left in him: it was called BEN AMI, and it was about a European aristocrat who rediscovers his Jewish heritage and ends up as a farmer in Palestine. Adler bought the rights, but he lost interest; then Goldfadn asked if he could read it aloud to the company. That was a mistake.

 We see Allen as Goldfadn isolated in a spotlight, reading the script in pantomime; we hear a snickering crowd.

The reading was a disaster. Adler's troupe laughed at him. And one minor actor decided to tell Goldfadn exactly what they all thought.

 Steve stops playing and becomes the actor.

ACTOR What kind of old-fashioned garbage is this? It doesn't even make sense! You don't even know what you put on the paper! You're senile, grandpa!	*Vus iz dus? Vus far an alte skhoyre derlangste inz? Vus far a farfoylte vetshere? Es leygt zikh afile nisht afn seykhl! In di veyst shoyn nisht vus di host aleyn geshribn. Bist ingantsn oyver butl! S'iz shoyn oys mit dir!*

Goldfadn was devastated. For months afterward he begged his wife and his friends to reassure him.

GOLDFADN Is it true, Paulina? Am I senile? Tell me the truth, I'm begging you...

Zug mir, zug mir, Paulina—Iz dus emes? Bin ikh take oyver butl gevorn? Zug mir dem emes, ikh beyt dir...

 Eventually he decided to try again. He went to Adler and got back the rights to BEN AMI, and arranged to read it to Thomashefsky's company. This time it went beautifully, and Thomashefsky decided to produce it.

Opening night was a triumph. Thunderous applause, cheering, tons of flowers; the old man was praised to the skies, and a crowd of fans followed him back to his doorstep. He adjusted a huge garland that hung around his neck and walked in.

GOLDFADN Look, Paulina, look! I'm not senile! I'm not sen—

Kik, Paulina, kik vus zey hobn mir gegebn! Ikh bin nisht oyver butl! Ikh bin nisht oyver...

 Goldfadn silently breaks down.

 He attended every performance of BEN AMI and watched, beaming, from a box. Then three weeks later, in his sleep, Avrom Goldfadn passed away.

Thirty thousand mourners went to his funeral. And BEN AMI ran for months and months.

 Lights change

 Okay, now let's talk about crap.

 A lot of people who don't know anything about Yiddish theatre think that it was all trashy melodramas. Of course it wasn't, but those kinds of plays did exist. They were called *shund*.

 Shund is "crap" in Yiddish. No question, plenty of Yiddish theatre was—and is—crap. But that's only sensible. Most theatre in general is crap.

 And why not? Most fiction is crap.

 Most poetry is crap.

 Most paintings are crap.

 Most movies are crap.

 Most music is crap.

Practically everything on television is crap. So what?

 & & This next scene which we will present to you is: crap.

Blume, the shoemaker's daughter, refuses to follow her parents' advice and marry Borukh, the gentle fruit peddler, who has long loved her silently from afar. Instead she marries Walter Steinfeld, the debonair bon vivant and man-about-town, who promises to take her out of her parents' humble basement apartment and introduce her to a more sophisticated lifestyle. This scene is from Act Two; they've been married for eight months.

DEM SHUSTER'S TOKHTER
The Shoemaker's Daughter

by Nahum Rakov (?)

☞ In the Steinfeld apartment.

BLUME (Yelena) Weren't we planning to go to Long Beach for dinner?

Valter… Mir hobn gezolt forn nokh Long Beach in dort hobn diner. Azoy gloyb ikh hosti haynt gezogt—?

WALTER (Steve) I can't go. I have to see someone important.

Ikh ken haynt nisht forn nokh Long Beach. Ikh hob tsi zeyn a vikhtige perzon.

BLUME Business?

WALTER Yes, business.

BLUME You're always busy…

Di verst imertsu bize in ovent.

Is this the marriage a young girl dreams of? I don't even know what you do for a living!

Iz dos di heyrat fin velkhe a meydl troymt ir gantse yugnd? Di bist mayn man in ikh veys afile nit vos iz mayn man'z basheftigung!

WALTER That's not your concern. If you lacked for anything, then you might complain—but you don't lack, you have too much!

Mayn basheftigung darf dikh nisht interesirn. Ven dir vet feln, dan vesti hobn a rekht tsi baklogn zikh. Dir felt nor nisht—di host fil, tsi fil.

I believe the move from beggary to extravagance has unsettled you. You're confused. That basement—

Ikh gloyb az di pletslikher ibergang fin ormut tsi luksus hot dikh baroysht. In di veyst shoyn aleyn nisht vos di vilst. Der beysment—

BLUME Again the basement! Stop reminding me of the basement! I was happy in the basement! My parents loved me in the basement! But here—

Vider der beysment! Nor dos haltsti mikh in eyn dermonen! In beysment bin ikh geveyn gliklekh. Ikh hob dort genosn di libe fun a foter, a muter, in do hob ikh es nisht—

You're stealing my soul from me! My parents must hide like thieves when they try to visit their only child!

Di roybst fin mir avek mayn gayst. Vi ganovim darfn mayne eltern bahaltn zikh ven zey viln kumen aher zeyn zeyer blit in fleysh, zeyer eyntsik kind.

WALTER I loathe your parents. I can't abide them. They nauseate me. I don't want them or their friends in my home. And so long as you bear my name, forget the basement! Forswear the cobblery!

Ikh has zey. Ikh ken zey nisht dulden. Zeyere banemungen, zeyere ziten eklen mikh. Ikh vil nisht zey in vil nisht zeyere fraynt hobn do in hoyz. In ikh vil as di, zolang di trogst mayn nomen, zolsti fargesn in beysment. In shister-tishl.

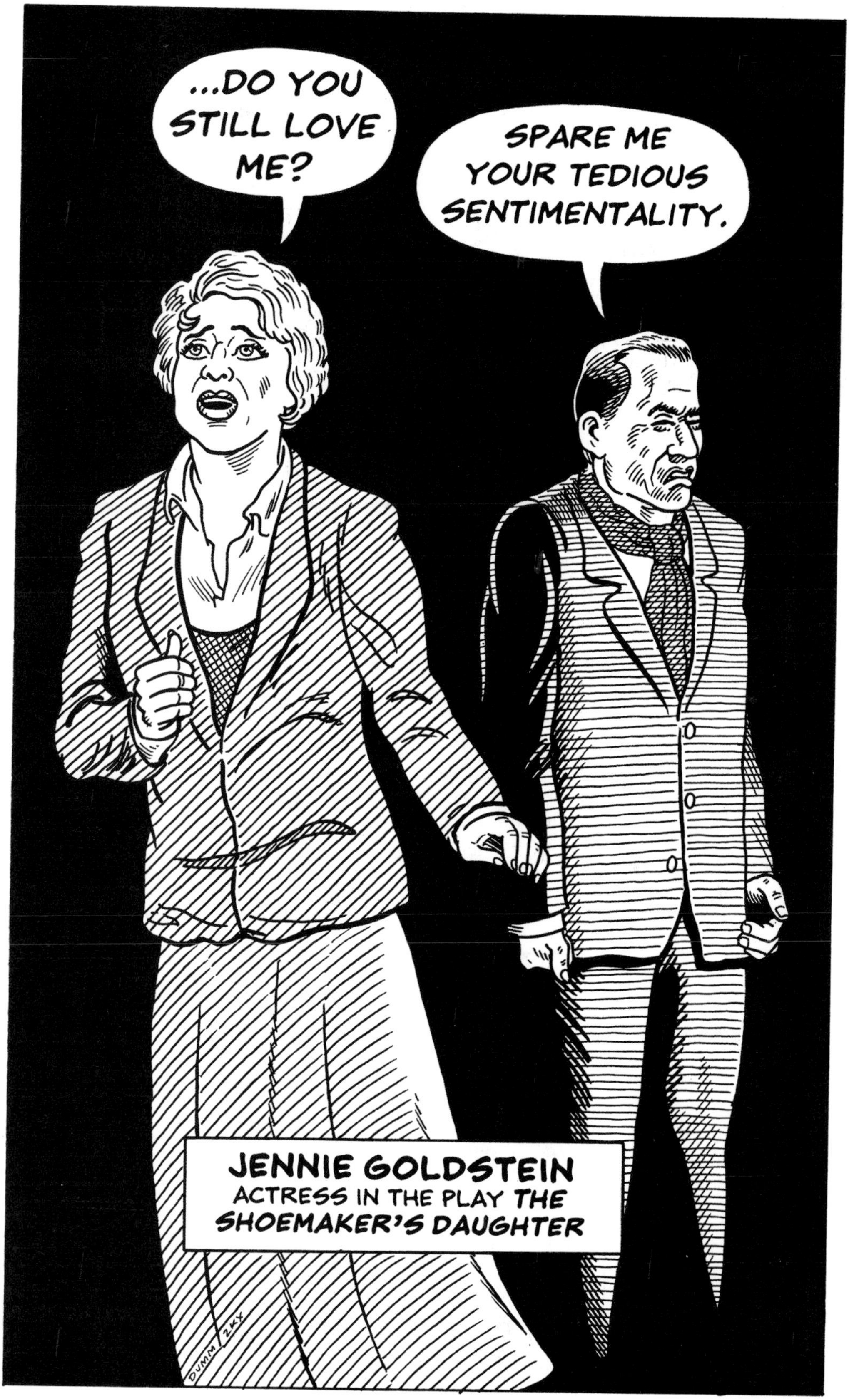
...DO YOU STILL LOVE ME?
SPARE ME YOUR TEDIOUS SENTIMENTALITY.
JENNIE GOLDSTEIN
ACTRESS IN THE PLAY THE SHOEMAKER'S DAUGHTER
DUMM 2KX

WALTER (cont'd) You must erase your former life.

Iberhoypt mek oys ingantsn di fargangenhayt fin dayn lebn.

BLUME Do you still love me?

Walter, libst mikh nit mer?

WALTER Spare me your tedious sentimentality.

Vi di langvaylegst mikh mit dayn narishen sentimentalizm!

BLUME Walter, I'm...I'm going to have a baby.

Walter...Ikh fil...Ikh...Ikh gey bald vern muter fin dayn kind.

WALTER Oh, hell.
Wretched little calf...

Shleperisher gayst glaykht kinder...

(to her) Now listen carefully: I don't like children. You go see Dr. Weinmann, and he will—

Di beser...Di farshteyst mikh vos ikh vil zogn. Ikh glaykh nisht kayn kinder. Baret zikh deriber mit Doktor Vaynmann in er vet—

BLUME Brute! Scoundrel! (starts to exit)

Brut! Shuft! Kanalie!

WALTER Take that back— (grabs her arm)

Tsi tsirik dayne verter—

BLUME No! Let me go! You're a disgusting parasite!

Keyn mol...Loz mikh geyn. Di ekelst mikh. Di bist a parazit.

WALTER The more that I disgust you, the more will I command you. You have no rights—my desire is your desire!

Vos mer ikh vel dikh eklen alts mer vel ikh dikh bahershen. Di host keyn rekht tsi hobn an eygenem viln. Mayn viln iz dayn viln—

BLUME Let me go!

Loz mikh geyn—

WALTER I don't want your soul—it's your body that intoxicates me! That's why I took you from that filthy basement!

Ikh darf nisht dayn gayst. Dayn kerper reytst mikh. Tsulib dayn kerper hob ikh dikh aroysgenimen fin beysment. Fin ormut. Fin shmuts.

And I've paid you for it with opulence and plenitude! You are my property, to do with as I wish!

Ikh hob dir derfar batsolt mit raykhtum. Mit luksus. Dayn sheyner kerper iz mayn eygntum in ikh ken im hobn ven ikh vil in vi azoy ikh vil.

He kisses her and cackles psychotically.

WALTER Now you know what you are!

Itst veysti vus di bist! Itst veysti ver di bist!

BLUME Tyrant!

Tiran!

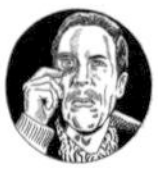
Then she runs off and the maid enters.

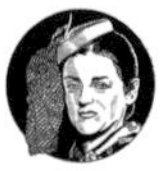
Ladies and Gentlemen—crap.

They bow.

Shund is a very strange kind of escapism. In conventional American crap—think of, say, Mary Pickford movies, or B musicals—the poor girl marries the rich man and lives happily ever after. In *shund* the poor girl marries the rich man and he turns out to be an abusive drunken gambler.

 That's entertainment. Jennie Goldstein was a big star of those plays—my grandmother was crazy about her—and she specialized in playing working girls whose lives were absolute hell-on-earth. The *New York Times* once wrote about her, quote, "Miss Goldstein counts that day on stage lost in which she does not spend a little time either in the gutter or in a psychopathic ward." Her husband used to write those parts for her… Yeah, that must've been a healthy marriage.

 In one of Herman Yablokoff's plays there was a scene where he was in prison. So, naturally, of course, he has to sing about it. He lets himself out of his cell, walks downstage, sings something like "Oy, I Hate Being in Prison," then goes back upstage and locks himself back in.

 Speaking of Herman Yablokoff—how many people here have had occasion to use that phrase in a conversation? show of hands?—He's probably best remembered as the man who wrote "Papirosn."

 "Papirosn" is the most shamelessly maudlin song ever written by anybody.

 Remember "Alone Again Naturally"? Okay, multiply that by ten.

 Let me play it for you. (sits at piano and plays)

 Let me sing it for you.

 Allow me to translate.

PAPIROSN
Cigarettes
from Papirosn

——•——

by Herman Yablokoff

 It is a dark and stormy night.

A sad young man looks around.

He holds out a little basket and pleads with his eyes—

"I have no more strength to wander the streets!

I'm hungry! and I'm soaking wet!

Please buy my cigarettes.

 A kalte nakht a regndike finster imetim

Shteyt a yingele fartroyert un kikt zikh arim

Fin regn shtist im nor a vant, a koshikl halt er in hant, in zayne oygn betn yedn shtim

"Ikh hob shoyn nisht kayn koyekh mer arimtsigeyn in gas

Hingerik in upgerisn fin dem regn nas

Kupitye koyft-zhe, koyft-zhe papirosn,

| They're dry. | *Trikene fin regn nisht fargosn.* |
| | |

| They're cheap. Buy them. Pity me. I'm starving." | *Koyft-zhe bilig benemunes, Koyft, oy hot af mir rakhmunes, Ratevet fin hinger mikh atsind…"* |

 It goes on.

| "My father lost his hands in the war. | *Mayn tate in milkhome hot farloyrn zayne hent,* |

| Mom couldn't take it. | *Mayn mame hot di tsores mer oys-haltn nisht gekent.* |

| She died young, leaving me miserable, and lonely as a rock. | *Ying in keyver zi getribn, bin ikh af der velt farblibn, imgliklekh in elnt vi a shteyn.* |

| I live on crumbs that I gather up in the marketplace. | *Breklekh klayb ikh af tsim esn af dem kaltn mark,* |

| I sleep on a bench in the park. It's cold. | *A harte bank iz mayn geleger in dem kaltn park.* |

| And policemen beat me with swords, despite my begging them to stop. | *In dertsu di politsyantn, shlugn mikh mit shverdn, kantn, s'helft nit mayn betn, mayn geveyn.* |

Steve sings the chorus straight through as Allen translates.

| Buy my cigarettes, please…I'm starving …And I'm freezing…And I'm starving and freezing and my mother is dead and my father is dead and I'm dying and freezing and I'm soaking wet…" | *Kupitye koyft-zhe, koyft-zhe papirosn…"* |

 But wait, there's more.

| "I had a little sister once…" | *"Ikh hob gehat a shvesterl, a kind fin der natur…"* |

(pause) Anybody not see where this is heading?

| "She shlepped around with me a whole year. | *"Mit mir tsizamen zikh geshlept hot zi a gants yur.* |

| Then all of a sudden she got very, very sick. | *Mit amul gevorn iz zi shvakh in zeyer krank,* |

| I held her on a bench and she died. | *Af mayne hent iz zi geshtorbn af a gasn-bank.* |

| I wish I was dead, too. | *In az ikh hob zi farloyrn, hob ikh ales ungevoyrn, zol der toyt shoyn kimen oykh tsi mir.* |

| Buy my cigarettes, please…" | *Kupitye koyft-zhe, koyft-zhe papirosn…"* |

 There are razor blades at the concession stand for those who feel the need… Everybody, sing! (Etc., and it ends.)

And now for something competely different—the shtetl plays.

 By World War One the European Jews had been in America for decades. They knew that life here could be frantic, like Menakhem-Yoysef, or cynical, like Walter Steinfeld, or just plain phony, like "Papirosn." And many of them started feeling nostalgic about the villages that they, or maybe their parents, had left.

 The shtetl plays were about how people imagined home, imagined the past, imagined where they came from…like what we might think Orchard Street or Brownsville used to be like. They were stories about simple people who lived in tight-knit communities and thought the world would never change.

 Leon Kobrin's YANKEL BOYLE takes place in a community that's so small it's not even a shtetl—there aren't even enough Jews there for a minyan (a prayer quorum). Young Yankel is in love with a Gentile girl, and it frightens him.

YANKEL BOYLE

by Leon Kobrin

☞ In a prayer-house for fishermen.

YANKEL (Steve) What do you think, Khatse? | *Iz vozhe zogt ir, Reb Khatse, ha?*

KHATSE (Allen) *Hm…Vos?*

YANKEL When you sin with a *shiksa*? What happens? | *Ven men zindikt mit a goyishe shiksa? Iz vozhe, ha?*

KHATSE What happens after? Oh, mammy, that's even worse than if you sinned with a married Jewish woman! | *Mit a shikse ven men zindikt, vos kumt derfar? Oy, ikh meyn epes, nokh erger vi mit a yidisher eyshes ish!*

It's worse than stoning, burning, beheading, and strangling. Oh, mammy! | *Skile iz veynik far dem…Sreyfe, heyreg, v'kheynik zaynen a shpay far dem, ikh meyn epes!*

I once heard the Sage of Kelm give a talk about it. You should hear this— | *Ikh hob amol gehert vi der Kelmer Magid, zeykher tsadik levrukhe, hot vegn dem gedarshnt. Her oys, Yankele, meygste hern.*

☞ He takes on a Talmudic intonation as he begins quoting the Sage.

A Jew who sins with a Gentile woman in this world, what do they do to him in the next world? First he's covered with tar from head to toe and handed to the Death King. | *A yidn vos hot gezindikt mit a goye af der velt— vos hot men im geton beys er iz gekumen af yener velt? Men hot im, reyshis, oysgeshmirt ingantsn mit smole funem kop biz di fis un men hot im ibergegebn tsim Malekh Doyme in di hent arayn.*

And what does the Death King do? He sends for Lilith (may her name be erased)! Lilith, you know, is no dime-a-dozen cupcake—Oh, mammy! | *Un vozhe hot der Malekh Doyme geton? Er hot gelozt tsi zikh rufn di yefas-toyer Lilis, yemakh shemo vezikhro, un Lilis, farshteystu mikh, iz nit glat abi a nekeyve kay un shpay…Ikh meyn epes!*

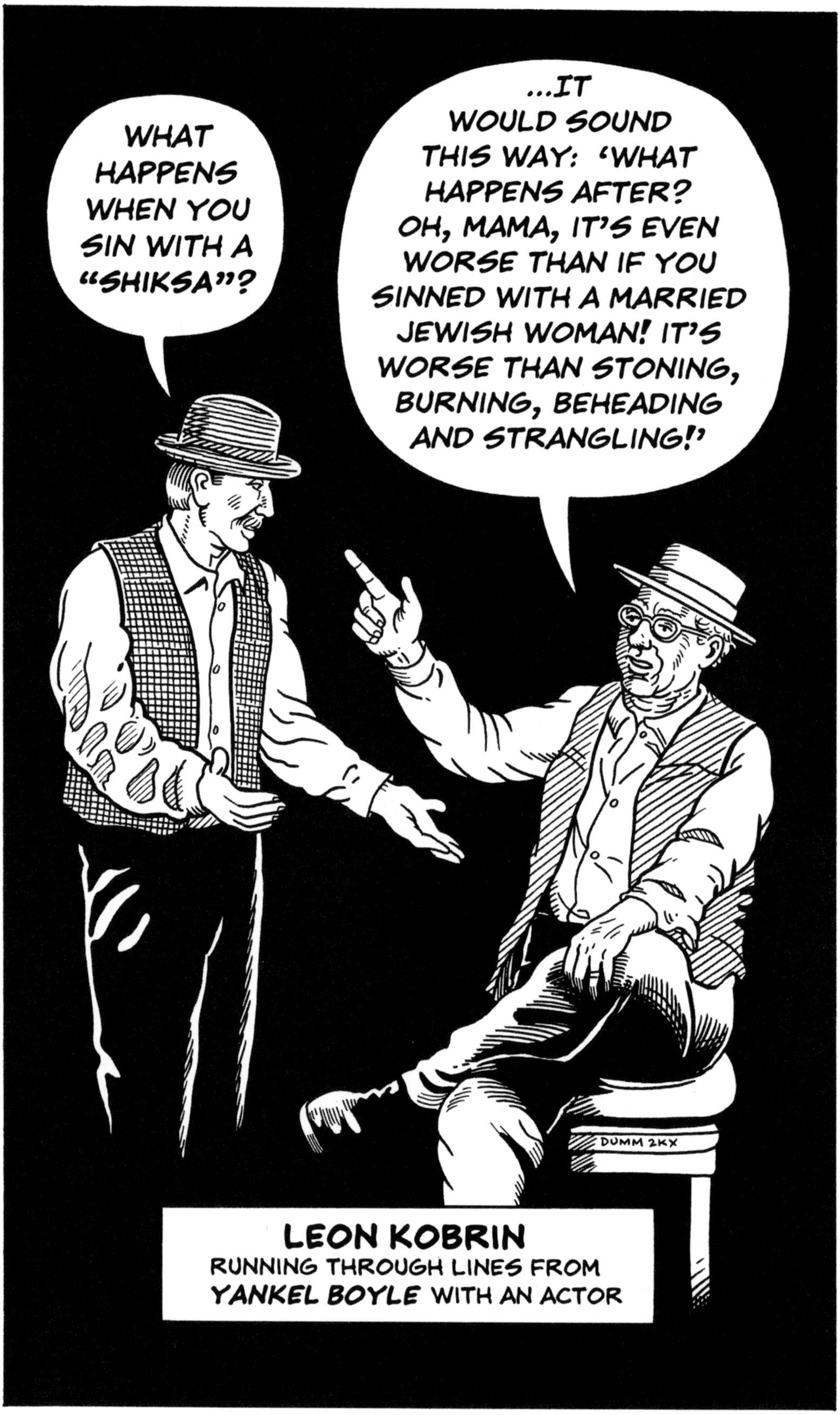
WHAT HAPPENS WHEN YOU SIN WITH A "SHIKSA"?
...IT WOULD SOUND THIS WAY: 'WHAT HAPPENS AFTER? OH, MAMA, IT'S EVEN WORSE THAN IF YOU SINNED WITH A MARRIED JEWISH WOMAN! IT'S WORSE THAN STONING, BURNING, BEHEADING AND STRANGLING!'
DUMM 2KX
LEON KOBRIN
RUNNING THROUGH LINES FROM *YANKEL BOYLE* WITH AN ACTOR

She's a pistol-hot floozie that no Jew should ever see. Screams like a banshee, eyes that flash lightning, and drop-dead gorgeous.	*Zi iz a nekeyve brand un fayer, az kayn yid zol zi nisht kenen. A lushn pekh un shveybl, oygn— fayerdike blitsn, un a yefas toyer iz zi, mamesh a gevald!*
The sun doesn't shine like she does. She's almost as beautiful as Jacob's wife Rachel. Oh, mammy!	*Di zun hot nit aza likhtik punim vi zi. Zi iz kimat aza yefas toyer vi unzer Muter Rukhl, Yankev Uvinu's vayb, ikh meyn epes!*
Just imagine how beautiful she must be— She's the right hand of The Evil Urge, she's the wife of Asmodeus, King of Ghouls…	*Du kenst dokh aleyn farshteyn vi sheyn zi iz, az zi iz di rekhte hant fun der yeytser hore, az zi iz di ployniste fun dem Ashmoday, fun dem meylekh fun ale sheydim un rikhes…*
Anyhow, Lilith (may her name be erased) grabs the Jew that sinned with a Gentile woman, gives him one look, and lightning sets fire to his brain…She says, "Hello, Jewboy," and a slaughterer's-knife pierces his heart…	*Hakitser, Lilis, yemakh shemo, tut zikh a nem tsum yidn vos hot gezindikt mit der goye af der velt…Tut af im a kuk, un a blits tsindt on zayn moyekh: tut im a zog "brukhim habuim a yid," un a sharfer khalef shnaydt durkh zayn harts…*
She's shameless, that Lilith, and she starts dancing a hoochie-koochie…	*Zi shemt zikh nit far a fremdn mansbil, Lilis, yemakh shemo, makht tsi im hultayske shtik…*

 He illustrates.

Then she starts to touch him…	*Tut im a glet do, dort, biz zi bakisheft im…*
And he comes unglued. Then he tries to touch her, and then—Oh, mammy!	*Er fargest af vos far a velt er iz un vil zi oykh a glet ton. Ot demolt, ikh meyn epes…*
She grabs him, tar and all, and Whammo—Into a burning oven! A BURNING OVEN!!!	*Tut zi im a khap on ot vi er shteyt azoy oysgeshmirt mit smole, un knak in brenendikn oyvn arayn, un knak in brenendikn oyvn arayn!…*
The flames lick him from all sides, he cries for mercy, and Lilith and a bunch of spooks dance around the oven, laughing, yelling—	*Dos fayer khapt im arum fun ale zaytn; er shrayt, bet zikh rakhamim, un zi, Lilis, mit a gantse khevre sheydim un leytsunim, tantsn kegn oyvn. Lakhn un reytsn zikh mit im:*
—"Oh-ho, sleep with a *shiksa*, will you?"	*"Ha, veste zindikn mit a goye, ha? Veste zindikn mit a goye?"*
YANKEL Please, please, STOP!	*Reb Khatse, Reb Khatse, genuk!*

 Meanwhile in the Soviet Union…

 Yelena plays "Volga Boatman" on the piano.

In the 1920s and 1930s some of the most exciting and innovative theatre in the world was being done by GOSET, the state Yiddish theatre in Moscow.

But before we get to that, let's pause for

ANOTHER IRRELEVANT INTERLUDE

 The catalog of Yiddish literature is enormous. Sholem Aleichem. I. L. Peretz. Asch. Singer. Manger. Sutskever. But in addition to all the works that were written in Yiddish, at one time or another, every kind of book published in other languages could also be found in Yiddish translation.

 Everything in world literature and world drama.

 Every kind of scientific text.

 Every economic work.

 Books about expressionist art.

 Vegetarian cookbooks.

 Grimm's Fairy Tales.

 The Bhagavad Gita, translated from the Sanskrit.

 Philosophy.

 Books about music. About poetry. About flowers.

 Leonid Brezhnev's autobigraphy.

 All published in Yiddish. You can download most of them when you get home.

 (holding up a book) Maybe the most surprising one is the one I've got right here. Anybody want to guess? (polls the audience) It's the New Testament, in Yiddish. Here, pass it around. (hands it to an audience member)

 That's just one version of it. There have been at least four different Yiddish translations of the New Testament.

 The New Testament—or, as they refer to it in rabbinical school, "The Sequel"— is different from the other books we mentioned. You see, the New Testament translations were not published for scholarly or literary purposes. No, these were published by Christian missionaries who figured they might convert a few people by handing them the New Testament in Yiddish. And they are still being published to this day. I'm not kidding. Yes, How to Win Friends and Influence People in Boro Park.

Ladies and Gentlemen, the King James Bible, in Yiddish. It goes something like this.

 She crosses (pardon the expression) to the piano and plays the Bach/Gounod "Ave Maria." Steve puts on a robe and crown of thorns. Allen kneels and faces him.

 And if your right eye offend you, pluck it out, and cast it from you.

In az dayn rekhte oyg zol dir shlekhts tin, rays es aroys fin kop in varf es avek fin dir.

 Oy! Oy!

 For it is profitable for you that one of your members should perish, and not that your whole body should be cast into hell.

Vayl s'iz beser az eyn shtik zol shtarbn eyder dayn gantser guf zol arayngevorfn vern in gehenem.

 Oy! Oy!

 And whoever shall smite you on your right cheek, turn to him the other also.

Az eymetser git dir a zets af der rekhter bak, derlang im di linke bak, zol er dir gebn a khmalye dortn.

 Gevalt!

 Blessed are the meek, for they shall inherit the earth.

Gebensht zaynen di nebekhdike, vayl zey veln zayn yorshim in yene velt.

 Amen!

Umayn!

 Blessed are the merciful, for they shall have mercy.

Gebensht zaynen di rakhmunesdike, vayl zey veln krign rakhmunes.

 Amen!

Umayn!

 Blessed are the pure in heart: for they shall see God.

Gebensht zaynen di reynhartsike, vayl zey veln zikh unkikn af dem riboynesheloylem.

 Oh, God!

Riboynesheloylem!

 (takes off thorns, points to Yelena) Ladies and Gentlemen, Miss Yelena Shmulenson, playing "Oyvey Maria."

 Yelena stops playing.

 (standing up) That's enough of that. Where were we?

We were in the Soviet Union.

Yelena plays "Volga Boatman."

In the 1920s and 1930s some of the most exciting and innovative theatre in the world was being done by GOSET, the state Yiddish theatre in Moscow.

GOSET's style was very experimental and very acrobatic, with constructivist sets, makeup designed by Marc Chagall, actors leaping and flying all over the stage...it was very, very visual. And when they toured the West in 1928, the Western theatre critics were stunned. They had never seen anything like it.

 It had a similar impact in Moscow: most of their audience didn't understand Yiddish, but they went to the shows anyhow.

 Many of their plays were classics from the Yiddish repertoire. But with a twist: The GOSET productions were mostly adaptations, and they had a very definite purpose: propaganda. The witch in DI KISHUFMAKHERIN became a capitalist; Sholem Aleichem's Menakhem Mendl became the enemy of the proletariat; and Perchik taught Tevye about dialectical materialism.

 And Shloyme Mikhoels himself, who ran GOSET for most of its life, was a true believer. He came here on a fund-raising tour in 1943, and when the actor Joseph Buloff offered to lend him a suit and tie to wear when he visited the State Department—instead of what he had been wearing, which was a torn shirt, sagging pants, and a rope belt—Mikhoels waved a roll of bills in his face and blew up at him.

☞ Pin spot on Steve as Mikhoels.

MIKHOELS You think my government didn't give me expense money? But I refuse to waste it on bourgeois suits and ties! Let your government see me as I am— a Soviet proletarian, who dresses like the workers!

Meynste az di sovetishe regirung git mir nisht kayn hetsues-gelt? Nor ikh vel es nisht oysbrengen af bourgeois kostyumen in kravatn! Zoln zey mikh zeyn vi ikh gey in shtey—vi an arbets-mensh fin ratn-farband, vus bakleydt zikh vi es darf tsi zayn!

 And he stomped off.

 GOSET's later pruductions were more naturalistic than their early ones, but the propaganda stayed.

 Propaganda or not, they were great Yiddish theatre. This song is from THE LUFTMENSH, which was based on Sholem Aleichem stories.

NIT BASHERT
Not Destined
—•—

words by Y. Dobrushin & N. Oyslender, music by Lev Pulver

 If it's not to be, it's not to be.
A million can be worthless too.

*Az nit bashert iz nit bashert
iz a milyon oykh gornit vert*

I had it right there in my hand, then 'bang'
and the whole world went bankrupt.

*Gehat in hant, ot bald, ot, ot
Itst, na dir, vert a velt bankrot*

It's a plague. Me, I'm a goat.
What's-his-name gets all the luck.

*Aza mageyfe. Bin ikh oykh a tsig
Nor Brodske hot gehat dos glik*

He gets a miracle.
Me? Just look. I'm half a corpse.

*Arofgeshprungen mit a nes
Un ikh, vi ir zet, a halber mes*

We're in a pretty pickle, auntie.	*A shlim-shlimazl iz durkhn tir*
	Oy, shvigerle, vos zogt ir?
But if it's not to be, it's not to be.	*Az nit bashert iz nit bashert*
…A million can be worthless too.	*iz a milyon oykh gornit vert*

 Mikhoels met Buloff in New York in 1943. In Europe at the same time…

Through the worst moments in human history there was still Yiddish theatre. Believe it or not. It seems almost too trivial to mention, but…it's something people need.

 In the ghetto, with disease and starvation all around, there were cabarets inside of apartments where they presented music and sketches. Audience members and performers couldn't go home afterwards—because of the curfew—so they stayed overnight.

 Amateur drama groups would bring their scenery and costumes with them—which they would make out of sheets, tablecloths, whatever they could get—and do full-length plays right there in the apartment buildings.

 In the Warsaw ghetto—which was the largest—there were even professional theatres going. Some of the actors who performed in them had performed in New York only a few years before…but then they went back home.

 Later, in the death camps, ordinary people—seamstresses, blacksmiths, factory workers—who remembered a monologue or song would climb down from their bunks at night and perform for their fellow prisoners.

 One play that was done in the ghettos was Goldfadn's BAR KOKHBA, which is about Jewish heroism during the Roman occupation. Imagine, if you can, hearing this song in the ghetto in 1943.

KLOG FUN TSION'S TEKHTER
Cry of the Daughters of Zion
from Bar Kokhba

words & music by Avrom Goldfadn

Weep together, daughters of Zion,	*Veynt-zhe ale Tsion's tekhter*
for the evil times that have befallen our land	*Klogt-zhe, kinder, ale baynand*
	af der noyt, der tsayt der shlekhter
	vos hot getrofn unzer land
Like the stars around the moon, we saw	*Azoy vi di shtern arum di levone*
ourselves reflected in her	*hobn mir zikh geshpiglt in ir;*
Now she is a widow and we are her orphans	*Oy, haynt heyst zi di almone*
	Un ire yesoymim zaynen mir
God, see our tears and our need and	*Got, zey unzere trern*
our suffering	*Unzer noyt un payn;*

Our weeping will continue until you help	*Veynen veln mir nit ofbern* *Biz dayn hilf vet zayn*
The widow Jerusalem sits defiled, her only child clasped to her breast	*Azoy zitst di almone Yerushalayim* *af der erd tsvishn mist* *Un ir eynsike kind Efrayim* *tulyet zi tsi ire brist*
"Dear God," she cries, "you have driven away my Jews and my Israel…	*"Fartribn hostu," veynt zi, "Got liber* *mayn Yidelen un Yisrol;*
…leave at least one child to remember me!"	*Oy, loz mikh khotsh dem kadish iber* *er zol mir gedenken khotsh amol!"*

Shortly before the war ended, on April 22nd, 1945, a group of soldiers marched into the concentration camp at Dachau. They were the Forty-second Infantry Division of New York. The soldiers, staring into the mouth of Hell, were too shocked to move; the wrecked half-people standing there stared at them and staggered about, terrified. A sergeant from Chicago fired five shots in the air to get their attention. Then, in a loud voice, he spoke to them all in Yiddish.

"I am an American soldier," he said. "I am a Jew. We are Americans. It will get better."	*"Ikh bin an Amerikaner soldat. Ikh bin a Yid. Ikh bin a Yid. Mir zaynen Amerikaner. Es vet zayn beser. Es vet zayn 'all right.'"*

Soon after, when it was all over…

In the Displaced Persons Camps, like food and clothing and medical attention, Yiddish theatre was there for those who had survived. They saw performances by visitors from America like Molly Picon and Herman Yablokoff; and there were amateur groups in most of the camps, producing plays, revues, everything.

Molly and her husband, Yankel Kalich, toured all over Europe doing concerts anywhere they could find an audience of survivors. At one concert a very small child started to cry; afterwards Yankel asked the mother why she had brought the child to the show. She said, "My baby is three years old and has never heard the sound of laughter. I don't want her to grow up without hearing people laugh."

The Jewish people did survive the war. So did Yiddish theatre.

In Paris after the war there were revivals of shtetl plays.

In Romania after the war the government began subsidizing Yiddish theatre; the Yiddish State Theatre in Bucharest survives to this day.

In Buenos Aires in 1949 Joseph Buloff premiered a Yiddish translation of a new play from Broadway. It was about the last days in the life of an ordinary man; the play was called DEATH OF A SALESMAN. Later on, when Buloff did his Yiddish version in New York, critics said that that must have been the original and that Arthur Miller had translated it into English.

In Poland in 1947 the comedy team of Dzigan & Schumacher, who had survived the war in a Russian slave labor camp, did a revue called ABI MEN ZEYT ZIKH (So Long As We See Each Other).

Here's a small sample of their style.

 Say, if they'd let me get into international politics, things would be different.

Ay, ay, ven m'lozt mikh araynmishn a bisele in der velt-politik, volt di lage andersh oysgezeyn.

 Why don't they?

Ver lozt dikh nisht, ver?

 Because I can't speak English! If I could speak English, I'd go to America, head straight for the U.N., walk right up to the Secretary General, and say—

Di shprakh, dus lushn! Ikh ken nisht kayn English! Oy, ven ikh volt gekent English azoy vi Yidish volt ikh ahingefurn kayn Amerike, kh'volt arayngegangen tsi dem Sekretar fin di Fareynikte Felker in kh'volt im gezugt af English: Mister Sekretar, zolt ir visn—

"Feh, feh, feh, feh, feh!"

 For this you need English?

Tsi deym darfste kenen English?

 I'd have gone to America when Professor Einstein did.

Volt ikh glaykh gefurn kayn Amerike in zelbikn tug fin Profesor Aynshtayn.

 What happened, something go funny with the cashbox?

Vusi, di kase iz nisht geveyn bay im in ordening?

 What?

Vus?

 Yeah, he pulled that stunt once before.

Nu, vus-vus, er hot dokh shoyn eyn mul gemakht di kunts, er.

 Who?

Ver?

 Weinstein, from the candy store.

Vaynshtayn, Vaynshtayn. Er hot a gesheft fin konfektsie.

 You dope! I'm talking about Einstein, the mathematician!

Meshigener, ikh red dokh gor vegn Aynshtayn, a profesor, a matematiker.

 Yeah? What'd *he* do?

Nu, vus hot er getin, vus?

 What did *he* do? He revolutionized science! Professor Einstein said that in this world there is time and there is space. And those two things are relative concepts. Do you know what "relative" means?

Vus hot er getin? Er hot gemakht an iberkerenish in der gantser visnshaft! Profesor Aynshtayn hot gezugt azoy: af der velt, hot er gezugt, zenen du tsvey zakhn, ort in tsayt, tsayt in ort. In di dozike tsvey zakhn, zugt er, dus zaynen relative bagrifn. Di veyst vus s'heyst "relativ"?

 Well…ahh…

Nu, a klal…Gey vayter, nu…

 I'll explain. For example, if you have seven hairs on your head, that's very few. But seven hairs in your milk, that's a lot.

Vel ikh dir balt geybn tsi farshteyn. Lemushl, az di host zibn hur afn kop iz zeyer veynik. In az di host zibn hur in di milkh iz zeyer a sakh.

He don't sell no milk. | *Er handlt dokh nisht mit kayn milkh.*

 Who? | *Ver?*

 Weinstein. | *Der Vaynshtayn.*

 Not Weinstein, Einstein! I'll give you another example. For example, he says, if you go sit naked on a hot oven— | *Vus far a Vaynshtayn? Aynshtayn! Vel ikh dir gebn tsi farshteyn di khokhme a tsveytn mushl. Lemushl, zugt er, az di zetst dikh avek naket mit a naketn kerper af a heysn oyvn—*

 Lemme give *you* an example— *you* go sit naked on a hot oven. | *Zets di dikh avek naket af a heysn oyvn. Vel ikh dir gebn a mushl.*

 Listen, it's just an example! See, if you sit naked on an oven for one minute, it feels to you like forever. But to the world it's one minute. | *Ober s'iz bloyz a mushl! Az di zetst dikh avek naket af a heysn oyvn af eyn minit, dakht zikh dir oys az di minit gedoyert af eybik—vi di gantse velt, gedoyert di minit.*

 Naturally. | *Nu, yo.*

 Understand? | *Farshteyst shoyn?*

 Not yet. | *Nokh nisht.*

 Oh, take me, Satan… | *Gevald geshrign…*

 Et cetera, et cetera, et cetera.

 Meanwhile, in the U.S.S.R.…

Shloyme Mikhoels had become the face of Jewish Russia, thanks to his traveling all over the world to represent his government at pro-Soviet rallies. In January 1948 they sent him to review a play in Minsk; it was a strange request, but he went. While there Mikhoels got a call in his hotel room from somebody claiming to be an old friend and he went out to meet the man.

Mikhoels's body was found in the snow.

Whether he had been beaten to death, deliberately run over, or poisoned is not certain; what is certain is that the Soviets gave medals to the policemen who "found the body"; the mortician who had embalmed Lenin was sent to remove any evidence of foul play; and communists abroad were told that Mikhoels had been murdered by American spies.

Shloyme Mikhoels was, as his old acquaintance Joseph Buloff put it, "slain by the hand he had blessed." A year later they closed his theatre.

Mikhoels's crime? He once said, in public, that he supported the idea of a Jewish state.

And four months after his murder, it came into being. After almost two thousand years of waiting, the Jews had a homeland again.

But in 1948 Israel was no friendlier to Yiddish theatre than the Soviet Union was. The Israelis hated Yiddish even more than the *yekes* used to. There are reports of people in Israel literally throwing bricks at gatherings of Yiddish speakers. At times in the 1950s producing Yiddish theatre there was absolutely, literally, prohibited by law. No other country in the world could make that claim. Just the Jewish homeland.

But the Yiddish essence could not be put down completely. There's an old Israeli joke: On a bus in Tel Aviv a mother's talking to her kid in Yiddish, and the kid keeps answering in Hebrew. The mother keeps trying to get the kid to answer in Yiddish, and finally an Israeli sitting next to them says, "Why don't you just let the kid speak Hebrew?" She says, "Because I don't want him to forget he's a Jew."

That extreme Israeli hostility to Yiddish couldn't last forever. It did diminish over time, and there was even the occasional Yiddish theatre breakthrough hit. In the '60s it was THE MEGILLA OF ITZIK MANGER, which was the story of Esther as told by Manger the poet. That show was so successful it even moved to Broadway.

This is one of Manger's poems that was later set to music by Dov Seltzer and became part of the show. The poem is about King Akhashverosh, who, if you remember the story, was an imbecile. Anybody know any Yiddish words for "imbecile"?

Just checking to see if you were paying attention.

Akhashverosh has just survived an assassination attempt, and he ponders the meaning of life.

DER MELEKH AKHASHVEROSH NOKH'N ATENTAT
King Akhashverosh After the Assassination Attempt

by Itzik Manger

The king stands at the window in his longjohns and contemplates.	*Der meylekh shteyt in di gatkes baym ofenem fenster un trakht.*
"The summer night is so full of stars…"	*"Azoy fil likhtike shtern farmogt di zumernakht…"*
He sighs deeply.	*Er otemt tif.*
"Living is a joy…drinking wine, whoring around, rattling a saber…"	*"S'a mekhaye, s'a mekhaye, tsu leybn oyf der erd. Tsu trinken vayn, un tsu hurn, un fokhen mit der shverd…"*
But what if that crazed young man had killed him? Then what?	*Oy, vos volt geveyn, a shteyger, ven der meshugener yunger man volt im oyf toyt derharget? Vos volt geveyzn dan?*
Instead of looking at the stars, and listening to the birds, he'd be laying in the ground…	*Er volt atsind geleygn nayn eyln tif indrerd, un volt nisht gezeyn di shtern un di feygl nisht gehert…*

His Esther would've mourned him for a year.	*Zayn Ester volt efsher gegangen a yor in troyer gehilt.*
Or maybe not, maybe she'd have found a new man right away…	*Un efsher nisht? Efsher teykef mit a tsveytn a libe geshpilt…*
And his dead ex-queen Vashti would come to him…	*Tsu im volt gekumen bloyz Vashti…*
"Well, if it isn't Himself!	*"S'kotsl kumt, mayn man!*
Who you been runnin' around with, bozo?"	*Vos makht epes mayn kanarikl? Un ver shpilt af mayn fortepyan?"*

 Meanwhile, in the United States…

 Most of the American Yiddish theatre in the '50s and '60s was featherweight *shund*. And rightly so. One hundred and forty thousand Holocaust survivors came here after the war, and they made up a significant part of the audience at that time. More than anything else, those people needed to know that life could be good again. They didn't need THE DYBBUK or THE JEWISH KING LEAR, they needed Mickey Mouse with a yarmulke. They needed musicals. Watching the eighty-year-old Jacob Jacobs chase younger women became, in a strange way, important.

KUPLET
Duet
from Bay Mir Bistu Sheyn

words by Jacob Jacobs, music by Sholom Secunda

HER (Yelena) So tell me, can you give a woman what she needs to be a regular wife?	*Zugt mir kent ir a vaybl gebn alts vus zi darft hubn tsim lebn—az zi zol zayn a balebuste vi es badarft tsi zayn?*
HIM (Allen) Of course I can. And if at first I don't succeed, I'll try, try again.	*Ikh ken, ikh vil. Kh'vel try-en gor un tsul. Vus ikh vel nit kenen eyn mul, vel ikh try-en nokh a mul.*
HER Can you give me absolutely everything? A nice mink coat, for example, that I can parade around in?	*Zugt kent ir gebn mir altsding? A sheynem coat gemakht fun mink, az ikh zol zikh firn laytish in ikh zol oyszeyen fayn?*
HIM Of course. What, you think I'm a drunk or something? Of course I can give you a mink. Or at least a skunk.	*Ikh ken, ikh vil. Vus meynsti, ikh bin a drunk? Oyb ikh vel nit kenen gebn dir a mink, vel ikh gebn dir a skunk.*
HER And after the wedding ceremony…is anything likely to happen?	*Ven ir vet mikh shoyn tsi der khipe firn… Denkt ir es ken epes nokh pasirn?*
HIM What, you think an old man has lost all desire?	*Vus meynst, an alter man farlirt in gantsn dem desire?*

HIM (cont'd) If you say so, then, my dear, you're a cockeyed liar!

	English	Yiddish

HER   Here's a question—   *Ikh vil aykh fregn epes—*

HIM   (spoken) *Vus?*

HER   Anything going on in the   *Vus hert zikh, zugt, mit* money?
        money department?   *Zugt iz epes du?*

HIM   Oh, yeah! It's all there! You betcha!   *S'iz du, s'iz du, s'iz du, s'iz du, s'iz du!*
        So much money!   *Zol ikh hobn azoy fil tozenter, vi fil gelt*
                                                   s'iz du!

HER   You have money—?   *Ir hot gelt, zogt ir—?*

HIM   Sure I have it. I just don't possess it.   *Ikh zug s'iz du—nor nit bay mir.*

HER   What are you talking about?   *Zugt-zhet mir, ikh beyt aykh, entfert mir—*
        What do you have?   *Vu-zhe fort azoyns hot ir?*

HIM   May all Jews have what   *Ikh hob, ikh hob, ikh hob in hob in hob!*
        I have!   *Af ale Yidn gezugt gevorn vus ikh hob!*

HER   (spoken) WHAT IS IT?!!   *VUS HOT IR?*

HIM   Social Security! A blessing for the elderly!   Social Security, *far alte layt a brukhe!*

HER   Social Security helps everybody!   Social Security *helft yedn aroys!*

HIM   Social Security is the family bank!   Social Security, *a bank far a mishpukhe!*

HER   Social Security is everywhere!   Social Security, *kimat in yedn hoyz!*

        Men used to want pretty wives…   *Amul a man fleg zikhn a sheyn vaybl,*
                                             a metsotse…

HIM   Now they only want women that have—   *Haynt art im gurnit ver zi iz, er vil nor*
                                             zeyn tsi hot zi—

BOTH   Social Security! You get a change of life?

        S'iz a bafrayer—you'll retire when you're sixty-five! (repeat)

The last few decades have seen Yiddish theatre popping up in some very surprising places. In Israel, exactly twenty years ago, a permanent Yiddish theatre, called "Yiddishpiel," was established in Tel Aviv. They have thirty-five actors in their company.

In the 1980s Yiddish theatre reappeared in, of all places, the Soviet Union. Among the plays presented by the new Moscow Yiddish Chamber Theatre was A BLACK BRIDLE FOR A WHITE HORSE, a story about the devil's enchanting a village, that was the Yiddish theatre's first-ever pop opera. No kidding.

TSUGN
Trains
from A Shvarts Tsayml Far A Vays Ferdl

words by Chaim Beyder, music by Yuri Sherling

 & &

Trains will be coming to Mirashne tomorrow	*Tsugn, tsugn kumen keyn Mirashne veln morgn*
And somebody's luck will change for sure	*Heyst es eymetsn vet opglikn gevis, gevis*
There will be no more worries for us	*Heyst es mer veln nit zayn bay unz keyn payn un*
The future will be sweet	*zorgn. Un der goyrl vet fun biter vern zis—zis, zis!*
—The train will bring me merchandise!	*—Mir der tsug vet brengen skhoyre!*
—Me, a golden menorah!	*—Mir a goldene menoyre!*
—I'll get wagons and corn!	*—Mir vagonen, vayts, un korn!*
—I'll have money!	*—Mir parnose ale yorn!*
—My business will be blessed!	*—Mir a brokhe in mayn handlen!*
—Wine and raisins and almonds!	*—Vayn un rozhinkes mit mandlen!*
—I'll get a bride with a big dowry!	*—Mir a kale vus a groysn nadn hot! Ot, ot!*
Trains are running to Mirashne	*Tsugn, tsugn, tsugn keyn Mirashne yogn, yogn*
The news is all over the world	*Ot di nays hot zikh tseshpreyt af gor der velt, der velt*
Good-bye to troubles	*Oys mit ale, ale shvere plogn, plogn, plogn*
And food and drink?	*Vos tsi esn, vos tsi trinken,*
Whatever you want, just ask!	*nor tseshtelt—tseshtelt!*

 And the Jewish State Theatre in Bucharest is doing just fine, thank you. Right now they have three Yiddish shows in their repertoire: THE KREUTZER SONATA by Jacob Gordin, THE BOOK OF RUTH by Mario Diament, and GIMPEL THE FOOL by Isaac Bashevis Singer.

 In New York it's been kinda 'spotty.' There were a number of interesting projects that didn't last long; there were a lot of brain-dead nostalgia shows, you know, like this—

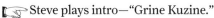

☞ Steve plays intro—"Grine Kuzine."

 (smiling) Remember the good old days when all those girls were burnt to a crisp in the Triangle Shirtwaist Factory? This was their favorite song!

 & &

(Steve plays) Oy, that, oy, that Yidishe Charleston
Oy, that, oy, that Yidishe Charleston. Dai dai dai dai…

 And then we had the flu epidemic!

 Yippee! Let's dance!

Steve plays the "button."

 —and then there was the Folksbiene, which was for decades run by the late Zypora Spaisman, a wonderful actress and a former midwife from Lublin, who, with the help of a few others, kept literary Yiddish theatre alive in New York for forty more years. It still exists, too, alongside its upstart competitor, the New Yiddish Rep.

 And there you have the entire history of Yiddish theatre up until (looks at watch) twenty after eight (or whatever) this evening.

 Now for the question we're all sick of hearing.

 & & What is the future of Yiddish theatre?

 It's tough to answer. On the one hand we have the opinion of Leo Weiner, the critic, who said, quote, "It is doubtful whether the Yiddish theatre can subsist in America another ten years," unquote.

On the other hand, Mr. Weiner said that in 1890, so...

 Ladies and Gentlemen, we now present our tribute to the late Leo Weiner.

 All "raspberry."

 The biggest part of the question is, of course, the language.

 Some people call Yiddish a "dead language."

 People called Hebrew a "dead language" for two thousand years. But it's doing all right now.

 Between one and four million people speak Yiddish today, and every one of them is alive.

 There are conflicting opinions about the actual number—We're talking about Jews here, you understand.

 Here's a thought: Did you know that speaking Yiddish today has become an act of rebellion? Strange But True.

 By going back to the language of their roots, younger people are rebelling against the older generation's crazy rush to give up their identity, to conform.

It's also an act of rebellion against history, against the Holocaust.

Speak Yiddish and the Germans lose.

Di reder dreyen zikh, certainly. The wheels turn. At my bar mitzvah the band was made up of three *alte kakers* who played sad, halfhearted rock 'n' roll in an attempt to keep up with the times. If you had told them that thirty years later hipsters would be listening to the klezmer music that had been played at their bar mitzvahs, they'd have said you were crazy.

So what is the *future* of Yiddish theatre?

 I know? | Ikh veys?

 Go know! | Gey veys!

 Who knows? | Ver veyst!

 I know a disease. | Ikh veys a krenk, ikh veys.

 The cholera knows! | Di kholerie veyst!

 May I know as much of troubles. | Zol ikh azoy visn fun tsures.

 If you know, you don't ask. | Az men veys aleyn, freygt men nisht kayn andere.

 I don't have my nightshirt. | Mayn pelts iz nisht bay mir.

 Ask me in Purgatory. | Freyg mikh bekheyrem.

 So nobody knows. But Jewish stories will always sound better in Yiddish. Because Yiddish has the essence.

 And like we say in Yiddish, *As men hot bitokhn, hot men af Shabes*; if you can believe...then you're doing all right.

YIDDISH
a.k.a. "Vaserl"

———————◆———————

words by Rukhl Schaechter & Paula Teitelbaum
music by Rukhl Schaechter

 & &

The stream that used to flow so brisk is still and frozen now | Shtil un farfroyrn zeyt oys der shtrom vos flegt azoy loyfn mit mut

The winter's force has wrapped it tight | Es viklt im ayn itst der mekhtiker vinter

The sleepy river, benumbed, lies quiet and rests | Der taykh ligt farshlofn, farglivert, un rut

But wait, hold fast, oh rivulet
The frost will go away | Vaserl, vaserl, gib nokh nisht uf
Es veln di frest fargeyn

The spring will soon be here	*Es kumt bald der friling tsu geyn*
No, do not think that all is hushed, there's buzzing in the deep	*Nor meyn nisht az alts iz ingantsn shoyn shtil, es zhumet nokh alts in der tif*
The pendulum, too long concealed, is now at last with all its strength for freedom crying out	*Der umru vos hot zikh azoy lang bahaltn un git itst mit koyekh tsu frayhayt a rif*
But wait, hold fast, oh rivulet The frost will go away	*Vaserl, vaserl, gib nokh nisht uf Es veln di frest fargeyn*
The spring will soon be here	*Es kumt bald der friling tsu geyn*
We wait for winter's thrall to end, for spring to melt the stream	*Men vart az tsum vinter zol kumen a sof, tseshmeltsn zol friling dem taykh*
For only then will waters flow and colorful and spirited his bounties will pour out	*Vayl demolt, nor demolt, vet er flisik vern. Mit gayst un kolirn vet er vern raykh*
Wait, hold fast, oh rivulet The frost will go away	*Vaserl, vaserl, gib nokh nisht uf Es veln di frest fargeyn*
The spring will soon be here.	*Es kumt bald der friling tsu geyn.*

CURTAIN

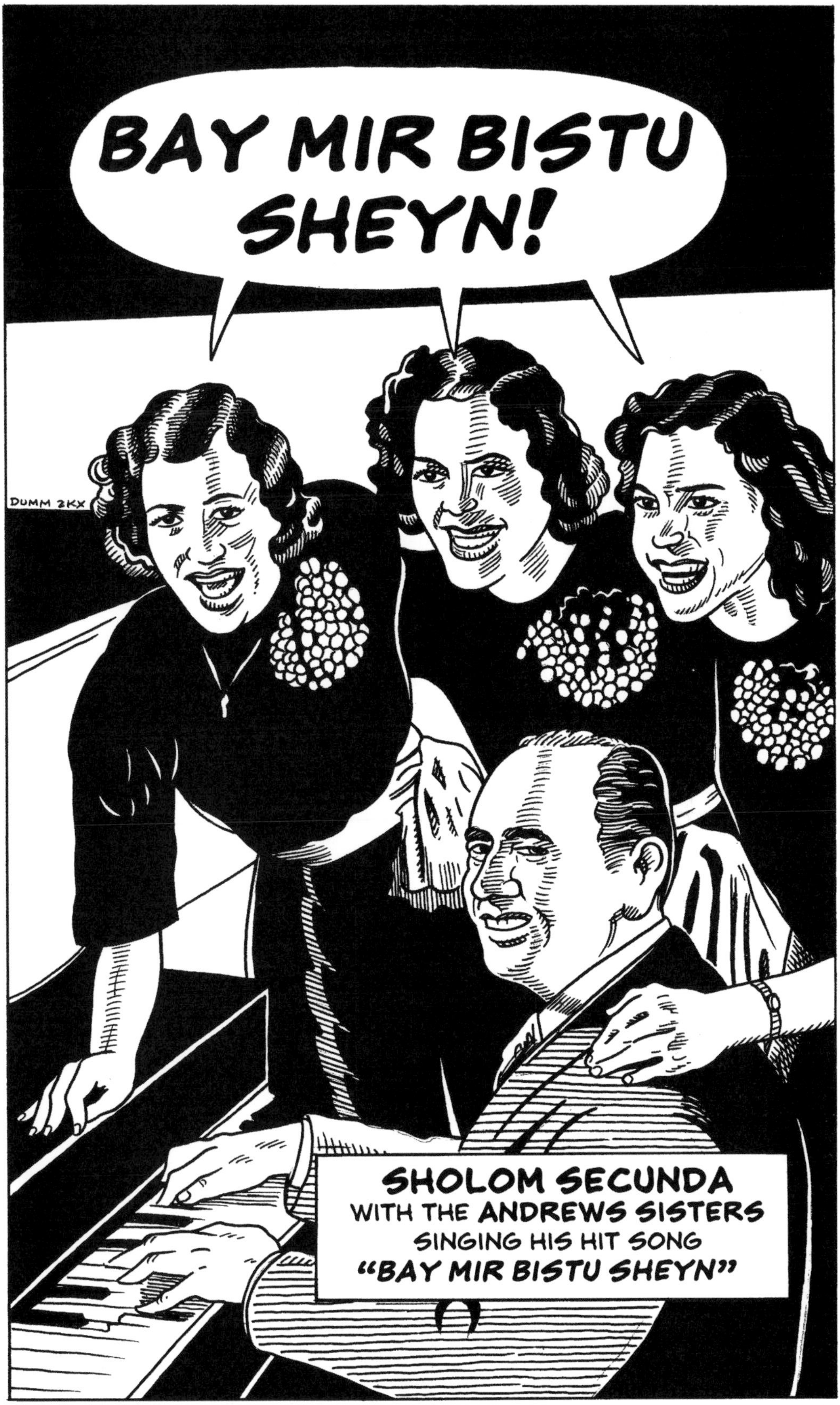
BAY MIR BISTU SHEYN!
DUMM 2KX
SHOLOM SECUNDA
WITH THE ANDREWS SISTERS
SINGING HIS HIT SONG
"BAY MIR BISTU SHEYN"

Masthead for *Der Groyser Kundes*. Passover Special Issue, April 14, 1911

Established by the melancholy poet Jakob Marinov, the weekly *Der Groyser Kundes* (*The Big Stick* or *The Big Prankster*), which was published from 1909 to 1927, was the American counterpart to the British *Punch* and German *Simplissimus*. *Der Groyser Kundes* supported Jewish working people (sometimes against Jewish employers) and opposed war, but its métier was weekly commentary on the passing scene of Jewish personalities, Jewish theater, and above all, the nature and sources of Jewish humor.

אונזער „אויבערשטע פון חריין"

נאָט אייך דעם מרור און נאָט אייך די חריין, אָט איז א ריב־אייזען — רייבט זיך אליין. (מיר רייבען זיי גענוג א גאַנץ יאָר).
אויבערשטע שורה: — בּאָראָגדעס, טאָמאַשעווסקי, י. אדלער, זעליקאָוויץ, שיף, מאַגנעט, קעסלער און מולער. צווייטע שורה: — קאַהאַן, מהאַמאַשעטפּסקי, זשיטלאָוופּסקי, ווינטשעווסקי, מאָסליאַנסקי און ראָזענפּעלד. אונטערשטע שורה : — ווינטשעווסקין, יהואַש, זעווין, זשאָלטקאָפּ און קאָהאַן.

"Our Cream of the Horseradish," April 14, 1911
Well-known literary, theatrical, and intellectual characters in the Yiddish-speaking community are offered to the public for grating on Passover. "Here's the bitter herbs. Here's the horseradish. There's a grater—do your own grating. (We grate on them enough all year long.)" The worthies include theatrical giants Jacob P. Adler and Boris Thomashefsky, theorist Chaim Zhitlovsky, socialist poet Morris Winchevsky, editor Abraham Cahan, and the prolific poet known as Yehoyish (Yehoash), who also translated the Hebrew Bible into Yiddish.

צווישען יצר הרע און יצר טוב

אידישער אַקטיאָר (מיט מוזיק): „איך האָב צוויי שעהנע מיידלעך װאָס
פּלאָגען מיר טאָג און נאכט: איינע מיט איהר עלטער, די צוױיטע מיט איהר
פּראכט". לאָמיך אזוי וויסען פון א ליטעראַרישע ראָלע, ווי איך וױיס וואו
צו גההן נעקסטען זיסאָן.

"Between the Good and Evil Impulses," 1911
The actor must choose between the elderly Yiddish Theater and the lovely Yiddish Variety Show,
i.e., between art and mere entertainment. "Yiddish Actor (music plays underneath): Two attractive
women torment me day and night, one with her age (dignity), the other with her beauty. I wish I knew
as much about finding a true literary role for myself as I do about where I will be onstage next season."

מיט דעם אויער צוגעבויערט צו דער טיר פון „פּיפּלס טהעאַטער", וועט שוין ז. ליבין פאר נעקסטע צוויי י א ה ר
וויינינגסטענס נאָך ט י ע פ ע ר אין אבגרונד נ י ט קענען קריכען.

"Boris Thomashefsky Engages Zalman Libin," 1911
Thomashefsky, notorious star/producer of *shund* (lowbrow commercial theater) performs the Old
Testament ritual of boring a hole through an indentured servant's ear to guarantee the loyalty of the
newly hired playright. The caption reads: "With his ear affixed to the door of the People's Theater,
playwright Zalman Libin will, for the next two years at least, be unable to descend deeper into the
abyss."

צו יעקב גאָרדין׳ס יאָהרצייט

יעקב גאָרדין׳ס ביוסט: כע־כע־כע! — מען דארף זיין פון גראַניט
און ניט פון מאַרמאָר, אום זיך צוריקצוהאַלטען פון לאַכען, הערענדיג די „סטאָמפּ-

"For Yankif (Jacob) Gordin's Yortsayt (death anniversary)," 1911
Journalist Louis Miller (who published the daily *Varhayt* [*Truth*], competing with the daily *Forverts*)
bangs the table, while Gordin's marble bust laughs, saying, "Heh-heh-heh! One needs to be of granite,
not marble, to keep from laughing at that 'stump speech.'" [Note: Yiddish text above is incomplete.]

די (אַהער-אוּן) „הינריכטוּנג"

"The (Back and Forth) Execution," 1911

Theatrical figures Rudolph Schildkraut, Moritz Morrison, and Boris Thomashefsky stand in judg-
ment over *Shund* (lowbrow commercial theater). Schildkraut and Morrison, both associated with literary theater, condemn *Shund*—but she flirts with Thomashefsky, who had recently forsaken such
plays as *The Green Millionaire*, *Ikey the Devil*, and *Alexander, Crown Prince of Jerusalem* in favor of *Hamlet*
(note his costume).

Chayale Ash's DAY IN COURT

STORY BY JOEL SCHECHTER

ART BY SPAIN

CHAYALE ASH, THE YIDDISH ROMANIAN ACTRESS, ARRIVED IN ISRAEL IN 1948. THERE WAS A SHORTAGE OF MALE ACTORS, SO SHE PLAYED SOME MEN'S ROLES IN TOP HAT AND TAILS.

ALMOST AT ONCE, ASH AND HER TROUPE IN HAIFA WERE ARRESTED FOR PERFORMING IN YIDDISH.

YIDDISH THEATER of HAIFA

CLOSED DUE TO POPULAR DEM...

WHAT DO YOU WANT, TO CUT OUT OUR TONGUES?

IN GERMANY WE EXPECTED THIS!

AZ MEN LEBT, DERLEBT MEN ZIK ALTS*

BEN-GURION, ISRAEL'S PRIME MINISTER, WAS AFRAID YIDDISH WOULD OVERTAKE HEBREW, THE NATIONAL LANGUAGE, ASH SAID. THE AUDIENCE WAS MOSTLY YIDDISH-SPEAKING SURVIVORS FROM RUSSIA, POLAND AND ROMANIA.

WITHIN 24 HOURS OF THEIR ARREST, THE ACTORS FORMED A UNION AND SUED THE GOVERNMENT.

ZAYN ODER NISHT ZAYN?**

WHAT CAN YOU DO? DOS IZ UNZER MAZL.***

THE ACTORS WON IN COURT AND CONTINUED PERFORMING. YIDDISH PLAYS BECAME SO POPULAR THAT HABIMA, ISRAEL'S NATIONAL THEATER, ALSO STAGED THEM — IN HEBREW.

✱✱ TO BE OR NOT TO BE

✱✱✱ THIS IS OUR FATE

ROBESON SINGS YIDDISH

STORY: JOEL SCHECHTER

ART: SPAIN

1943. THE GREAT AFRICAN-AMERICAN ACTOR PAUL ROBESON MEETS SOVIET YIDDISH THEATER DIRECTOR SHLOYME MIKHOELS AND POET ITZIK FEFFER AT A POLO GROUNDS RALLY IN NEW YORK.

AT LAST, AN AMERICAN ACTOR CONCERNED WITH POLITICS.

1949. IN MOSCOW TO PERFORM A CONCERT, ROBESON ASKS TO SEE HIS JEWISH FRIENDS.

REGRETTABLY COMRADE FEFFER HAS GONE ON VACATION. MIKHOELS DIED IN AN AUTOMOBILE ACCIDENT.

YIDDISH AND NEGRO MUSICIANS HAVE MUCH IN COMMON.

HIDDEN MICROPHONE

IN FACT, ITZIK FEFFER WAS IN PRISON; HE AND OTHER JEWISH WRITERS AND ARTISTS HAD BEEN ARRESTED, AS ROBESON LEARNED WHEN HE MET THE POET DURING A BRIEF REUNION AT THE HOTEL.

ROOM WIRED. MIKHOELS MURDERED BY SECRET POLICE

OPPRESSION FOR EXAMPLE!

AT HIS CONCERT THAT NIGHT, ROBESON, WHO IS FLUENT IN RUSSIAN, DEDICATES THE LAST SONG OF THE EVENING TO MIKHOELS.

IN CASE YOU DON'T SPEAK YIDDISH, HERE ARE THE LYRICS— "NEVER SAY YOU HAVE REACHED THE VERY END. WHEN LEADEN SKIES A BITTER FUTURE MAY PORTEND. THE TIME FOR WHICH WE YEARN WILL YET ARRIVE AND OUR MARCHING STEPS WILL THUNDER: WE SURVIVE!"

ZOG NIT KEYNMOL AZ DU GEYST DEM LETSTN VEG, KHOTSH HIMLEN BLAYENE FARSHTELN BLOYE TEG; KUMEN VET NOKH UNDZER OYSGEBENKTE SHO, S'VET A POYK TON UNDZER TROT-MIR ZAYNEN DO

ROBESON DOES NOT OVERTLY PROTEST STALIN'S REPRESSION OF JEWS, FOR FEAR OF INFLAMING ANTI-SOVIET PASSIONS BACK IN AMERICA, BUT AFTER HIS PERFORMANCE OF THE PARTISAN HYMN, HIS MOSCOW AUDIENCE KNOWS WHERE HE STANDS. SOME OF THEM WEEP. MOST GIVE A STANDING OVATION.

SONG LYRICS TRANSLATED BY AARON KRAMER

Nadir's MESSIAH in AMERICA

STORY BY JOEL SCHECHTER

ART BY SPAIN

1933, MOISHE NADIR, A GREAT YIDDISH SATIRIST, SEES HIS PLAY "MESSIAH IN AMERICA" STAGED BY ARTEF'S ACTORS ON THE LOWER EAST SIDE.

IN THE PLAY, A FALSE MESSIAH ARRIVES ON A MOTORCYCLE.

IR DARFT A MESHIEKH?

THE MESSIAH IS HIRED BY A CONEY ISLAND SIDESHOW PRODUCER WHO SELLS TICKETS TO ALL SEEKING REDEMPTION.

A RIVAL PRODUCER HIRES AN OLDER FALSE MESSIAH, COMPLETE WITH WHITE BEARD, TO SHARE IN THE MESSIAH MARKET.

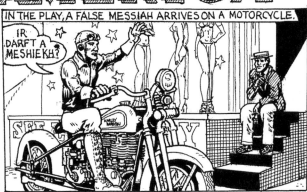

FRUM, HEYLIK, VI A GREYSER REBBE*

A BOXING MATCH IS ARRANGED TO DECIDE WHO IS THE TRUE MESSIAH.

WHY DO YOU PUT THIS IN MY GLOVE?

IT'S FOR GOOD LUCK!

THE OLDER MESSIAH WINS!

2005, NADIR'S PLAY IS ALMOST FORGOTTEN, BUT FALSE MESSIAHS STILL ARRIVE, AND COMPETE IN MORE DANGEROUS ARENAS.

KAMINSKA'S Mother Courage

ART: SPAIN

STORY: JOEL SCHECHTER

WARSAW, 1957: YIDDISH ACTRESS IDA KAMINSKA PERFORMS BRECHT'S PLAY, "MOTHER COURAGE". THE JEWISH MOTHER PULLS A CANTEEN WAGON ACROSS BATTLEFIELDS AND TRIES TO KEEP HER CHILDREN OUT OF THE ARMY.

VI KENEN MIR FIRN A MILKHOME VEN S'ZAYNEN NITO KAYN SOLDATEN?*

OBER ZEY DARFIN NIT ZAYN MAYNE**

** DO THEY HAVE TO BE MINE?

KAMINSKA'S MOTHER, THE FAMOUS ACTRESS ESTER-ROKHL KAMINSKA, COULD NOT KEEP HER DAUGHTER OUT OF WAR OR THEATER. IN 1916 IDA, AT AGE 17, PORTRAYED ISAAC IN GOLDFADN'S "THE BINDING OF ISAAC" WHILE GERMAN TROOPS OCCUPIED WARSAW.

IN 1941, KAMINSKA'S COURAGEOUS YIDDISH TROUPE PERFORMED GOLDFADN'S "THE TENTH COMMANDMENT" WHILE BOMBS FELL ON ROVNO.

WHAT ABOUT THE SIXTH COMMANDMENT?

AFTER THE WAR KAMINSKA DIRECTED THE ONLY STATE YIDDISH THEATER IN POLAND. BUT MOST YIDDISH THEATERGOERS WERE GONE. POLISH CRITIC JAN KOTT LAMENTED THIS TRAGEDY WHEN HE SAW KAMINSKA'S "MOTHER COURAGE" IN WARSAW.

HARDLY ANYONE THERE COULD UNDERSTAND YIDDISH. THE TRAGEDY OF "MOTHER COURAGE" WAS NOT PERFORMED ON THE STAGE. THE SPECTATORS MAKE THE THEATER AS MUCH AS THE ACTORS DO.

1967. KAMINSKA'S MOTHER COURAGE SPOKE YIDDISH IN NEW YORK, TOO, AS THE ACTRESS PULLED THE COURAGE CANTEEN INSIDE THE BILLY ROSE THEATER ON BROADWAY.

HOW LONG WON'T YOU STAND FOR INJUSTICE, ONE HOUR? OR TWO?

AFTER BRAVING ANTI-SEMITISM IN POLAND AND PERFORMING OVER 150 DIFFERENT ROLES THERE, KAMINSKA EMIGRATED TO NEW YORK, WHERE SHE HOPED TO START A NEW YIDDISH THEATER BEFORE SHE DIED IN 1980.

BRAVERY! IN A GOOD COUNTRY, SUCH VIRTUES WOULDN'T BE NEEDED. WE COULD ALL BE COWARDS AND RELAX.

IT CAN'T HAPPEN HERE
IN YIDDISH

STORY BY: JOEL SCHECHTER   ART BY: SPAIN

ON OCTOBER 27, 1936, FASCISM ARRIVED IN THE UNITED STATES, AT LEAST ON STAGE. THAT NIGHT THE FEDERAL THEATER PROJECT OPENED A PLAY BASED ON SINCLAIR LEWIS'S NOVEL ABOUT THE ELECTION OF A FASCIST PRESIDENT. "IT CAN'T HAPPEN HERE" WAS PERFORMED IN ENGLISH AT THE ADELPHI THEATER AND IN YIDDISH AT THE BILTMORE THEATER IN NEW YORK. (IT SIMULTANEOUSLY OPENED IN 16 OTHER AMERICAN CITIES)

HALLIE FLANAGAN, ARTISTIC DIRECTOR OF THE FEDERAL THEATER PROJECT, SAW ACT ONE OF THE PLAY IN ENGLISH AND ACT TWO IN YIDDISH ON OPENING NIGHT. AFTERWARDS SHE SAID:

THE YIDDISH PRODUCTION INCLUDED SEVERAL SCENES, NOTABLY THE CONCENTRATION CAMP SCENE, OMITTED AT THE ADELPHI. AND ON THE WHOLE I THOUGHT IT A BETTER SHOW.

THE AMERICAN CONCENTRATION CAMP PRISONERS WHO SPOKE YIDDISH INCLUDED DOREMUS JESSUP, A NEWSPAPER EDITOR ARRESTED FOR PROTESTING AGAINST THE COUNTRY'S FASCIST PRESIDENT, BUZZ WINDRIP. JESSUP, PORTRAYED BY ACTOR JULIUS ADLER, ESCAPED FROM HIS PRISON CELL TO JOIN A RESISTANCE MOVEMENT IN CANADA.

ZEY VELN MIKH NIT KHAPN-NIT A LEBEDIKN * *

JESSUP ESCAPES BY IMPERSONATING A PRISON DOCTOR

LATE IN JOINING THE ANTI-FASCIST MOVEMENT, JESSUP ADMITS: "THIS TYRANNY ISN'T PRIMARILY THE FAULT OF BIG BUSINESS OR OF THE DEMAGOGUES. IT'S THE FAULT OF ALL THE RESPECTABLE DOREMUS JESSUPS THAT LET THE CROOKS COME IN WITHOUT A PROTEST."

MARK TWAIN TRANSLATED

STORY: JOEL SCHECHTER   ART: SPAIN

SKULNIK ON STRIKE

STORY: JOEL SCHECHTER
ART: SPAIN

1932. YIDDISH ACTOR MENASHA SKULNIK JOINS A UNION OF KOSHER CHICKEN CUTTERS AND GOES ON STRIKE—IN A STAGE PLAY. SKULNIK (1890-1970) PORTRAYS A SHLEMIEL, A NAIVE, UNLUCKY CHARACTER, IN A HAT TOO SMALL FOR HIS HEAD. SOME CRITICS CALL HIS COMIC PLAYS "SHUND"—LITERARY TRASH; BUT THE PUBLIC LOVES HIM.

NO ORDINARY SHLEMIEL, SKULNIK AS GETZEL IS A CHICKEN FLICKER WHO DREAMS OF BECOMING A CHICKEN CUTTER AND MAYBE A SULTAN. HE LEADS A STRIKE AGAINST THE WHOLESALE CHICKEN MARKET OF HIS WIFE'S BROTHER, HIS MARRIAGE SURVIVES AND THE UNION WINS TOO.

LATER, IN THE WORLD BEYOND THE STAGE, OTHER STRIKES FOLLOW. BY 1934, THE AMERICAN LABOR MOVEMENT IS STAGING HUGE MARCHES, PICKET LINES AND FACTORY OCCUPATIONS ACROSS THE COUNTRY.

SKULNIK'S SUCCESS IN THIS PLAY LEADS HIM TO NEW ROLES ON RADIO, TELEVISION AND BROADWAY. THE SHLEMIEL'S IMPERVIOUSNESS TO THE ODDS AGAINST HIM, AND HIS NAÏVE FAITH IN OTHERS, WIN THE DAY.

Modicut's DYBBUK

STORY BY JOEL SCHECHTER   ART BY SPAIN

FROM 1925 TO 1933, YOSL CUTLER AND ZUNI MAUD'S YIDDISH COMMUNIST PUPPET THEATER, MODICUT, THRIVED ON THE LOWER EAST SIDE. ON THEIR SMALL STAGE, ANCIENT RABBIS DANCED FOR JOY, TENANTS WON RENT STRIKES AND HITLER BARED HIS FANGS.

MAUD AND CUTLER TOURED THEIR PUPPET SHOWS TO ACCLAIM IN VILNA, WARSAW, LONDON, PARIS, MOSCOW AND THE CATSKILLS.

IN NEW YORK, THEY STAGED MOISHE NADIR'S IRREVERENT PLAY "THE OTHER WORLD" IN WHICH GOD ASKS "WHO IS GREAT?" AND THE ANGEL GABRIEL REPLIES "YOU ARE".

FUN VANEN VEYSTU?*

DU HAST MIR ALEYN GEZOGT. **

* HOW DO YOU KNOW? ** YOU TOLD ME SO YOURSELF.

IN MODICUT'S 1930s PARODY OF "THE DYBBUK", THE BRIDE IS MAE WEST. FDR AS THE RABBI FAILS TO VANQUISH THE SPIRIT (DYBBUK) IN MAE.

IN THE NAME OF WPA, NRA, CCC, I COMMAND YOU DYBBUK **GO AWAY!**

IS THAT AN EXCOMMUNICATION IN YOUR POCKET?

MODICUT DISBANDED IN 1933. BUT A NEW RADICAL PUPPETRY IN ANTIWAR PARADES AND YIDDISHKEIT PLAYS KEEPS ALIVE THE RESISTANT SPIRIT OF MAUD AND CUTLER'S COMIC DYBBUK.

RIVINGTON STREET

STORY: JOEL SCHECHTER TRANSLATION: HARVEY FINK ART: SPAIN

ONE NIGHT WE HEARD THE BILLY TIPTON MEMORIAL SAXOPHONE QUARTET PLAY IN "TONIC", A LOWER EAST SIDE JAZZ CLUB WHICH USED TO BE A KOSHER WINE CELLAR.

EXIT

WALKING HOME ALONG RIVINGTON STREET, IN THE DAMP NIGHT AIR, I SAW AN OLD YIDDISH PEDDLER WITH A BASKET ON HIS ARM.

GOT HOT FARLOYRN DOS BODN UNTER ZIKH, UN BENK KRAKHN.*

* GOD HAS LOST HIS FOOTING AND BANKS ARE COLLAPSING.

I HAD SEEN HIM BEFORE. BILL GROPPER DREW HIS PORTRAIT FOR NADIR'S EPIC POEM "RIVINGTON STREET." HE WAS A CLOAK MAKER BEFORE THE 1929 CRASH REDUCED HIM TO SELLING FRUIT AND HALVAH ON THE STREET.

NOW THAT'S WHAT I CALL WORK, BROTHER! ONCE EVERYONE EXPECTED TO WORK.

I STILL REMEMBER RIVINGTON STREET FROM THE TIME GALICIAN JEWS FRESH OFF THE BOAT... PUSHED THE "PEYES" BACK BEHIND THEIR EARS AND PEDDLED LEMONS ON THE STREETS FOR SO LONG UNTIL GOD CAME TO THEIR AID THEN THEY OPENED SWEATSHOPS AND GAVE YOUNG GIRLS FROM THEIR HOMETOWNS A SHOVE TO WORK FOURTEEN, FIFTEEN HOURS A DAY.

WHEN NADIR MET THE PEDDLER, RIVINGTON STREET WAS UNDER REPAIR. NEAR THEM THE ASPHALT CRUMPLED. NO WONDER GOD LOST HIS FOOTING.

THE PEDDLER DESCRIBED THE OLD LOWER EAST SIDE HE KNEW: THE JEWISH GANGSTERS, TAILORS CARRYING THEIR OWN SEWING MACHINES, UNTRANSLATED POETS, ACTIVISTS AND POPULAR ACTORS IN A CAFE.

IN THE ROLE OF HIRSH LEKERT I'M A GOD.

THEN YOU CAN AFFORD TO PAY THE CHECK.

HE HAD SEEN OTHER PEDDLERS CLIMB THE LADDER OF SUCCESS.

OUT INTO WIDE OPEN AMERICA, TO UPTOWN, TO THE RICH YAHODIM, TO FIFTH AVENUE, TO RIVERSIDE DRIVE, TO MORNINGSIDE, TO THE PALISADES... ATLANTIC CITY, LAKEWOOD, ASBURY PARK... MIAMI, PALM BEACH

A TIP OF THE YARMULKE TO PAUL BUHLE

OCCASIONALLY THE SUCCESSFUL ENTREPRENEURS RETURNED TO RIVINGTON STREET.

...THEY COME IN THEIR BEIGE COLORED LIMOUSINES THESE DAYS ON "SLUMMING TOURS" THROUGH THE LOWER EAST-SIDE SNEAKING OFF FROM THE CHAUFFEURS TO RUN AND EAT SOME GARLIC-WURST, ROMANIAN MAMELIGE, DELICIOUS KNISHES, AND KASHA.

NO FRIEND OF THE RICH, THE PEDDLER ONCE KNEW FAMOUS YIDDISH ANARCHISTS.

I STILL REMEMBER HOW JOHAN MOST BROUGHT OUT THE FIRST PAPER, AND WHEN ASKED: "WHO MAKES THE CONSTITUTION OF THE UNITED STATES?" HE ANSWERED: "JAY GOULD AND ROCKEFELLER."

YO MIR HOBN KAYN BANANAS*

* YES, WE HAVE NO BANANAS

ONCE THE PEDDLER AND OTHER YIDDISH IMMIGRANTS SAW PROMISE IN AMERICA. BUT BY 1932, HE TOLD NADIR:

HOW MUCH UNEMPLOYMENT DO WE HAVE THESE DAYS? TWELVE MILLION? SIXTEEN MILLION?... AND STOCKS FALLING AND FALLING AND FALLING. THE ONLY ARTICLE THAT'S ON THE RISE IS POVERTY. WHAT IS IT THEY SING IN THE YIDDISH THEATER? "OY PO-VER-TY, HOW I LOVE YOU FROM A DISTANCE OY POVERTY, PLEASE REMIND ME OF BETTER TIMES.

AT ONE TIME I HAD TALENT. I COULD'VE BEEN A POET OR A WATCH MAKER, AND NOW I'M A SICK JEW WITH A BASKET... BUT GOD HIMSELF... HAS PROBLEMS OF HIS OWN - NO DEPENDING ON SUCH A HAS-BEEN GOD LIKE THAT... IT'S MUCH BETTER TO WALK WITH A BASKET SHOUTING: HALVAH.

LISTEN, SOMETIMES IT SEEMS TO ME THAT I MYSELF AM THE OLD RIVINGTON STREET... TORN UP, RUINED AND DEPRESSED... I HAVEN'T PAID MY RENT... AND THEY CAN PUT ME OUT ON THE STREET WITH ALL MY WORLDLY POSSESSIONS.

THE RAIN INCREASED, THE PEDDLER VANISHED. ALONE ON RIVINGTON STREET, I WALKED PAST ABC NO RIO, VERLAINE, OTHER CLUBS AND THE NEW HIGH RISE WHERE SHMULKA BERNSTEIN'S DELICATESSEN ONCE STOOD. RIVINGTON STREET NO LONGER LOOKED LIKE THE PLACE NADIR DESCRIBED; HE CLOSED HIS POEM WITH A VISION OF THOUSANDS ON THE MARCH, PEOPLE INFLAMED WITH THE FERVOR FOR CHANGE, UNITED TO REPAIR THE WORLD.

NO JIM CROW

4 HOUR DAY

I.W.W. AN INJURY TO ONE IS AN INJURY TO ALL INDUSTRIAL WORKERS OF THE WORLD

A FLAME RISES FROM YOUR HOME FACTORY, FROM YOUR NEEDLE SHOPS AND FUR SHOPS AND STORES AND OFFICES AND CELLARS AND ATTICS, FROM PUSHCARTS AND TAXIS. A FLAME THAT WILL UNITE WITH ALL THE FLAMES OF THE WORLD; THAT WILL RISE OVER THE CITADELS OF POVERTY, OVER THE FORTRESSES OF WORK; THAT WILL COVER THE PUS-FILLED SPECTERS OF HUNGER, OF NEED, AND OF BLOOD, AND WILL FLAME THE LENGTH AND BREADTH OF THE WORLD AND FLUTTER, AND FLUTTER, AND FLUTTER.

Illustration by Sharon Rudahl

MOLLY PICON:
GODDESS OF SECOND AVENUE

M olly Picon, the leading figure of the Yiddish stage, was famed for her sprightliness, her humor, her diminutive stature, and her cross-dressing. She was an incredibly versatile actress, onstage or in front of the camera, from 1904, at age six, to 1984, at age eighty-six. Picon was also an icon of almost unimaginable importance in conveying to audiences across the world her love of Yiddish and the subtle meanings of *Yiddishkeit*.

Born Malka Opiekun, on February 28, 1898 in New York City, daughter of a seamstress in the local Yiddish theater, she was discovered at age six , singing, dancing, and doing somersaults, by Boris Thomashefsky's sister-in-law. She soon began performing as a novelty "movie star" in the two-reel silent nickelodeons as Baby Margaret, the International Comedienne. On the vaudeville circuit years later, she met Jacob Kalich, manager of Boston's Grand Opera House. Husband, constant companion, and savant, he continued to write some of her best material and to produce her works, almost until his death in 1975.

The two embarked on transatlantic tours of the 1920s, helping to bind an always fragmented Yiddish world together. Back in the United States, Picon starred in a string of hits, nearly taking over the Second Avenue Theater, later renamed the Molly Picon Theater and one of the key locations of Yiddish Broadway. She and Kalich nevertheless headed back to Europe once more, to be closer to the homeland of *Yiddishkeit*. Her mission lay in Yiddish film as well. She debuted in *Das Judenmädel* (*The Jewish Girl*) in Austria in 1921, but became notorious in *East and West*, shot in Vienna two years later. The Americanized jazz baby with stylishly bobbed hair and bee-stung lips made a smashing appearance in shtetl life in this latter film, teaching yeshiva boys how to shimmy, and also crashing a wedding dressed as a boy, dancing in pajamas, and demanding her own wedding! A hit in Europe, the film opened in New York in 1924 under the title *Mazel Tov* and set off a storm of disapproval.

Picon's Yiddish film career was destined to be cut short. She starred in *Mamela* (1938), very nearly the final Yiddish film made in Poland, but her lasting triumph would remain *Yidl mitn Fidl* (*Yiddle with His Fiddle*) in 1936, created expressly for her, with the best score of any Yiddish film ever made. Her signature song, "Oy Mame, Bin Ikh Farlibt" ("Oh Mama, I'm in Love"), was a worldwide Yiddish hit. *Yidl mitn Fidl* notably offered a kind of documentary about the living conditions of Eastern European Jews, seen by their American relatives not only as from another continent but as if from another century. According to *Variety*, *Yidl mitn Fidl* combined all of Picon's verbal, musical, and acrobatic moves in film, theater, stage, and radio (where she had her own program from 1936 onward). Between films, Picon remained the highest-paid Yiddish stage performer in the world. No longer the glamorous youth, she became most famous during the 1940s for touring and performing, first on U.S. military bases, then after the war in refugee centers. Her troupe frequently reached the displaced persons camps as the first entertainers.

Picon later returned to the fading Yiddish stage as the star of a 1959 hit, *The Kosher Widow*, otherwise mostly acting in television, adopting the persona of a loving and very, *very* Jewish grandma, "the little yente with the big, expressive talent." Most

Illustration by Sharon Rudahl

memorably, at least to sitcom watchers, she was Mrs. Bronson on the most Yiddish-accented show ever aired, *Car 54, Where Are You?* Picon also played herself on the late-night show circuit, from *Toast of the Town* (the original *Ed Sullivan Show*) to the *Tonight Show* with Johnny Carson. The sharp-witted and lively, if aging, typically female Jewish "personality," Molly Picon represented a generation and a sensibility. Her return to film success, after *Yidl mitn Fidl*, came first as the yenta and matchmaker in the Frank Sinatra vehicle *Come Blow Your Horn* (1963). Then she was Yente in the film adaptation of *Fiddler on the Roof* (1971) and, in the same year, a madame, Mrs. Cherry, in the Barbra Streisand screwball comedy *For Pete's Sake* (1974). The Molly Picon room, an entire area of New York City's famed Second Avenue Deli, was filled with her memorabilia after her death in 1992—perhaps the most appropriate tribute of all.

1927~ SOPHIE TUCKER AND MOLLY PICON
SHARE THE PLAYBILL AT NEW YORK'S
HIGH-TONED PALACE THEATER.

Illustration by Sharon Rudahl

Illustration by Sharon Rudahl

EDGAR G. ULMER & GREEN FIELDS

T he most successful Yiddish film ever produced, and perhaps ever likely to be produced, owed its creation to many things, Yiddish theater first of all. But its existence is also due to the indefatigable determination of the director Edgar G. Ulmer (1904–72). An auteur of the vernacular and a determined escapee from the Hollywood studio system, Ulmer produced more Yiddish American feature films than anyone else. He also remains one of the most eccentric figures in all of film history.

Born in Bohemia, the son of a socialistic wine merchant, Ulmer grew up mostly in Vienna, where he eventually studied architecture at the distinguished Academy of Arts and Sciences. Homeless and impoverished by war, Ulmer was more or less adopted by the family of later famed actor Joseph Schildkraut.

Ulmer began in the film industry as a set builder. Late in life he insisted that his true introduction to the industry had been when he was working on *The Golem* (1920). Ulmer came to Hollywood in 1923 and, dividing his time between Los Angeles and Berlin, worked with many film greats for the next decade, including F. W. Murnau, Erich Von Stroheim, Emil Jannings, and Ernst Lubitch. After directing minor westerns and the first solid documentary about the danger of venereal disease, Ulmer made the expressionist horror classic *The Black Cat* (1934), pairing Boris Karloff and Bela Lugosi for the first time. Sickened by Hollywood and introduced to Yiddish art theater by attending Second Avenue Broadway, Ulmer quickly found his métier: film adaptations of Yiddish stage dramas, comedies, and musicals, employing Yiddish theatrical veterans while he oversaw the process.

Raising money from needle trades unions, from former Yiddish actor Paul Muni, and from the Household Finance Corporation on the collateral of his own mortgaged home, Ulmer filmed *Grine Felder* (*Green Fields*) in New Jersey during 1937. Based on a hit play by Peretz Hirshbein, it was suffused with nostalgia for a folkish collectivity and an evocation of nature's bounties. The young rabbi who visits this distant spot learns about redemption beyond the power of his Torah and falls in love to boot. The audience responded with their own version of spiritual enthusiasm: At the Times Square opening, they refused to leave their seats and had to be escorted out so as to allow seating for the next showing. Perhaps a million Jews worldwide saw this film. Ulmer insisted that he earned all of three hundred dollars for his work, and also claimed to have consciously followed the style of Sholem Aleichem and Marc Chagall, blending folklore and fantasy.

During the next three years, Ulmer also completed *Yankl der Shmidt* (*The Singing Blacksmith*), *Di Klyatsche* (*The Light Ahead*), and *American Shadkhn* (*The Marriage Broker*)—none as successful as *Grine Felder* in artistic or financial terms, but nevertheless sturdy examples of the last wave of Yiddish cinema. Together with the writers, technicians, and the actors themselves, Ulmer had succeeded in creating something literally out of time, a fantasy version of Jewish life of the Pale unseen in Hollywood until *Fiddler on the Roof*.

Ulmer went on to produce more than a hundred other films, some of them shot in a single weekend. None had notably Jewish content, but *Detour* (1945) was a classic of the noir genre, anticipating disillusionment in the great hopes for the era to follow victory over fascism, and his late films (including warnings against nuclear war, and *The Naked Venus*, a curious nudist camp–based feature in 1959 without his name on the credits) frequently urged redemption from war, hatred, and philistinism. *Grine Felder* remains his monument.

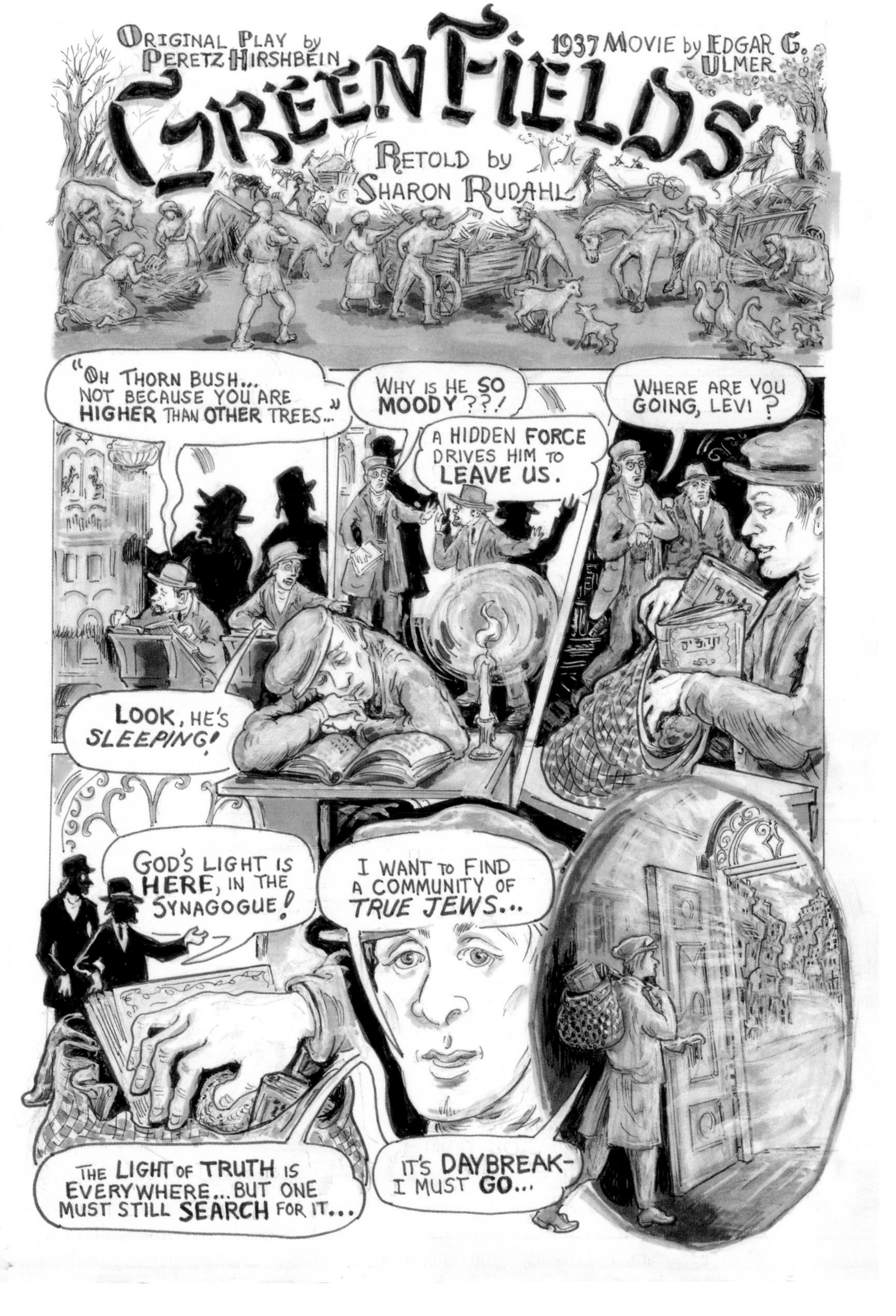
ORIGINAL PLAY by PERETZ HIRSHBEIN
GREENFIELDS
1937 MOVIE by EDGAR G. ULMER
RETOLD by SHARON RUDAHL
"OH THORN BUSH... NOT BECAUSE YOU ARE HIGHER THAN OTHER TREES..."
WHY IS HE SO MOODY??!
A HIDDEN FORCE DRIVES HIM TO LEAVE US.
WHERE ARE YOU GOING, LEVI?
LOOK, HE'S SLEEPING!
GOD'S LIGHT IS HERE, IN THE SYNAGOGUE!
I WANT TO FIND A COMMUNITY OF TRUE JEWS...
THE LIGHT OF TRUTH IS EVERYWHERE... BUT ONE MUST STILL SEARCH FOR IT...
IT'S DAYBREAK- I MUST GO...

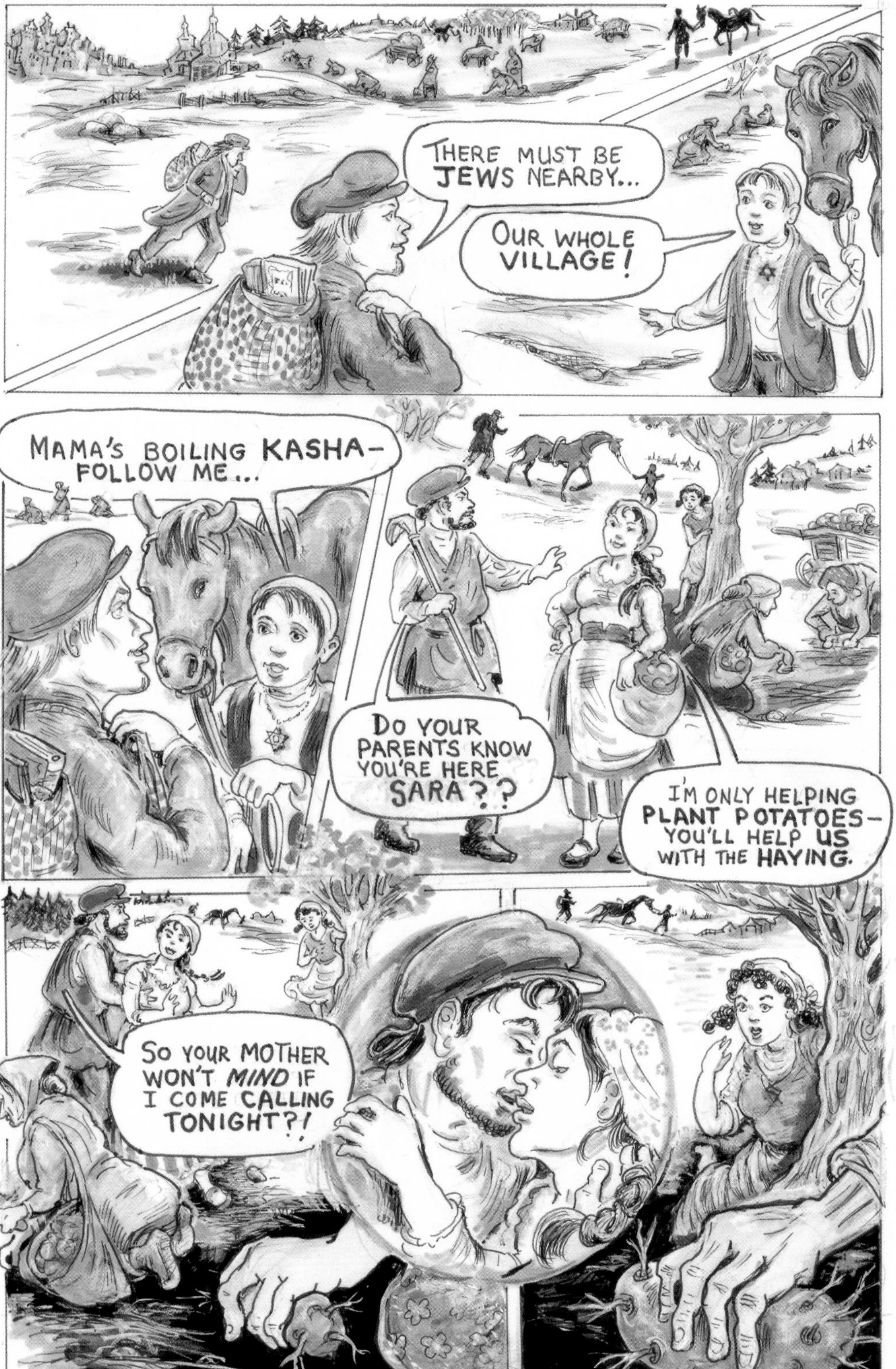
THERE MUST BE JEWS NEARBY...
OUR WHOLE VILLAGE!
MAMA'S BOILING KASHA-FOLLOW ME...
DO YOUR PARENTS KNOW YOU'RE HERE SARA??
I'M ONLY HELPING PLANT POTATOES-YOU'LL HELP US WITH THE HAYING.
SO YOUR MOTHER WON'T *MIND* IF I COME CALLING TONIGHT?!

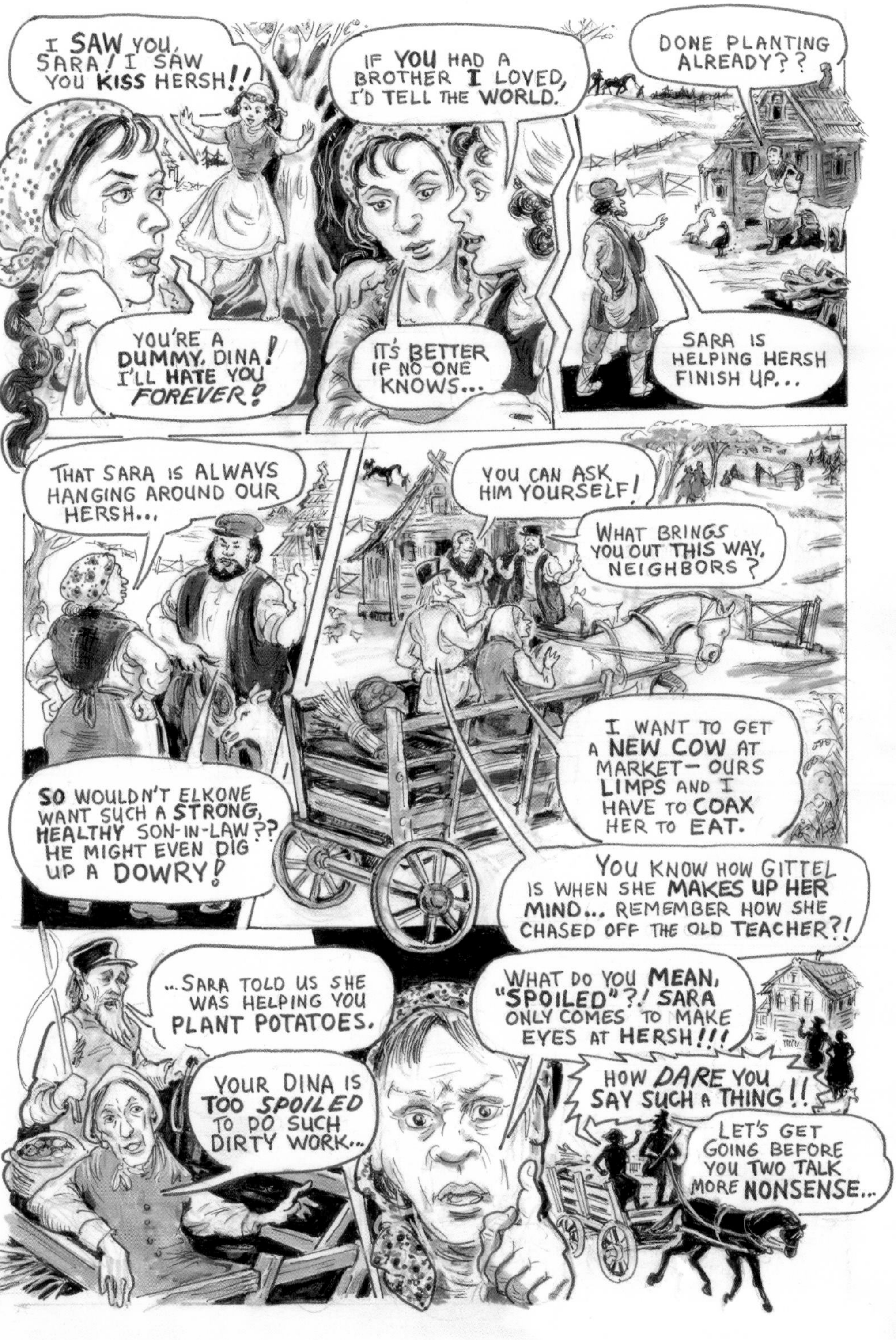
I SAW YOU, SARA! I SAW YOU KISS HERSH!!
YOU'RE A DUMMY, DINA! I'LL HATE YOU FOREVER!
IF YOU HAD A BROTHER I LOVED, I'D TELL THE WORLD.
IT'S BETTER IF NO ONE KNOWS...
DONE PLANTING ALREADY??
SARA IS HELPING HERSH FINISH UP...
THAT SARA IS ALWAYS HANGING AROUND OUR HERSH...
SO WOULDN'T ELKONE WANT SUCH A STRONG, HEALTHY SON-IN-LAW?? HE MIGHT EVEN DIG UP A DOWRY!
YOU CAN ASK HIM YOURSELF!
WHAT BRINGS YOU OUT THIS WAY, NEIGHBORS?
I WANT TO GET A NEW COW AT MARKET— OURS LIMPS AND I HAVE TO COAX HER TO EAT.
YOU KNOW HOW GITTEL IS WHEN SHE MAKES UP HER MIND... REMEMBER HOW SHE CHASED OFF THE OLD TEACHER?!
...SARA TOLD US SHE WAS HELPING YOU PLANT POTATOES.
YOUR DINA IS TOO SPOILED TO DO SUCH DIRTY WORK...
WHAT DO YOU MEAN, "SPOILED"?! SARA ONLY COMES TO MAKE EYES AT HERSH!!!
HOW DARE YOU SAY SUCH A THING!!
LET'S GET GOING BEFORE YOU TWO TALK MORE NONSENSE...

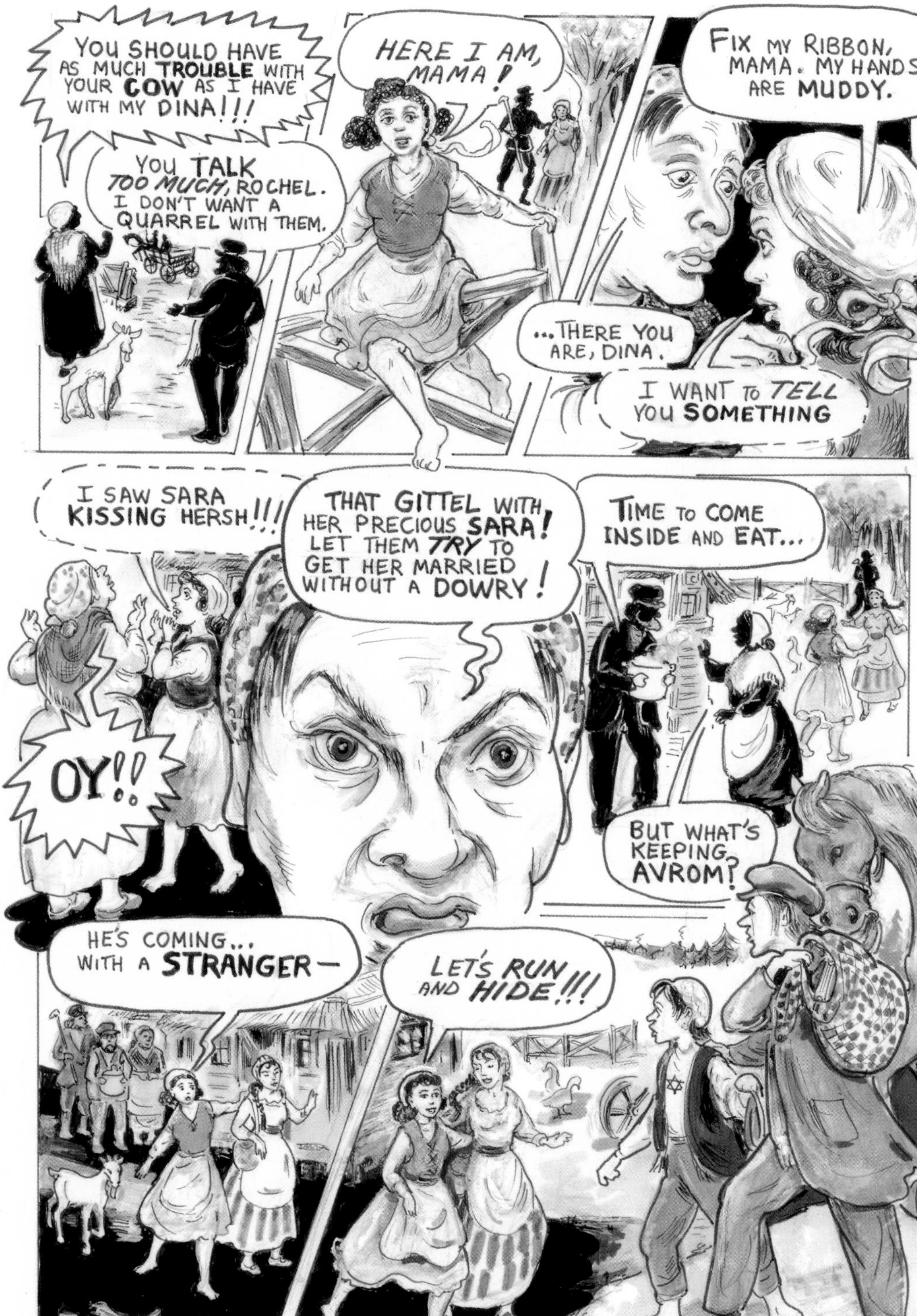

YOU SHOULD HAVE AS MUCH TROUBLE WITH YOUR COW AS I HAVE WITH MY DINA!!!
YOU TALK TOO MUCH, ROCHEL. I DON'T WANT A QUARREL WITH THEM.
HERE I AM, MAMA!
FIX MY RIBBON, MAMA. MY HANDS ARE MUDDY.
...THERE YOU ARE, DINA.
I WANT TO TELL YOU SOMETHING
I SAW SARA KISSING HERSH!!!
OY!!
THAT GITTEL WITH HER PRECIOUS SARA! LET THEM TRY TO GET HER MARRIED WITHOUT A DOWRY!
TIME TO COME INSIDE AND EAT...
BUT WHAT'S KEEPING AVROM?
HE'S COMING... WITH A STRANGER—
LET'S RUN AND HIDE!!!

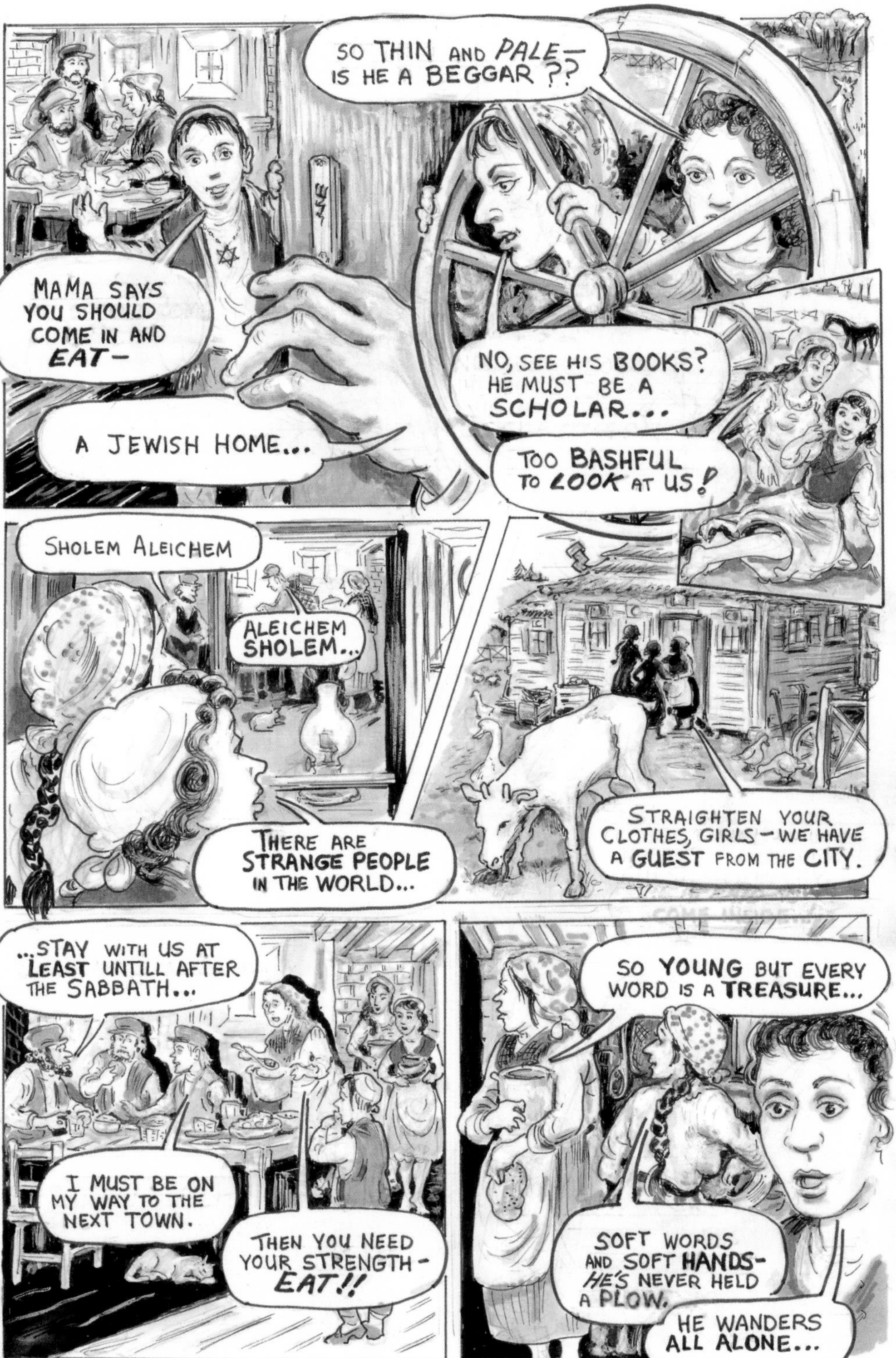
SO THIN AND PALE—
IS HE A BEGGAR ??
MAMA SAYS YOU SHOULD COME IN AND EAT—
A JEWISH HOME...
NO, SEE HIS BOOKS? HE MUST BE A SCHOLAR...
TOO BASHFUL TO LOOK AT US!
SHOLEM ALEICHEM
ALEICHEM SHOLEM...
THERE ARE STRANGE PEOPLE IN THE WORLD...
STRAIGHTEN YOUR CLOTHES, GIRLS—WE HAVE A GUEST FROM THE CITY.
...STAY WITH US AT LEAST UNTILL AFTER THE SABBATH...
I MUST BE ON MY WAY TO THE NEXT TOWN.
THEN YOU NEED YOUR STRENGTH-EAT!!
SO YOUNG BUT EVERY WORD IS A TREASURE...
SOFT WORDS AND SOFT HANDS-HE'S NEVER HELD A PLOW.
HE WANDERS ALL ALONE...

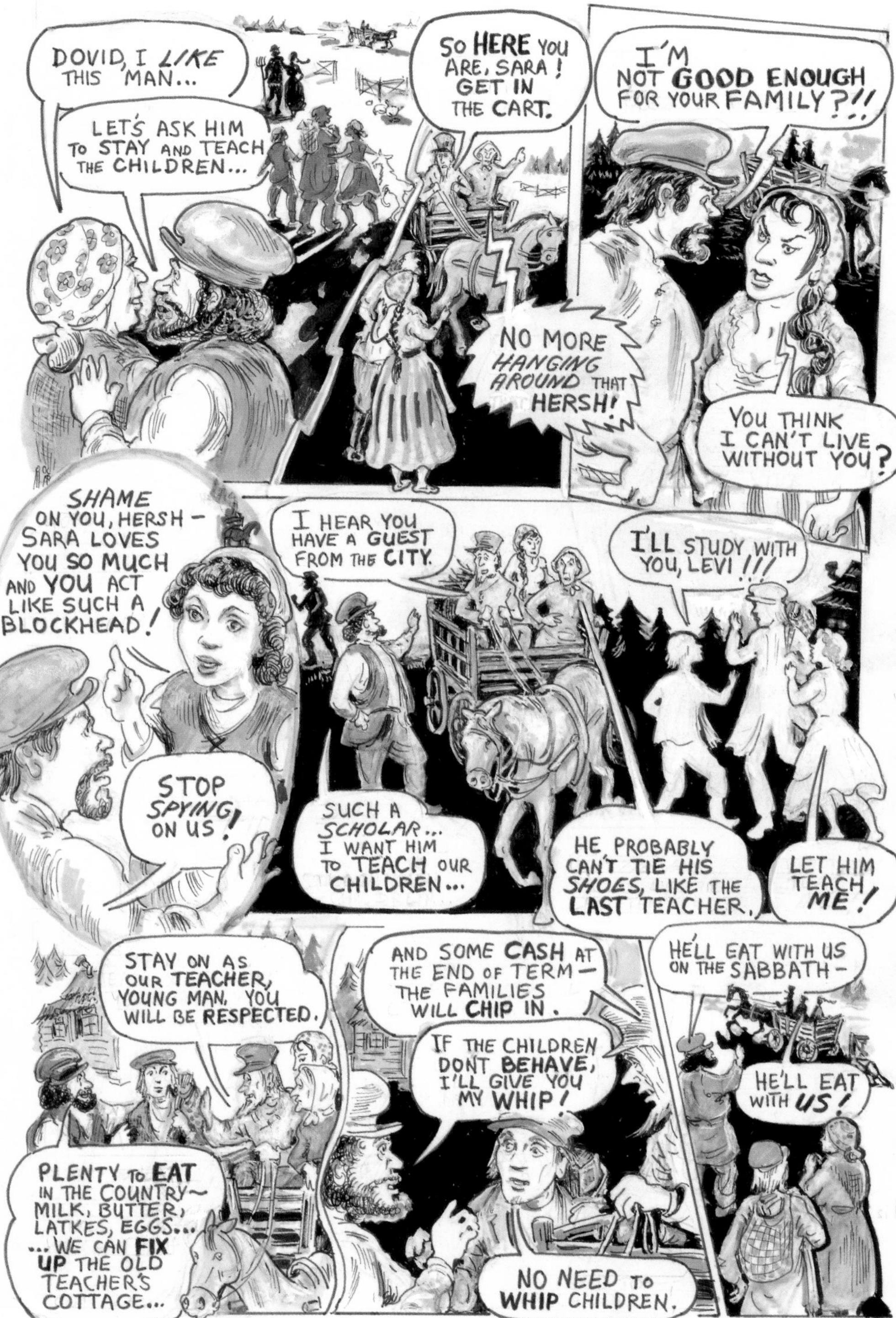
DOVID, I LIKE THIS MAN...
LET'S ASK HIM TO STAY AND TEACH THE CHILDREN...
SO HERE YOU ARE, SARA! GET IN THE CART.
NO MORE HANGING AROUND THAT HERSH!
I'M NOT GOOD ENOUGH FOR YOUR FAMILY?!!
YOU THINK I CAN'T LIVE WITHOUT YOU?
SHAME ON YOU, HERSH – SARA LOVES YOU SO MUCH AND YOU ACT LIKE SUCH A BLOCKHEAD!
STOP SPYING ON US!
I HEAR YOU HAVE A GUEST FROM THE CITY.
SUCH A SCHOLAR... I WANT HIM TO TEACH OUR CHILDREN...
HE PROBABLY CAN'T TIE HIS SHOES, LIKE THE LAST TEACHER.
I'LL STUDY WITH YOU, LEVI!!!
LET HIM TEACH ME!
STAY ON AS OUR TEACHER, YOUNG MAN. YOU WILL BE RESPECTED.
PLENTY TO EAT IN THE COUNTRY~ MILK, BUTTER, LATKES, EGGS... ...WE CAN FIX UP THE OLD TEACHER'S COTTAGE...
AND SOME CASH AT THE END OF TERM – THE FAMILIES WILL CHIP IN.
IF THE CHILDREN DONT BEHAVE, I'LL GIVE YOU MY WHIP!
NO NEED TO WHIP CHILDREN.
HE'LL EAT WITH US ON THE SABBATH –
HE'LL EAT WITH US!

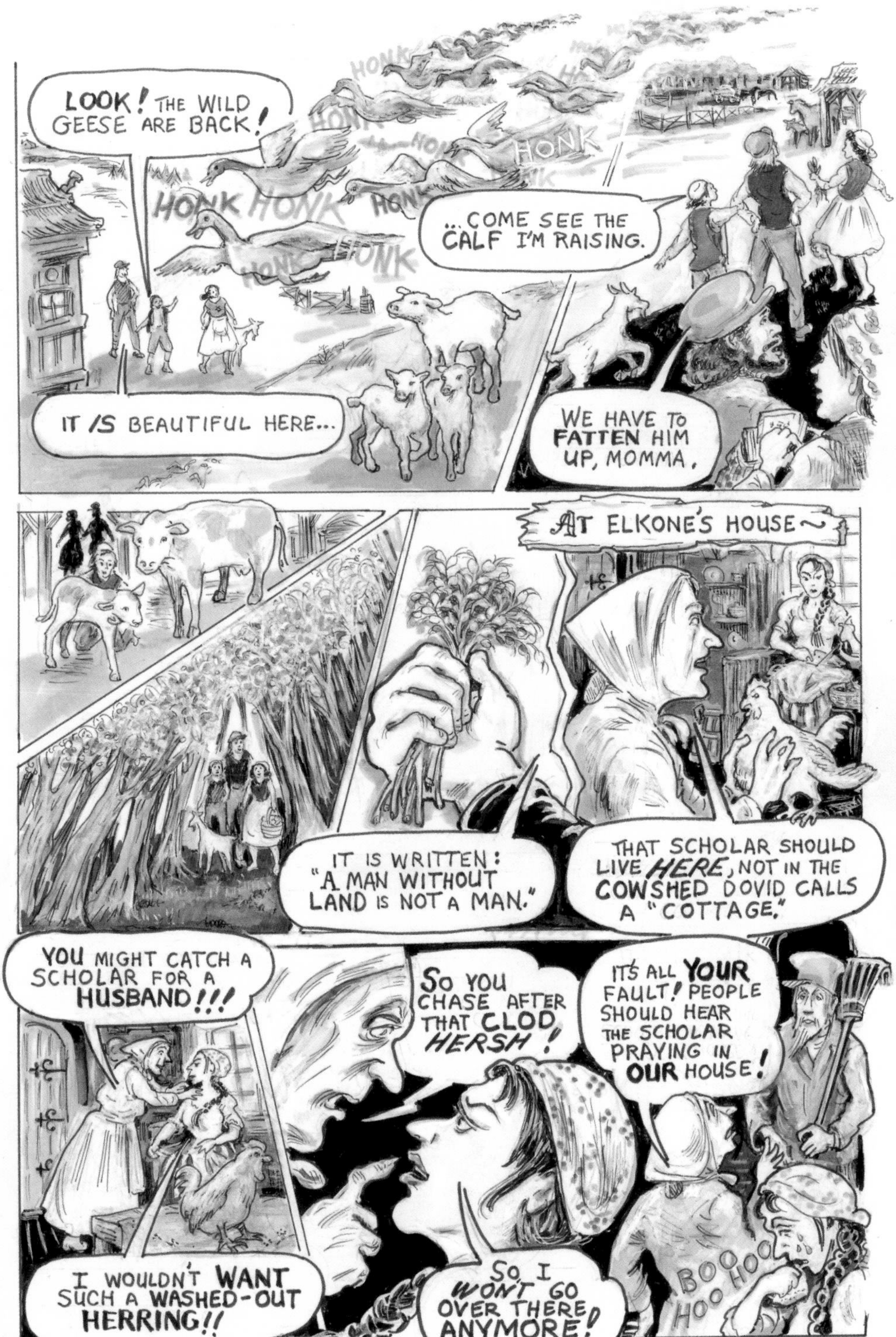
LOOK! THE WILD GEESE ARE BACK!
HONK HONK HONK HONK HONK HONK HONK
IT IS BEAUTIFUL HERE...
...COME SEE THE CALF I'M RAISING.
WE HAVE TO FATTEN HIM UP, MOMMA.
AT ELKONE'S HOUSE
IT IS WRITTEN: "A MAN WITHOUT LAND IS NOT A MAN."
THAT SCHOLAR SHOULD LIVE HERE, NOT IN THE COWSHED DOVID CALLS A "COTTAGE."
YOU MIGHT CATCH A SCHOLAR FOR A HUSBAND!!!
I WOULDN'T WANT SUCH A WASHED-OUT HERRING!!
SO YOU CHASE AFTER THAT CLOD HERSH!
SO, I WON'T GO OVER THERE ANYMORE!
IT'S ALL YOUR FAULT! PEOPLE SHOULD HEAR THE SCHOLAR PRAYING IN OUR HOUSE!
BOO HOO HOO

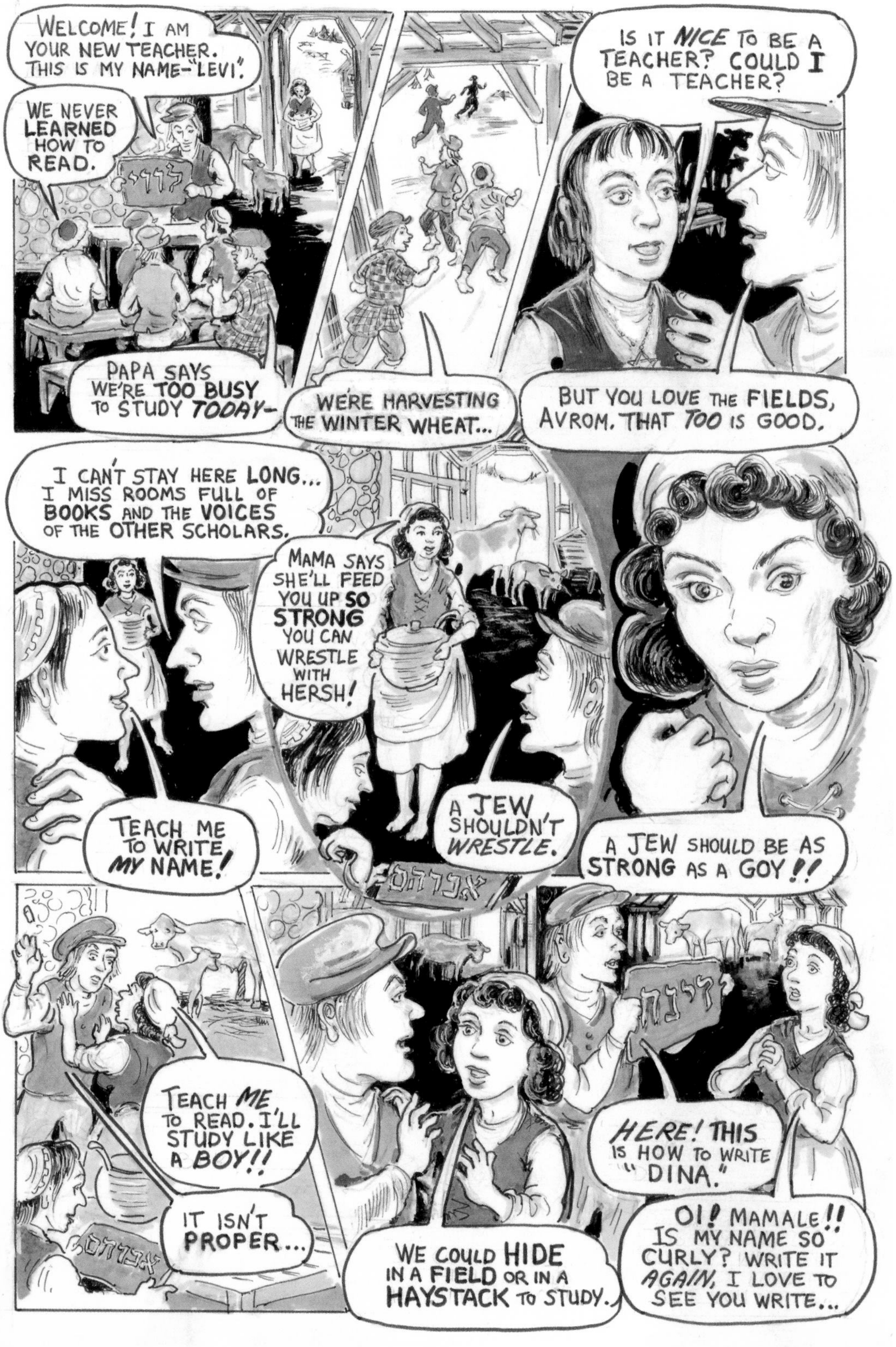
WELCOME! I AM YOUR NEW TEACHER. THIS IS MY NAME-"LEVI".
WE NEVER LEARNED HOW TO READ.
PAPA SAYS WE'RE TOO BUSY TO STUDY TODAY-
WE'RE HARVESTING THE WINTER WHEAT...
IS IT NICE TO BE A TEACHER? COULD I BE A TEACHER?
BUT YOU LOVE THE FIELDS, AVROM. THAT TOO IS GOOD.
I CAN'T STAY HERE LONG... I MISS ROOMS FULL OF BOOKS AND THE VOICES OF THE OTHER SCHOLARS.
TEACH ME TO WRITE MY NAME!
MAMA SAYS SHE'LL FEED YOU UP SO STRONG YOU CAN WRESTLE WITH HERSH!
A JEW SHOULDN'T WRESTLE.
A JEW SHOULD BE AS STRONG AS A GOY!!
TEACH ME TO READ. I'LL STUDY LIKE A BOY!!
IT ISN'T PROPER...
WE COULD HIDE IN A FIELD OR IN A HAYSTACK TO STUDY.
HERE! THIS IS HOW TO WRITE "DINA."
OI! MAMALE!! IS MY NAME SO CURLY? WRITE IT AGAIN, I LOVE TO SEE YOU WRITE...

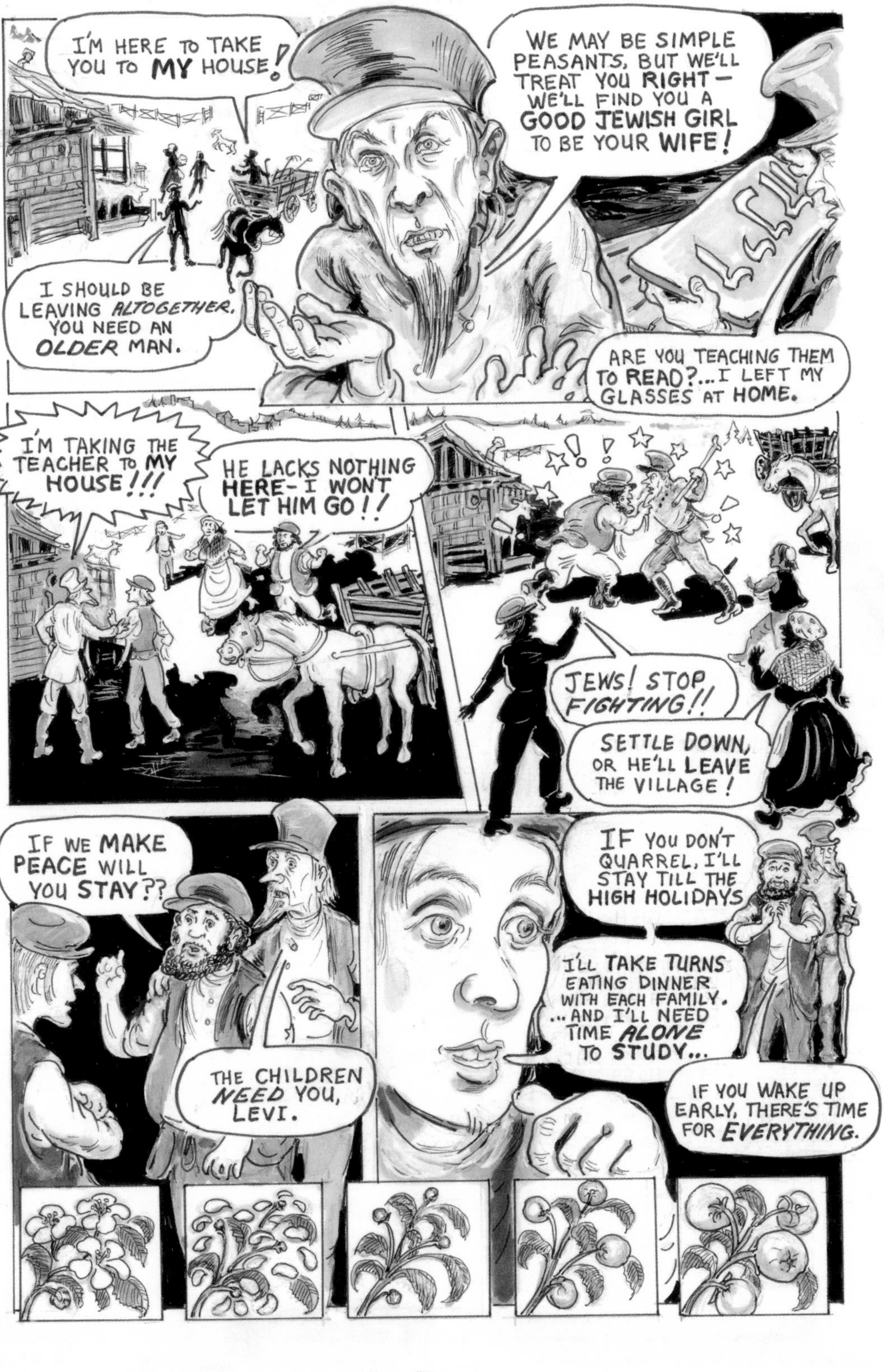
I'M HERE TO TAKE YOU TO MY HOUSE!
WE MAY BE SIMPLE PEASANTS, BUT WE'LL TREAT YOU RIGHT— WE'LL FIND YOU A GOOD JEWISH GIRL TO BE YOUR WIFE!
I SHOULD BE LEAVING ALTOGETHER. YOU NEED AN OLDER MAN.
ARE YOU TEACHING THEM TO READ?...I LEFT MY GLASSES AT HOME.
I'M TAKING THE TEACHER TO MY HOUSE!!!
HE LACKS NOTHING HERE— I WON'T LET HIM GO!!
JEWS! STOP FIGHTING!!
SETTLE DOWN, OR HE'LL LEAVE THE VILLAGE!
IF WE MAKE PEACE WILL YOU STAY??
THE CHILDREN NEED YOU, LEVI.
IF YOU DON'T QUARREL, I'LL STAY TILL THE HIGH HOLIDAYS
I'LL TAKE TURNS EATING DINNER WITH EACH FAMILY. ...AND I'LL NEED TIME ALONE TO STUDY...
IF YOU WAKE UP EARLY, THERE'S TIME FOR EVERYTHING.

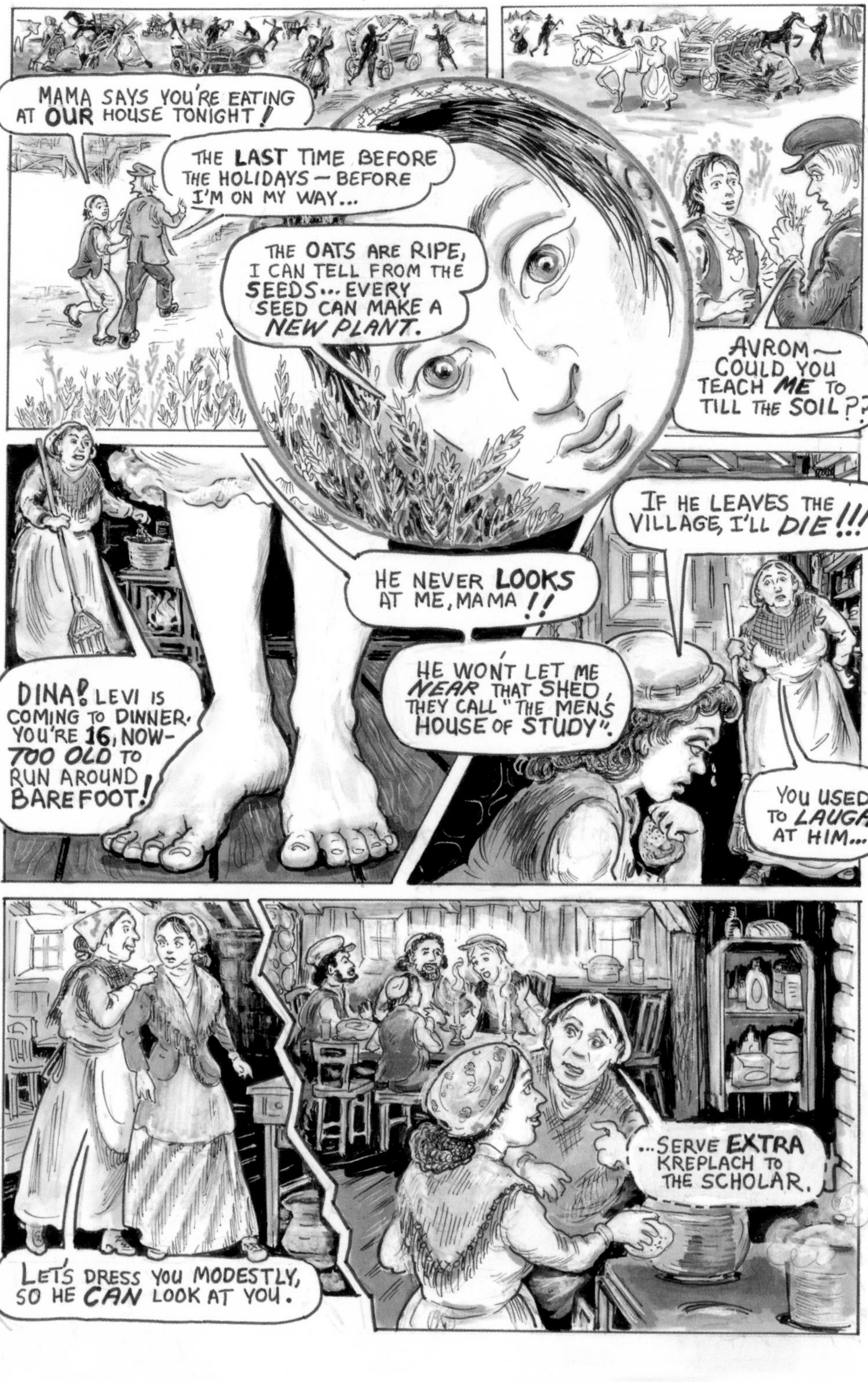

MAMA SAYS YOU'RE EATING AT OUR HOUSE TONIGHT!
THE LAST TIME BEFORE THE HOLIDAYS — BEFORE I'M ON MY WAY...
THE OATS ARE RIPE, I CAN TELL FROM THE SEEDS... EVERY SEED CAN MAKE A NEW PLANT.
AVROM — COULD YOU TEACH ME TO TILL THE SOIL??
DINA! LEVI IS COMING TO DINNER. YOU'RE 16, NOW — TOO OLD TO RUN AROUND BAREFOOT!
HE NEVER LOOKS AT ME, MAMA!!
HE WON'T LET ME NEAR THAT SHED, THEY CALL "THE MEN'S HOUSE OF STUDY".
IF HE LEAVES THE VILLAGE, I'LL DIE!!!
YOU USED TO LAUGH AT HIM...
LET'S DRESS YOU MODESTLY, SO HE CAN LOOK AT YOU.
...SERVE EXTRA KREPLACH TO THE SCHOLAR.

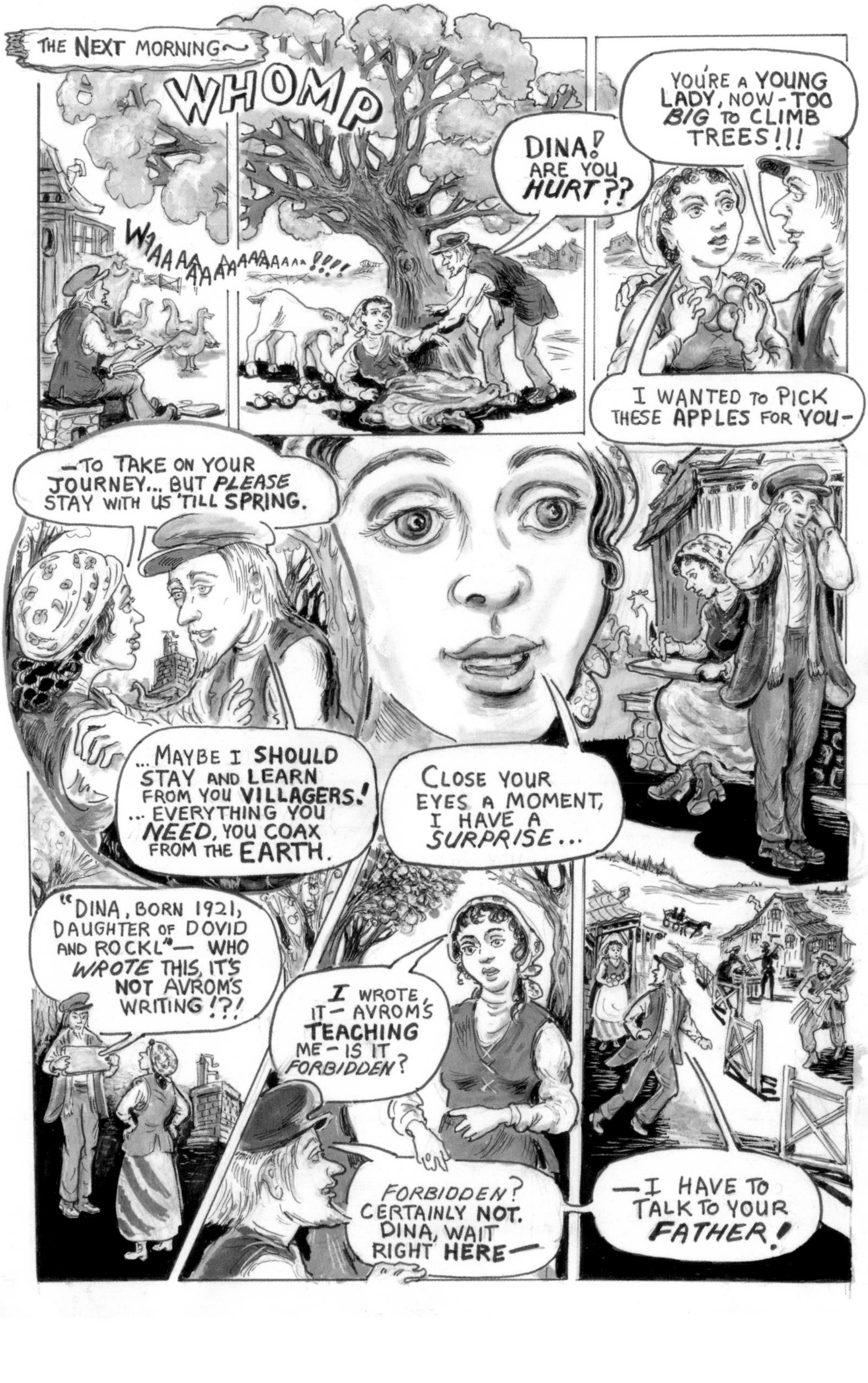
THE NEXT MORNING~
WHOMP
WAAAAAAAAAAAAAAAA!!!!
DINA! ARE YOU HURT??
YOU'RE A YOUNG LADY, NOW - TOO BIG TO CLIMB TREES!!!
I WANTED TO PICK THESE APPLES FOR YOU-
—TO TAKE ON YOUR JOURNEY... BUT PLEASE STAY WITH US 'TILL SPRING.
...MAYBE I SHOULD STAY AND LEARN FROM YOU VILLAGERS! ...EVERYTHING YOU NEED, YOU COAX FROM THE EARTH.
CLOSE YOUR EYES A MOMENT, I HAVE A SURPRISE...
"DINA, BORN 1921, DAUGHTER OF DOVID AND ROCKL"— WHO WROTE THIS, IT'S NOT AVROM'S WRITING!?!
I WROTE IT— AVROM'S TEACHING ME—IS IT FORBIDDEN?
FORBIDDEN? CERTAINLY NOT. DINA, WAIT RIGHT HERE—
—I HAVE TO TALK TO YOUR FATHER!

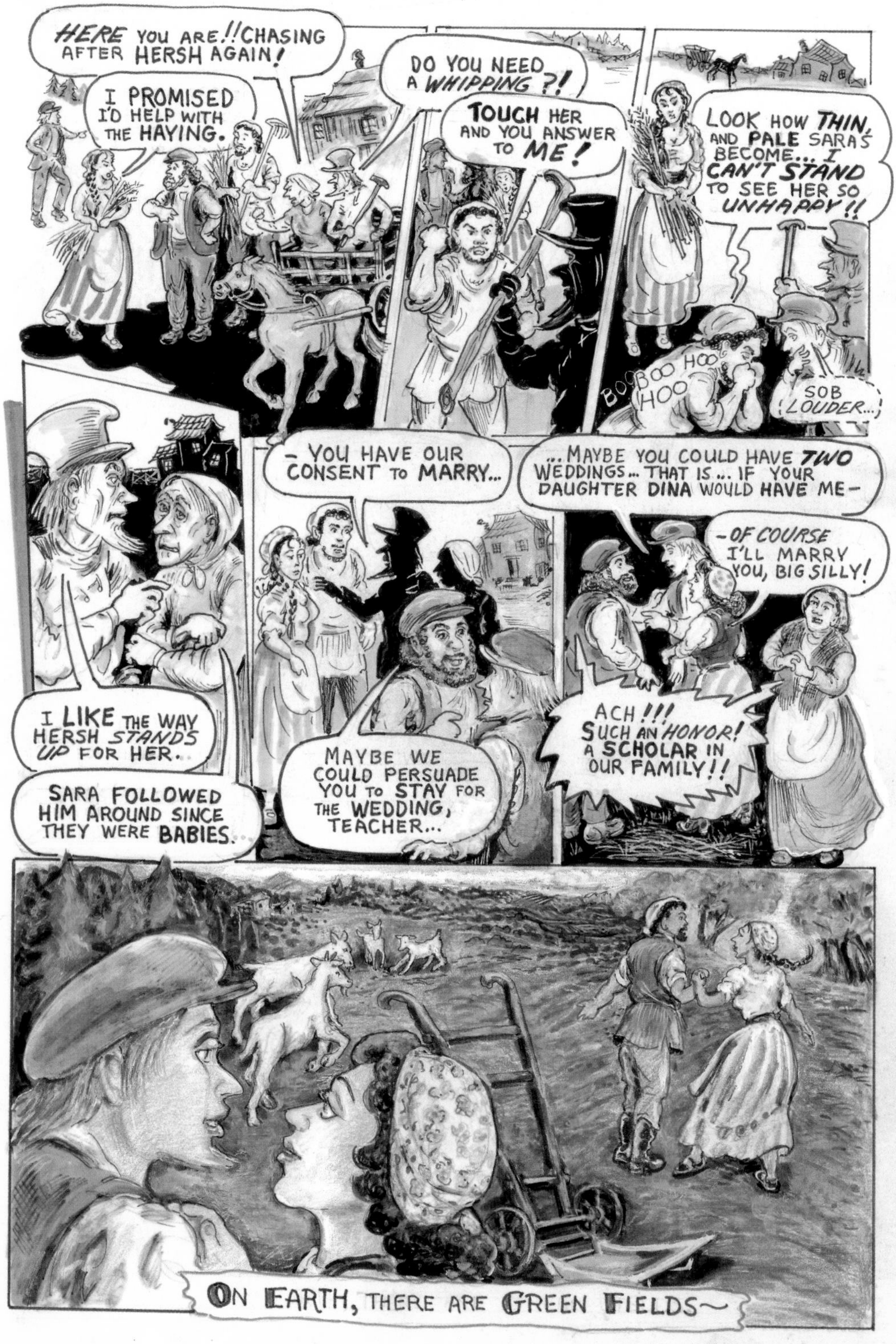
HERE YOU ARE!! CHASING AFTER HERSH AGAIN!
I PROMISED I'D HELP WITH THE HAYING.
DO YOU NEED A WHIPPING ?!
TOUCH HER AND YOU ANSWER TO ME!
LOOK HOW THIN, AND PALE SARA'S BECOME... I CAN'T STAND TO SEE HER SO UNHAPPY!!
BOO BOO HOO HOO
SOB LOUDER...
I LIKE THE WAY HERSH STANDS UP FOR HER..
SARA FOLLOWED HIM AROUND SINCE THEY WERE BABIES..
- YOU HAVE OUR CONSENT TO MARRY...
MAYBE WE COULD PERSUADE YOU TO STAY FOR THE WEDDING, TEACHER...
...MAYBE YOU COULD HAVE TWO WEDDINGS... THAT IS... IF YOUR DAUGHTER DINA WOULD HAVE ME-
- OF COURSE I'LL MARRY YOU, BIG SILLY!
ACH!!! SUCH AN HONOR! A SCHOLAR IN OUR FAMILY!!
ON EARTH, THERE ARE GREEN FIELDS~

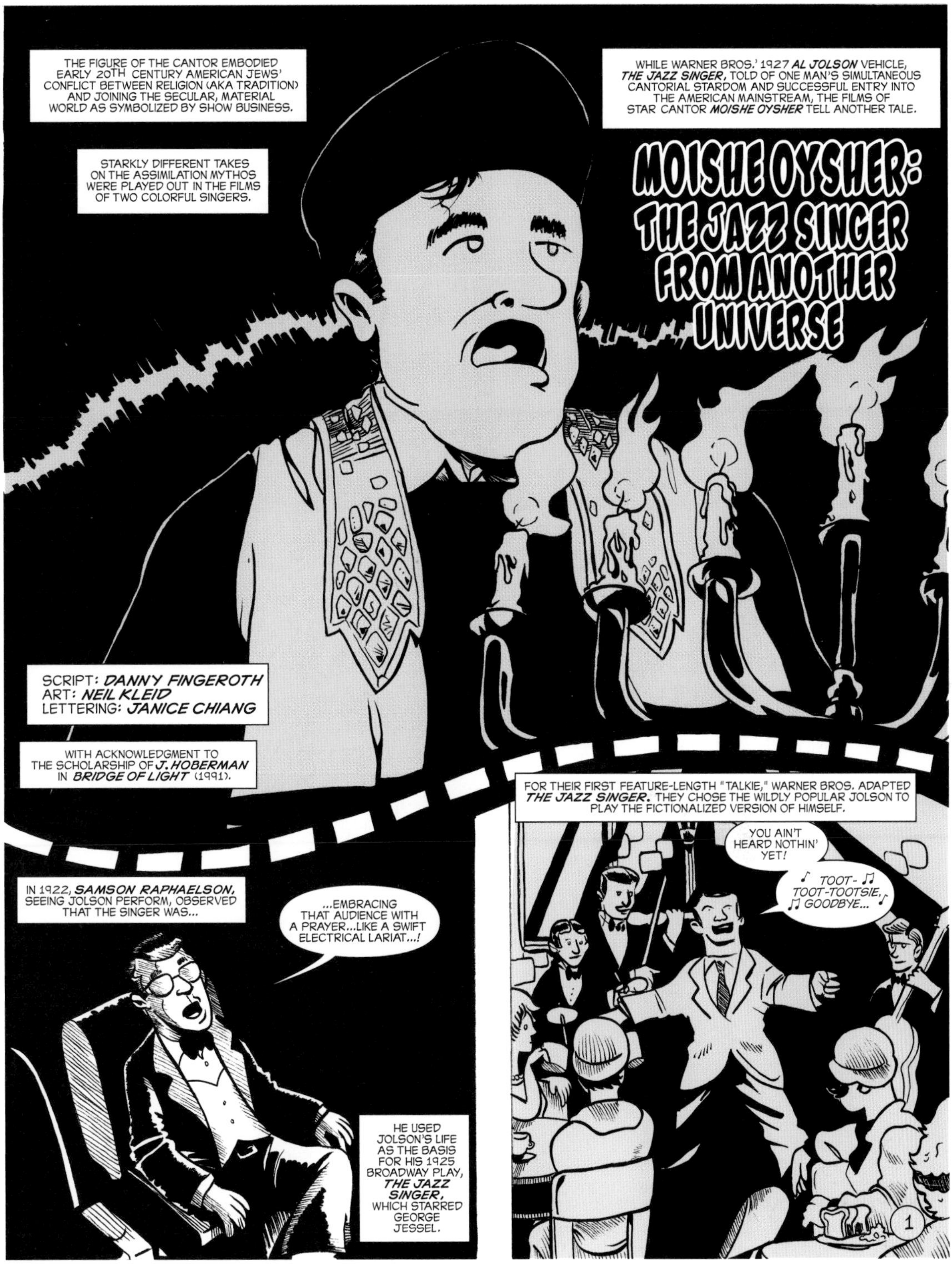
THE FIGURE OF THE CANTOR EMBODIED EARLY 20TH CENTURY AMERICAN JEWS' CONFLICT BETWEEN RELIGION (AKA TRADITION) AND JOINING THE SECULAR, MATERIAL WORLD AS SYMBOLIZED BY SHOW BUSINESS.
STARKLY DIFFERENT TAKES ON THE ASSIMILATION MYTHOS WERE PLAYED OUT IN THE FILMS OF TWO COLORFUL SINGERS.
WHILE WARNER BROS.' 1927 AL JOLSON VEHICLE, THE JAZZ SINGER, TOLD OF ONE MAN'S SIMULTANEOUS CANTORIAL STARDOM AND SUCCESSFUL ENTRY INTO THE AMERICAN MAINSTREAM, THE FILMS OF STAR CANTOR MOISHE OYSHER TELL ANOTHER TALE.
MOISHE OYSHER: THE JAZZ SINGER FROM ANOTHER UNIVERSE
SCRIPT: DANNY FINGEROTH
ART: NEIL KLEID
LETTERING: JANICE CHIANG
WITH ACKNOWLEDGMENT TO THE SCHOLARSHIP OF J. HOBERMAN IN BRIDGE OF LIGHT (1991).
IN 1922, SAMSON RAPHAELSON, SEEING JOLSON PERFORM, OBSERVED THAT THE SINGER WAS...
...EMBRACING THAT AUDIENCE WITH A PRAYER...LIKE A SWIFT ELECTRICAL LARIAT...!
HE USED JOLSON'S LIFE AS THE BASIS FOR HIS 1925 BROADWAY PLAY, THE JAZZ SINGER, WHICH STARRED GEORGE JESSEL.
FOR THEIR FIRST FEATURE-LENGTH "TALKIE," WARNER BROS. ADAPTED THE JAZZ SINGER. THEY CHOSE THE WILDLY POPULAR JOLSON TO PLAY THE FICTIONALIZED VERSION OF HIMSELF.
YOU AIN'T HEARD NOTHIN' YET!
♪ TOOT- ♫ TOOT-TOOTSIE, ♫ GOODBYE... ♪
1

JOLSON PLAYS JACK ROBIN (BORN JAKIE RABINOWITZ), WHOSE CANTOR FATHER BANISHED HIM FOR HIS LOVE OF POP MUSIC: *JAZZ!* RETURNING TO NEW YORK FOR HIS BROADWAY DEBUT, JACK VISITS HOME...

MOMMA, WE'RE GONNA MOVE TO THE BRONX—A LOT OF GREEN GRASS THERE...!

♪ BLUE SKIES...♪

♪...SMILIN' AT ME—♪

STOP!

I NEVER WANT TO SEE YOU AGAIN!

THE YEARS HAVE NOT SOFTENED CANTOR RABINOWITZ.

ALSO FEATURED IN THE MOVIE IS THE FAMOUS *CANTOR JOSEPH ROSENBLATT,* WHO JACK GOES TO SEE PERFORM.

ROSENBLATT IS IN THE MOVIE FOR NO OTHER REASON THAN TO ATTRACT CANTORIAL FANS OF THE ERA.

SPECIAL MATINEE
LAST CHICAGO
CONCERT
♪ CANTOR ♪
ROSENBLATT

ONE CAN SCARCELY IMAGINE WHAT GENTILE VIEWERS MADE OF ALL THESE MUSICAL JEWS.

EVENTUALLY, FORCED TO CHOOSE BETWEEN HEADLINING A MUSICAL AND SINGING *KOL NIDRE* IN PLACE OF HIS DYING FATHER, IT SEEMS LIKE JACK WILL PICK THE BROADWAY DEBUT...

HE SINGS AT THE REVUE'S FINAL REHEARSAL, MERE HOURS BEFORE YOM KIPPUR...

♪ MOTHER, I'M SORRY...♪

THE SONGS OF ISRAEL ARE TEARING AT MY HEART...

WHILE MANY WHITE ENTERTAINERS OF THE ERA PERFORMED IN BLACKFACE, JOLSON IS TODAY THE ONE MOST IDENTIFIED WITH IT. PARADOXICALLY, HE WAS KNOWN FOR SEEING THAT HIS BLACK COLLEAGUES WERE TREATED WELL.

NONETHELESS, BLACKFACE, FROM A MODERN PERSPECTIVE IS, AT THE VERY LEAST, *WEIRD.*

IN HIS DRESSING ROOM, JACK REALIZES...

HE LEAVES, DESPITE THE PLEAS OF MARY DALE, HIS GENTILE GIRLFRIEND (AND CO-STAR), AND HIS PRODUCER'S THREATS...

2

JACK GETS TO THE SYNAGOGUE IN TIME...

♪ ...KOL NIDRE VE'ESAREI... ♪

CANTOR RABINOWITZ DIES CONTENT, FORGIVENESS IN HIS HEART. THIS IS WHERE THE PLAY *THE JAZZ SINGER* ENDS.

THE MOVIE ADDS AN EXTRA FINAL SCENE, WITH JACK ROBIN BACK ON BROADWAY...

♪ ...I KNOW WHERE... ♪

♪ ...THE SUN SHINES BEST... ♪

HIS MOTHER BEAMS IN THE AUDIENCE.

MARY ALSO WATCHES THE SINGER ADORINGLY. JACK—AND THE WARNER BROS.—HAVE THEIR SCHMALTZ AND EAT IT, TOO.

WHEN A POLISH COMPOSER OFFERS TO MAKE HIM A WARSAW OPERA STAR, YOEL'S FATHER-IN-LAW AND THE SYNAGOGUE'S RABBI ARE ENRAGED THAT HE EVEN CONSIDERS THE OFFER...

WHAT EVIL HAVE I DONE TO DESERVE SUCH THANKS?

YOU WILL STAND BETWEEN BOTH WORLDS. YOU WILL BE NOWHERE.

MOISHE OYSHER WAS KEPT FROM MAINSTREAM SUCCESS BY BELIEFS THAT WOULDN'T ALLOW HIM TO PERFORM ON *SHABBOS*.

HUGELY POPULAR AMONG FANS OF CANTORIAL MUSIC AND YIDDISH RADIO, THEATER, AND MOVIES, IN 1940'S *OVERTURE TO GLORY*, HE'S CANTOR *YOEL STRASHUNSKY*.

♪ HINENI, HEANI MIMA'AS... ♪

BUT STRASHUNSKY'S WIFE SUPPORTS HIS DECISION TO LEAVE HER AND THEIR SON, *PERETZ*, AND THEIR NATIVE VILNA, LITHUANIA...

I'M *CHOKING* HERE! I WILL RUN AWAY!

I PRAY TO GOD THAT HE WATCHES YOUR STEPS SO YOU DON'T STUMBLE. BE SUCCESSFUL.

③

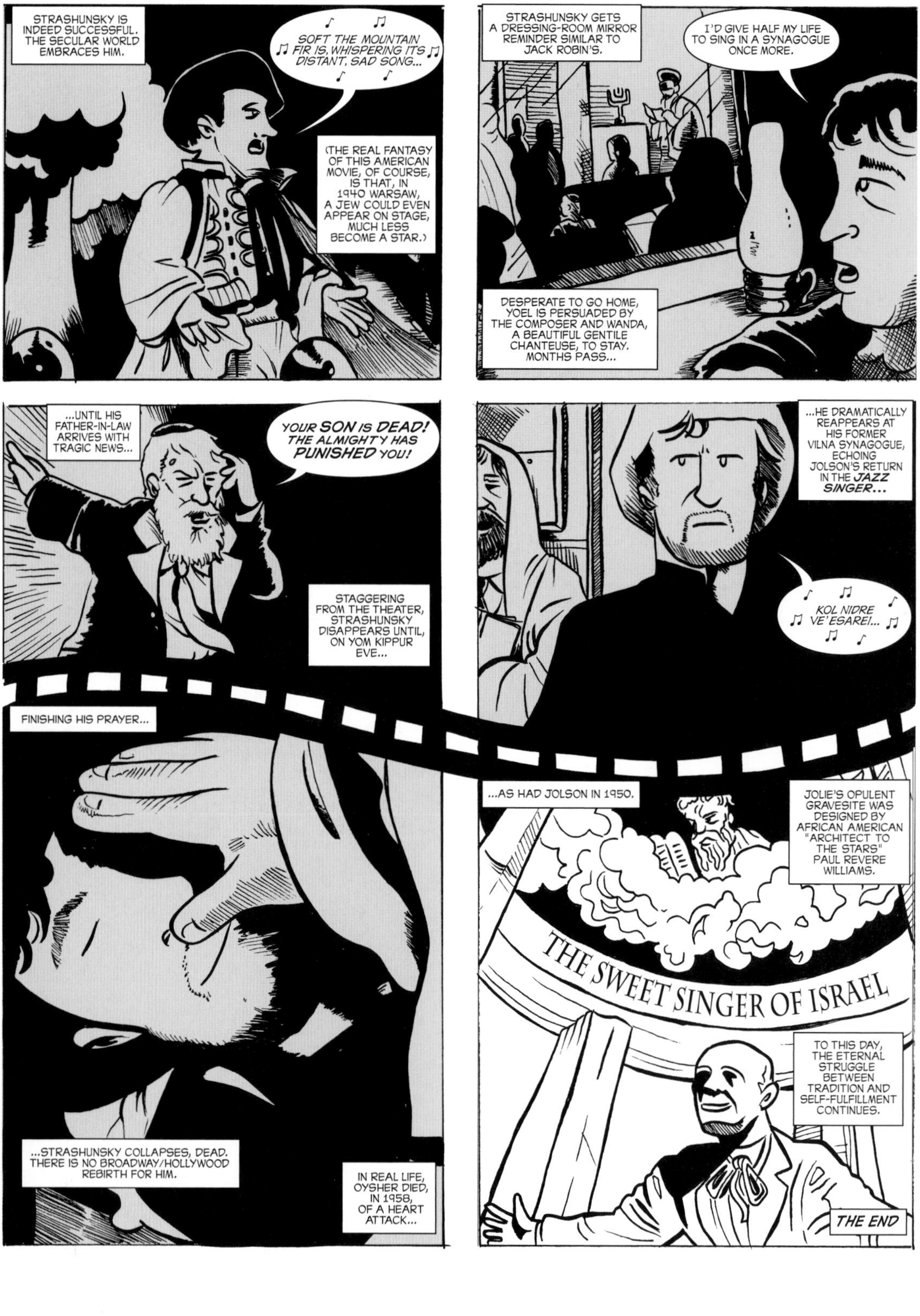
STRASHUNSKY IS INDEED SUCCESSFUL. THE SECULAR WORLD EMBRACES HIM.
SOFT THE MOUNTAIN FIR IS, WHISPERING ITS DISTANT, SAD SONG...
(THE REAL FANTASY OF THIS AMERICAN MOVIE, OF COURSE, IS THAT, IN 1940 WARSAW, A JEW COULD EVEN APPEAR ON STAGE, MUCH LESS BECOME A STAR.)
STRASHUNSKY GETS A DRESSING-ROOM MIRROR REMINDER SIMILAR TO JACK ROBIN'S.
I'D GIVE HALF MY LIFE TO SING IN A SYNAGOGUE ONCE MORE.
DESPERATE TO GO HOME, YOEL IS PERSUADED BY THE COMPOSER AND WANDA, A BEAUTIFUL GENTILE CHANTEUSE, TO STAY. MONTHS PASS...
...UNTIL HIS FATHER-IN-LAW ARRIVES WITH TRAGIC NEWS...
YOUR SON IS DEAD! THE ALMIGHTY HAS PUNISHED YOU!
STAGGERING FROM THE THEATER, STRASHUNSKY DISAPPEARS UNTIL, ON YOM KIPPUR EVE...
...HE DRAMATICALLY REAPPEARS AT HIS FORMER VILNA SYNAGOGUE, ECHOING JOLSON'S RETURN IN THE JAZZ SINGER...
KOL NIDRE VE'ESAREI...
FINISHING HIS PRAYER...
...STRASHUNSKY COLLAPSES, DEAD. THERE IS NO BROADWAY/HOLLYWOOD REBIRTH FOR HIM.
IN REAL LIFE, OYSHER DIED, IN 1958, OF A HEART ATTACK...
...AS HAD JOLSON IN 1950.
JOLIE'S OPULENT GRAVESITE WAS DESIGNED BY AFRICAN AMERICAN "ARCHITECT TO THE STARS" PAUL REVERE WILLIAMS.
THE SWEET SINGER OF ISRAEL
TO THIS DAY, THE ETERNAL STRUGGLE BETWEEN TRADITION AND SELF-FULFILLMENT CONTINUES.
THE END

His parents were lovely people. Very religious. Everyone looked up to Israel and Celia.

Childhood neighbor

Such smart people! They both spoke many languages, but around the home it was Yiddish or English.

Back then, before the shows and the movies and all that, no one called him "Zero."

He was named Samuel, but we all just called him Sammy. Little Sammy Mostel.

THE LEGEND OF ZERO

The first play Sammy ever saw? "King Lear" in Yiddish, starring Boris Thomashefsky.

Lifelong friend

Sometimes we worked as extras in the Yiddish theaters. They'd pay us a buck or two, but we did it because we liked it.

Those old Yiddish actors ... so outsized! Hilarious one second, tragic the next. The goyim never saw anything like it.

Well, not until Sammy started acting, anyhow.

Sammy was such a smart boy! Israel and Celia were sure they had a future rabbi on their hands.

Even Sammy himself didn't think of acting. All that kid thought about was painting.

One day he finally told his parents, "Ikh ken nit zayn keyn rebe. Ikh vel zayn a kinstler."

In English? It means ... Uh ... "I can't be a rabbi. I'm going to be an artist."

Written and illustrated by Barry Deutsch

In the late thirties, Sammy got a WPA job giving museum tours. It paid lousy money, something like $20 a week.

Now, Sammy knew everything about art. But he couldn't resist throwing in jokes and ad-libs.

And he'd have all those museum patrons falling down, they were laughing so hard!

No one ever moved on a stage like he did! Big like a rhino, *moved* like a ballerina.

Theater historian

He could hypnotize an audience with just a finger waggle, or spread his arms and take up the whole room!

His films never captured the way he moved...

Cafe Society hired Sammy to do stand-up for $40 a week. They called him "Zero," for how broke he was.

How good was he? Within a year, Sammy was making $4,000 a week! But the Zero name stuck.

In 1952, Zero was subpoenaed by the House Committee on Un-American Activities.

They ordered him to name some communists, but Zero wouldn't name names.

He just lectured them about his right to perform. "There is no crime in making anybody laugh," he told 'em!

Of course, no one would dare hire Zero after *that*.

So he tried to eke out a living selling his paintings.

Actress, colleague

A Catskills resort offered Zero a measly $500 to perform.

But once he drove all the way there, they said they'd only pay $250.

So he got on that stage and cursed out the audience in Yiddish.

The audience thought it was an act. They howled with laughter.

Zero would say "I am a man of a thousand faces. All of them blacklisted."

In 1962, the blacklist was mostly over, and Zero starred in a new musical, "A Funny Thing Happened on the Way to the Forum."

The show was flopping! The producers wanted to bring in this famous director, Jerry Robbins, to save the show.

But Robbins had cooperated with HUAC and gotten a lot of people blacklisted. Zero loathed him.

So they very nervously asked Zero—who had a famous temper—if they could bring in Robbins.

And Zero asked "Do I have to eat with him?" They said not if he didn't want to.

So Zero said to hire Robbins. He told them, "We of the left do not blacklist!"

After three consecutive Tony Awards for best actor, Zero was more famous than ever.

Zero in "Fiddler on the Roof" is *legend!* An all-time great live performance!

Zero always said he understood "Fiddler" so well because he knew the original Yiddish stories it was based on.

Zero starred in some movies, a few good, many bad. That's how it goes, I guess.

All this talking about Sammy... Wanna watch "The Producers" again?

CHAPTER 3.

Not Quite Assimilation:
Yiddish & American Popular Culture

◆►◀●▬●◄●►◀◆►◀◆►

Y iddish has had a long life of deceiving those who predicted its demise. Like per-
secuted Jews themselves within assorted populations, but for somewhat different reasons, a disguise or semi-disguise suited Jewish performers of all kinds.
In order to make a living as an actor, let alone become a star in the booming popular
entertainment of 1910–60 and perhaps after, a Gentile name was preferable, just for
starters. And there were other reasons, more political and artistic, for becoming Ev-
eryman or Everywoman rather than an immediately identifiable Jew on stage, screen,
and television.

One reason bespoke two purposes: political and artistic. The Jewish writer or actor
needed to reach a Gentile audience in order to achieve universality, and also in order
to make a contribution to the transformation of a class- and race-divided, often bru-
tally warlike society. Jewish playwrights adopted Konstantin Stanislavky's Method
acting, and Jewish drama coaches taught varieties of Method (the effort at encour-
aging a "thinking" actor rather than a mere physical stand-in for the director's de-
mands) for everyone willing to struggle for real stage art. Humanistic novelists made
and still make the same choice, whether actually coming from lower-middle-class
Yiddish culture in time past or from the comfortable and assimilated middle class of
normal Jewish American life today.

This move did not, however, eliminate the precious corners of a distinctly Jewish
and Yiddish culture, including Yiddish-framed memories that remained crucial to
any sort of meaningful, positive Jewish identity. In recent stages, recuperation has become a selective art of memory, picking up significant details and weaving them into
fresh pictures. Even the process of recuperating who was a Yiddish speaker is part
of a larger game of lost and found, a game destined for generations ahead to continue.

E. Y. "YIP" HARBURG
& THE DEPRESSION EPIC

E. Y. "Yip" Harburg, one of the most successful lyricists of the twentieth century ("Somewhere Over the Rainbow," "April in Paris," "Only a Paper Moon," and many others), broke into the big time with a Depression lyric considered by many to be dangerously subversive. The song was "Brother, Can You Spare a Dime?"

Born on New York's Lower East Side on April 8, 1896 to Russian Jewish immigrants, Yip grew up speaking Yiddish and going with his Orthodox father to the Thalia Theatre at 46–48 Bowery, where some of the greatest Yiddish theater was being performed. He also loved vaudeville, and his boyhood pals included the Gershwin brothers, Ira and George.

Yip became a businessman for a few years after graduating from City College, but threw himself full-time into songwriting after the stock market crash of 1929. He teamed up with a composer of similar background, Jay Gorney. Together, they were part of a generation that began writing songs with a story suited for the evolving stage musical, and then for sound films. "I'm Yours" was a big hit for Yip in 1930 (with music by Johnny Green), but Yip's real breakthrough was created for a minor 1932 Broadway musical called *New Americana*. As Yip told historian Studs Terkel decades later, he was walking around Manhattan and noticed the lines of the unemployed waiting for food. Yip had personally shared the best dreams of America, the land free of oppression and hunger. Then the system fell apart—but the ordinary fellow was not in anything like revolt. Instead, as bitterness sank in, the pointlessness of World War I and its human sacrifice came back with a vengeance, along with the other accumulated grievances of having worked hard and gained so little.

No small part of the instant hit "Brother, Can You Spare a Dime?" was Gorney's music, with its inflection of Eastern European sadness, a continuity from music associated with Jewish immigrants, among others. But the strength of the song was its lyric sense of hope gone badly awry, with falling minor chords, especially in the chorus, making the point for a popular audience that rarely heard such.

Reviewers were ecstatic, bands played it, Al Jolson, Rudy Valée, and Bing Crosby sang it, and Republicans facing the fall election warned radio officials to take it off the air. They were too late. It was a huge and continuing success, arguably *the* saga of the Depression.

Harburg's biggest success thereafter were the lyrics for *The Wizard of Oz*, a film production that appeared doomed until his lyrics wove a narrative that could be successfully developed, unifying the film. Harburg's political spirit was definitely left-wing, and he was informally blacklisted from the movies by 1950. But he remained the buoyant, diminutive fellow whom I met at a reception in the late 1970s, and who was always looking for a rainbow (the word, by the way, did not exist in the literary original of *The Wizard of Oz* by L. Frank Baum; it was Harburg's key addition and, right-wing critics accurately charged, implied an idyllic socialism). Yip Harburg died on March 5, 1981, at the age of eighty four. The Harburg Foundation has kindly given us permission to reprint the famed lyric for "Brother, Can You Spare a Dime?" on the following pages.

BROTHER CAN YOU SPARE A DIME

Lyrics by Yip Harburg · Tune by Jay Gorney · Pictures by Sharon Rudahl

"THEY USED TO TELL ME I WAS BUILDING A DREAM, AND SO I FOLLOWED THE MOB,

WHEN THERE WAS EARTH TO PLOW,

OR GUNS TO BEAR, I WAS ALWAYS THERE RIGHT ON THE JOB."

"THEY USED TO TELL ME I WAS BUILDING A DREAM, WITH PEACE AND GLORY AHEAD,

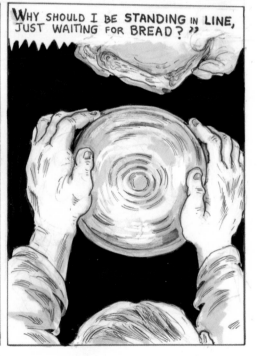

WHY SHOULD I BE STANDING IN LINE, JUST WAITING FOR BREAD?"

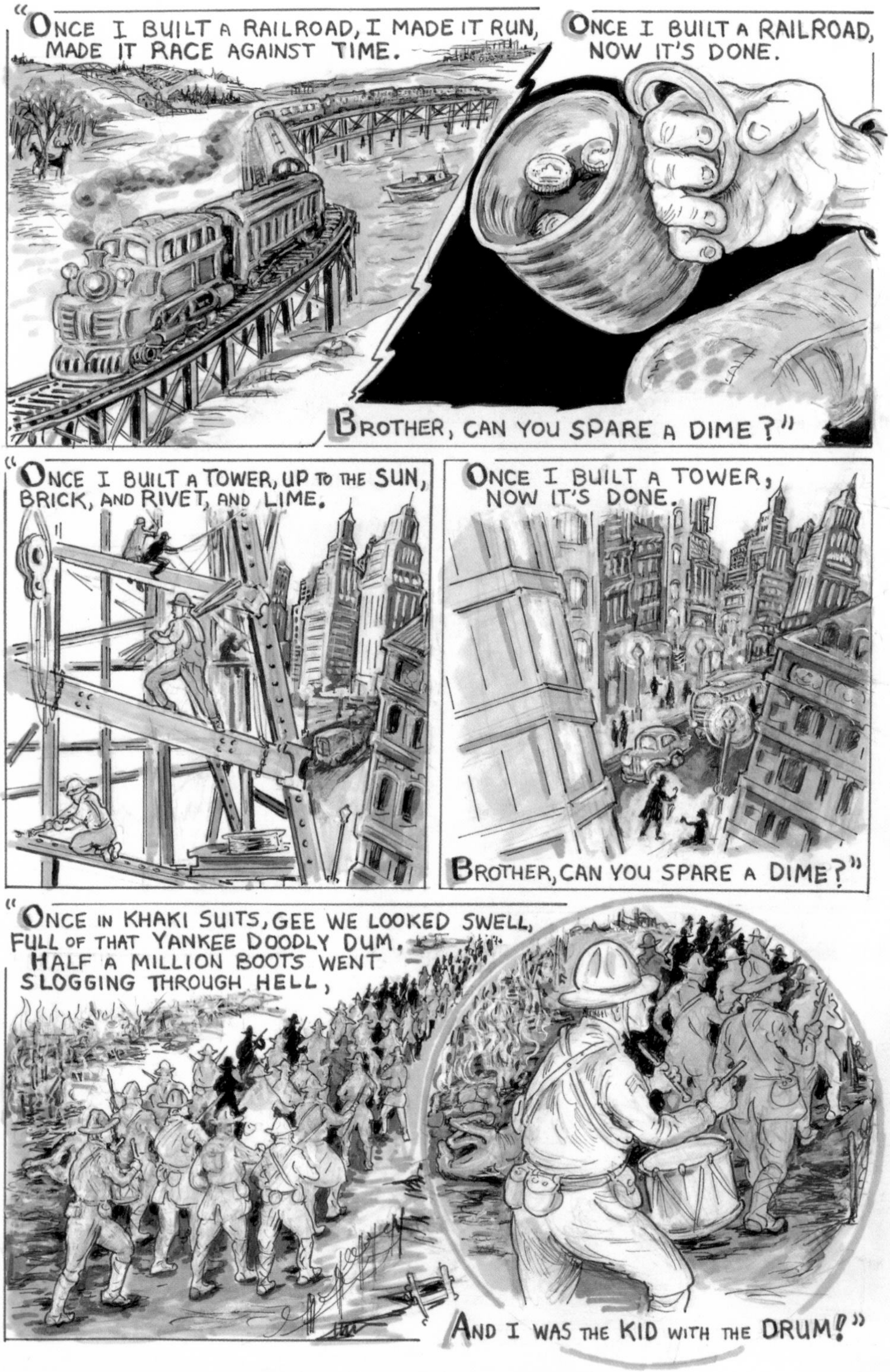
"ONCE I BUILT A RAILROAD, I MADE IT RUN, MADE IT RACE AGAINST TIME.
ONCE I BUILT A RAILROAD, NOW IT'S DONE.
BROTHER, CAN YOU SPARE A DIME?"
"ONCE I BUILT A TOWER, UP TO THE SUN, BRICK, AND RIVET, AND LIME.
ONCE I BUILT A TOWER, NOW IT'S DONE.
BROTHER, CAN YOU SPARE A DIME?"
"ONCE IN KHAKI SUITS, GEE WE LOOKED SWELL, FULL OF THAT YANKEE DOODLY DUM. HALF A MILLION BOOTS WENT SLOGGING THROUGH HELL,
AND I WAS THE KID WITH THE DRUM!"

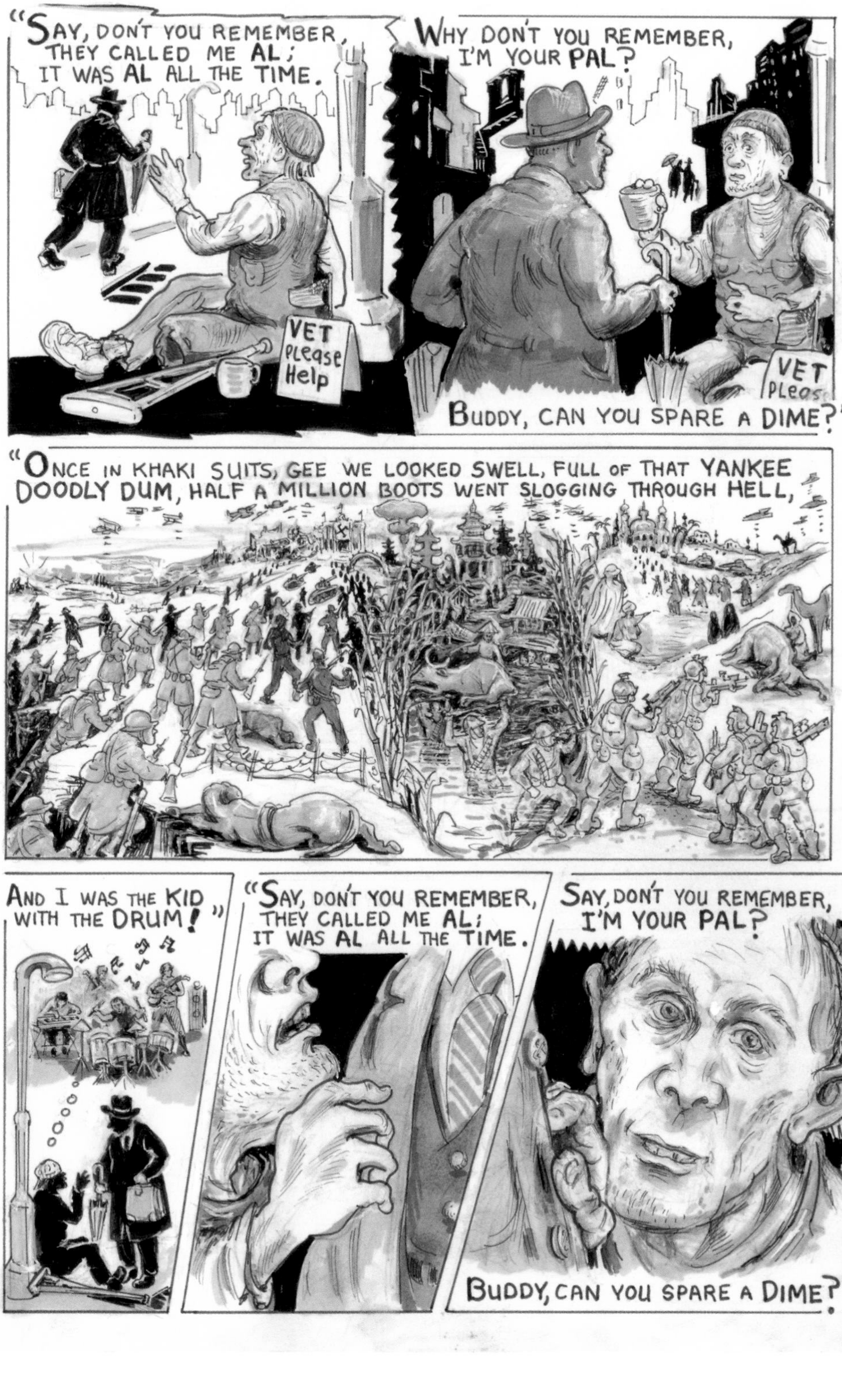
"SAY, DON'T YOU REMEMBER, THEY CALLED ME AL; IT WAS AL ALL THE TIME.
VET Please Help
WHY DON'T YOU REMEMBER, I'M YOUR PAL?
VET
BUDDY, CAN YOU SPARE A DIME?"
"ONCE IN KHAKI SUITS, GEE WE LOOKED SWELL, FULL OF THAT YANKEE DOODLY DUM, HALF A MILLION BOOTS WENT SLOGGING THROUGH HELL,
AND I WAS THE KID WITH THE DRUM!"
"SAY, DON'T YOU REMEMBER, THEY CALLED ME AL; IT WAS AL ALL THE TIME.
SAY, DON'T YOU REMEMBER, I'M YOUR PAL?
BUDDY, CAN YOU SPARE A DIME?"

Portrait of Uncle Benny by Marvin Friedman, 1976

THE MEMORY ART
OF MARVIN FRIEDMAN

O ne of the most vernacular of artists and most artlike of comics artists, Marvin Friedman may properly belong to a vanished era that won't stay forgotten. Born and raised in Chester, Pennsylvania, Friedman learned about art by looking at the magazines that arrived at his lower-middle-class Jewish home. He wanted to drop out of art school and help with the struggling family hardware store, but his dying father insisted on giving him tuition money to continue. In a few years Friedman moved to New York and made good, drawing for slick magazines including the *New Yorker, Playboy, Redbook, McCall's, Ladies' Home Journal, Boy's Life,* and the *Saturday Evening Post,* among others. He also worked at *Gourmet* magazine for seven years, illustrating the luxurious restaurants of New York City.

By the late 1950s and the early decline of the magazine trade, Friedman went into something like a total collapse. Perhaps his mother's long, tortured depression had caught up with him. For a time, he was institutionalized. Toward the middle 1980s Friedman emerged out of depression into a world of art that had changed dramatically. Memory, his own memory as a part of a larger social history, had become more important to him. So had Jewishness, not the semiofficial "Jewish history" encompassing an ancient Israel, commemorating the Holocaust, or celebrating an American upward mobility, but a different Jewish history, where an alternative and more personal nostalgia and sense of loss was common. Along with sadness regarding his family's troubles, there are also Atlantic City memories of summer days, memories of sex—or usually a craving for sex—and the other variously funny disproportions involved in a semi-assimilation. These were the kinds of memories not so likely to be treasured by others, but more likely seen as a confession of self-embarrassment far more painful than increased Jewish referencing in sitcoms. Unlike "funny characters" on such television shows as *Seinfeld,* Marvin Friedman reveals the sense of loss above all of the closeness that has vanished. He bears the weight of history rather than banishing it into some half-remembered, misunderstood past.

7 O'CLOCK. DINNER EATEN. ~~WE~~ DISHES WASHED AND AFTER EDWIN C. HILL AND THE HUMAN SIDE OF THE NEWS, MY FATHER WOULD LIGHT UP A ~~CIGAR~~ CIGAR AND WITH HIS HANDS FOLDED BEHIND HIM, HE'D WALK WITH ME TO ~~HUTCHINSON'S~~ HUTCHINSON'S DRUG STORE AND WHILE I TWISTED THIS WAY AND THAT ~~WAY~~ WAY ON THE COUNTER ~~STOOL~~ STOOL HE WOULD BUY ME A CONE OR A POPSICLE AND MAYBE A PINT OF ~~FRESHLY~~ FRESHLY DIPPED ~~~~ CHOCOLATE, VANILLA AND STRAWBERRY TO TAKE HOME TO MOM. IF HE HAD SOME EXTRA CHANGE, HE'D SPLURGE AND WOULD BUY A QUART AND UNCLE BENNY AND AUNT TANIA WOULD COME DOWN AND WE'D SIT ON THE FRONT STOOP AND EAT ICE CREAM AND DRINK ICE WATER IN THE SOFT EVENING LIGHT. AROUND ~~THE~~ MEMORIAL DAY, THE LIVING ROOM RUG WAS SPRINKLED WITH MOTHBALLS, ROLLED UP IN NEWSPAPERS AND SHLEPPED DOWN TO THE CELLAR AND ~~HUNG~~ HUNG UP. THEN WE SHLEPPED UP THE SUMMER ~~~~ WOVEN STRAW RUGS, HUNG THEM OVER THE CLOTHESLINE AND BEAT THEM AND ~~~~ SHLEPPED ~~~~ THEM INTO

THE LIVING ROOM AND PUT DOWN ON THE FLOOR. ~~~~ OUR FURNITURE WAS SHROUDED IN WHITE SHEETS LIKE SOMETHING OUT OF THE ~~WINGS~~ WINGS OF THE DOVE. HOT ~~~~ BORSCHT WITH MEAT VANISHED AND COLD GLASSES OF ~~SPINACH~~ SPINACH BORSCHT, DOLLOPED WITH SOUR CREAM, ~~WERE~~ WERE SERVED IN TALL ~~THICK~~ THICK GLASSES. THE EMERSON ~~~~ FAN, OR MAYBE IT WAS A ~~GE~~ GE FAN ~~WAS~~ WAS BROUGHT OUT OF THE CLOSET AND FLY SWATTERS, CATERPILLERS AND LILAC BUSHES MATERIALIZED. ~~ON~~ ON A SWEET SUMMER'S NIGHT WHEN I WAS TWENTYFOUR I BROUGHT JONNY HOME TO CHESTER TO MEET MY FOLKS. AUNT TANIA MADE STRAWBERRY JAM TEA AND BLACK RAISIN CAKE. MY ~~BODBA~~ BODBA MADE HER LUMPY MOHN COOKIES, SHE PRESSED OUT OF DOUGH WITH A DRINKING GLASS. SHE HELD JONNY'S HAND TO HER CHEEK AND SAID OH MY SWEET BEAUTIFUL CHILD. UNCLE BENNY KISSED HER HAND AND MY MOTHER HELD US CLOSE AND ~~GENTLY~~ GENTLY TOUCHED THE LAPEL OF MY ~~~~ JACKET

OUR APARTMENT WAS FILLED WITH STIFLING HEAT.
FANS BLEW AROUND HOT AIR, NO AMOUNT OF
ICE TEA WAS ENOUGH. 5:30 ON THE DOT, CHARLIE
WOULD TURN OUR CORNERS, BELLS TINKLING IN
HIS ICE CREAM TRUCK. IT WAS AN OLD
POST OFFICE TRUCK THAT HE PAINTED WHITE AND
COVERED IN BRIGHT RED LETTERS-"CHARLIE'S HERE".
HE WORE A WHITE SHIRT AND A WHITE APRON
AND A WHITE CAP. HE BROUGHT RELIEF IN 3¢
CHOCOLATE OR VANILLA CONES.
HE CAME AROUND AT 5:30 BECAUSE THAT'S WHEN
CAAAA APPTTTAINN MILDNNIGHT SIGNED OFF OF
WFIL. IF HE HAD COME EARLIER 2 GIRLS
WOULD HAVE SHOWN UP TO BUY 2 CONES.
I WAS NEVER ALLOWED TO BUY ICE CREAM
FROM CHARLIE BECAUSE WE'D EAT DINNER AT
6 O'CLOCK. MY MOTHER WOULD FROWN. GOYEM,
I DON'T UNDERSTAND GOYEM, WHEN DO THEY EAT?
I RAN UP SEIGLE STREET WITH
EVERYBODY ELSE AND WATCHED.

WHEN AUNT TANIA DIED I FOUND AN ANCIENT ~~ARTESE~~ SCUFFED SCRAPBOOK WITH A PICTURE OF TOLSTOY ON ITS COVER. RIFFLING THROUGH THE PAGES I FOUND POST CARDS FROM BEFORE THE ~~RUSSIAN~~ REVOLUTION AND DANDELIONS AND ROSES PRESSED PALE AND ~~BY~~ BROWN. THERE WERE STAINED LETTERS IN RUSSIAN AND YIDDISH AND PAGES TORN FROM ~~RED~~ ~~DICK~~ BOOKS WITH NOTATIONS IN FADED PENCIL IN THE MARGINS AND PHOTOS OF ~~A~~ STRANGERS IN EUROPE AND AMERICA I DIDN'T KNOW. AUNT SARAH POINTED OUT A FEW. "THIS IS COUSINS FROM GAUWNA-GUBERNA, RUMKOWSKY, I THINK THE NAME WAS. THIS IS SHIVA'S SISTER'S COUSIN. SHE HAD 3 BOYS, THEY ALL DIED IN A TYPHOID."

I CAME ACROSS AN OLD SEPIA PHOTOGRAPH OF A BEAUTIFUL, ELEGANTLY DRESSED YOUNG WOMAN WITH A SLY SIDEWAYS GLANCE HOLDING WHITE GLOVES. I ASKED AUNT SARAH WHO SHE WAS. "WHAT'S THE MATTER WITH YOU? THAT'S YOUR MUMMA." I'M STILL ASTONISHED BY THAT PHOTOGRAPH. I DON'T EVER REMEMBER MY MOTHER LOOKING LIKE THAT. A LIFETIME OF STRESS AND ILL HEALTH EXHAUSTED HER. BUT YOU KNOW SOMETHING FUNNY? ~~THERE~~ I DON'T HAVE ONE PHOTOGRAPH OF MY MOTHER WHERE SHE'S NOT SMILING OR LAUGHING. GO FIGURE. MY MOM WAS NEUROTIC AND ~~SO~~ SO AM I. THERE WAS A TIME FOR ME WHEN BEING NEUROTIC WAS PART OF A GAME. IT EXPLAINED PSUEDO-SUFFERING AND INTENSITY. I THINK I READ SOMETHING BY ALBERT CAMUS ~~WAS~~ ABOUT EXISTENTIALISM I HAD NO IDEA OF WHAT IT MEANT AND I'M ~~XXXX~~ NOT SO SURE ~~XXXX~~ I KNOW WHAT IT MEANS NOW.

THE JELLO PROGRAM STARRING JACK BENNY MARY LIVINGSTON, DENNIS DAY, PHIL HARRIS, ROCHESTER AND ME, DON WILSON... JACK AND MARY ARE ON A BUS GOING DOWNTOWN SO JACK CAN EXCHANGE A BIRTHDAY GIFT THAT HE BOUGHT 3 YEARS AGO. MARY: JACK, YOU'RE SO CHEAP. !

BUT IT COMES IN ~~THE~~ VERY HANDY ~~F~~ FOR ART STUDENTS. ONE DAY WHEN I WAS ~~DO~~ PSUEDO-SUFFERING, WE WERE EATING DINNER AND I ASKED WHY IS THIS A TABLE? MY MOTHER GAVE ME ONE OF HER LOOKS. MY MOTHER HAD A LOOK THAT COULD KNOCK YOU TO THE LINOLEUM. THEN THROUGH THE YEARS THERE ARE ~~SO~~ SO MANY DEVISTATING AND CONFUSING AND ~~A~~ HEART RENDING CIRCUMSTANCES THAT ALL OF OUR NEEDS, ALL OF OUR RITUALS, ALL OF OUR HABITS ARE DISRUPTED MOM. CALL MOM. WHATEVER GARBAGE IS ON YOUR HEAD MOM WILL USE EVERYTHING AVAILABLE TO HER TO ~~XXXX~~

MITIGATE AND LIGHTEN YOUR ~~G~~ GRIEF AND EMBELLISH YOUR JOY. MOMS DON'T HAVE TO BE STRONGER OR UNTROUBLED TO PUT THEIR PROBLEMS ON HOLD AND LISTEN ~~X~~ HEARTFULLY AND

NON JUDGEMENTALLY AND FOCUS ~~X~~ ON HER CHILD'S NEED. LISTEN, THROUGH THE AGES SMARTER PEOPLE THAN I HAVE BEEN DELIBERATING AND ANALYZING THE MOM THING, PROBABLY SINCE THE BIG BANG AND PEOPLE WILL CONTINUE SIFTING AND DISCUSSING THE MOM THING TILL THE FINAL BIG BANG. THESE ARE THINGS YOU DON'T UNDERSTAND TILL YOU ARE OLDER AND YOU'RE A PARENT YOURSELF. I WISH YOU WERE HERE, MOM SO I COULD GIVE YOU A BIG ~~XXX~~ KISS AND A BOX OF WHITMAN'S CHOCOLATES.

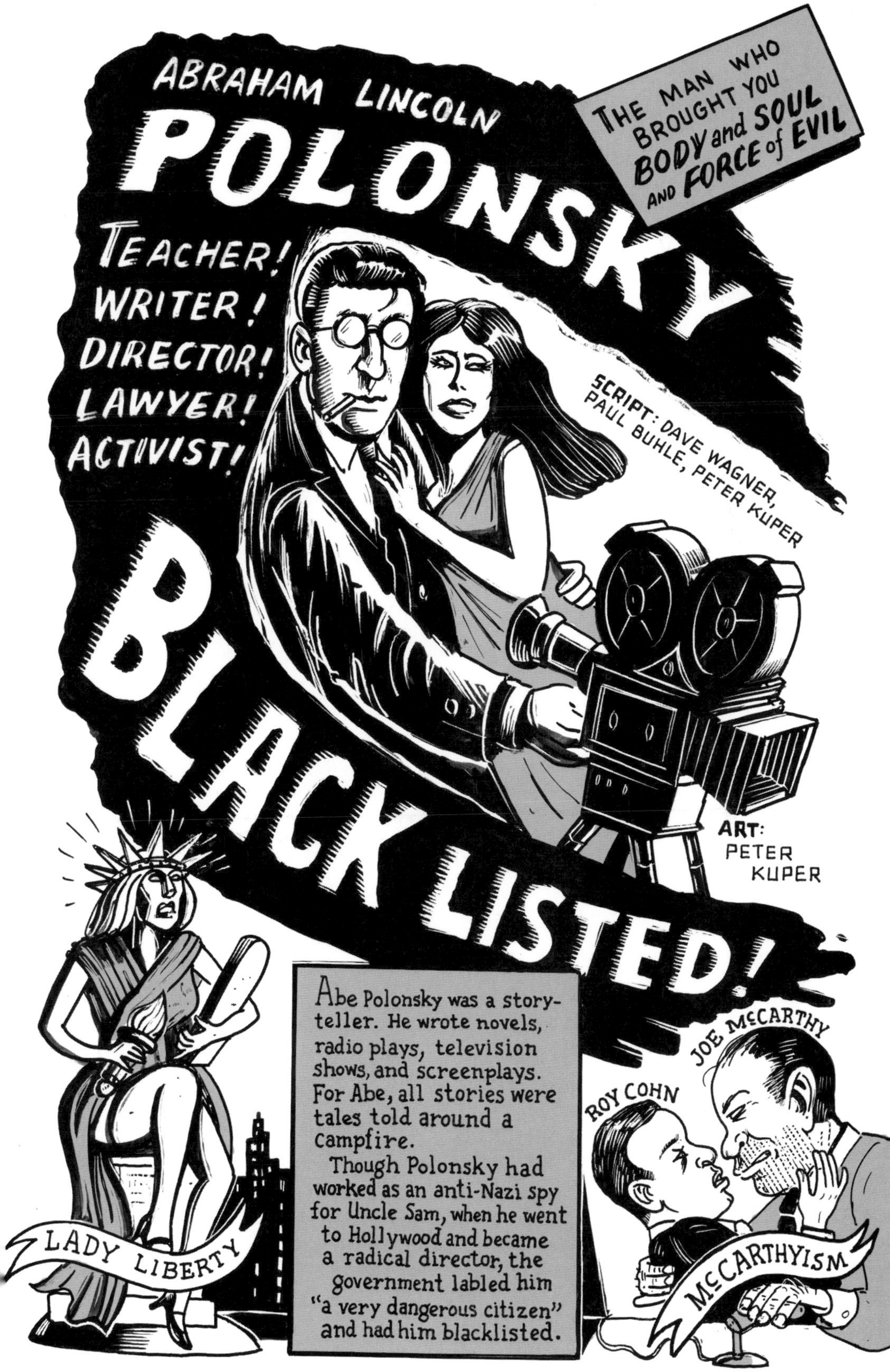
ABRAHAM LINCOLN
POLONSKY
THE MAN WHO BROUGHT YOU BODY and SOUL AND FORCE of EVIL
TEACHER! WRITER! DIRECTOR! LAWYER! ACTIVIST!
SCRIPT: DAVE WAGNER, PAUL BUHLE, PETER KUPER
BLACKLISTED!
ART: PETER KUPER
Abe Polonsky was a storyteller. He wrote novels, radio plays, television shows, and screenplays. For Abe, all stories were tales told around a campfire.
Though Polonsky had worked as an anti-Nazi spy for Uncle Sam, when he went to Hollywood and became a radical director, the government labled him "a very dangerous citizen" and had him blacklisted.
JOE McCARTHY
ROY COHN
LADY LIBERTY
McCARTHYISM

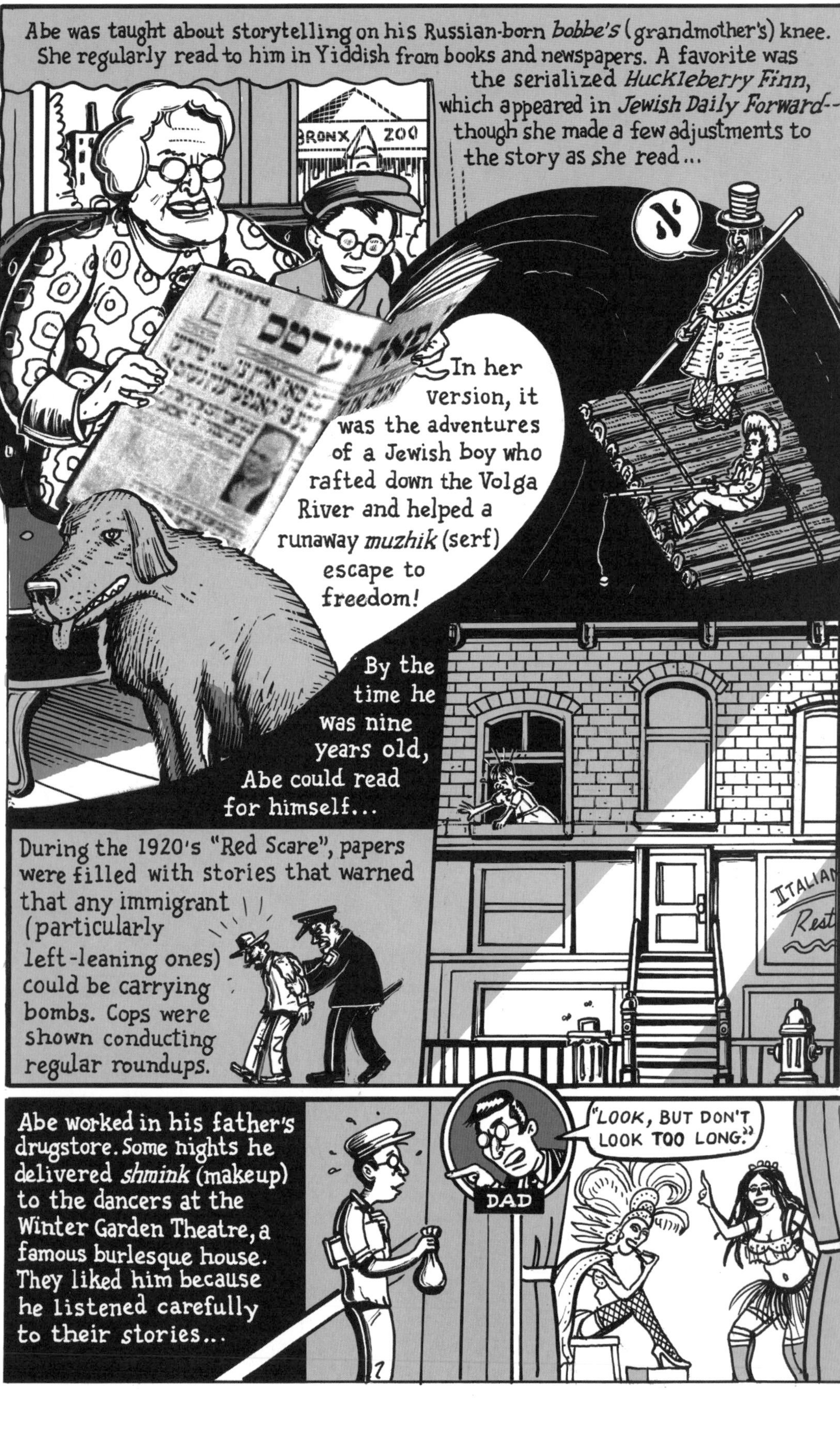

Abe was taught about storytelling on his Russian-born *bobbe's* (grandmother's) knee. She regularly read to him in Yiddish from books and newspapers. A favorite was the serialized *Huckleberry Finn*, which appeared in *Jewish Daily Forward*-- though she made a few adjustments to the story as she read...
BRONX ZOO
In her version, it was the adventures of a Jewish boy who rafted down the Volga River and helped a runaway *muzhik* (serf) escape to freedom!
By the time he was nine years old, Abe could read for himself...
During the 1920's "Red Scare", papers were filled with stories that warned that any immigrant (particularly left-leaning ones) could be carrying bombs. Cops were shown conducting regular roundups.
Abe worked in his father's drugstore. Some nights he delivered *shmink* (makeup) to the dancers at the Winter Garden Theatre, a famous burlesque house. They liked him because he listened carefully to their stories...
"LOOK, BUT DON'T LOOK TOO LONG."
DAD

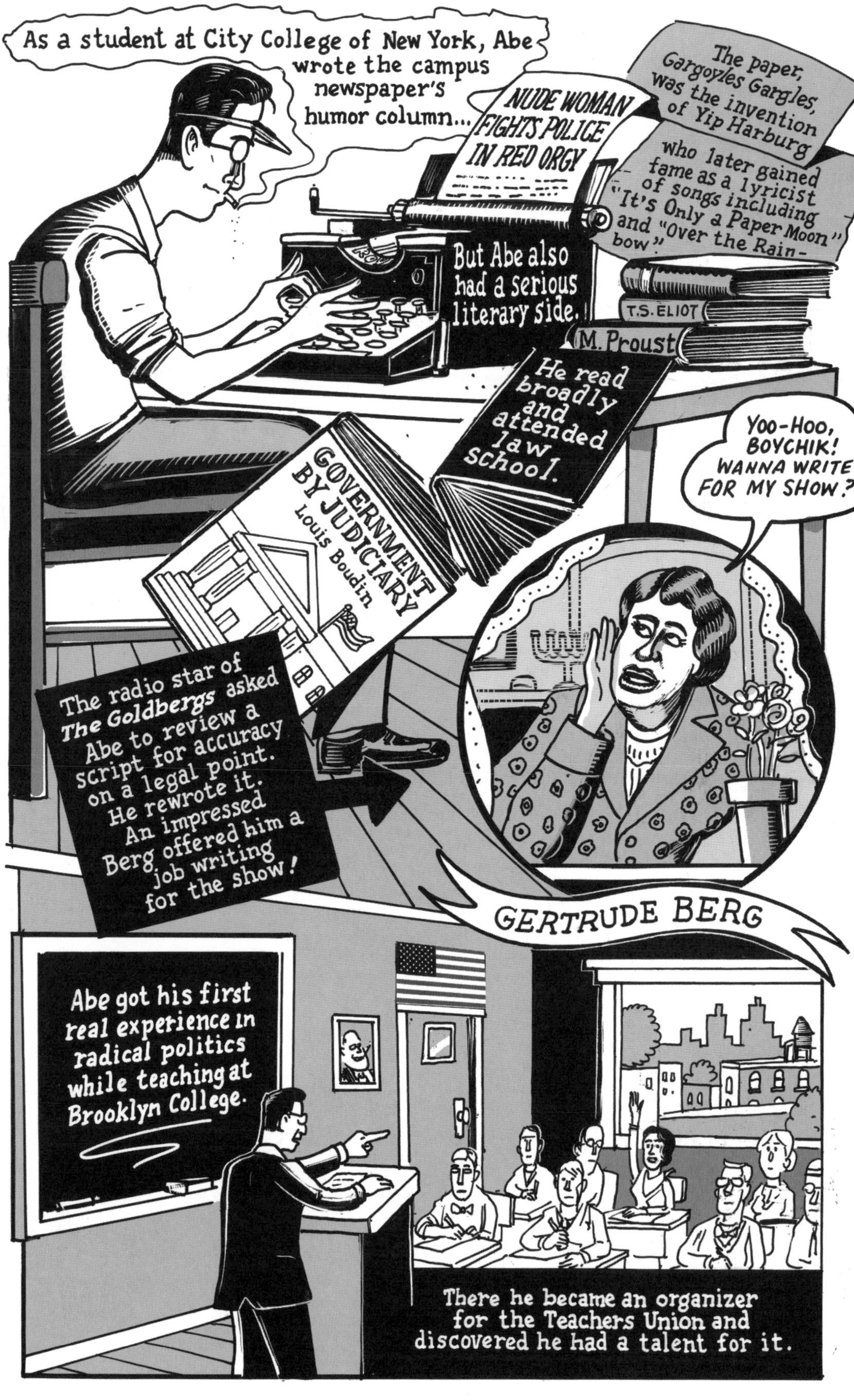
As a student at City College of New York, Abe wrote the campus newspaper's humor column...
NUDE WOMAN FIGHTS POLICE IN RED ORGY
The paper, Gargoyles Gargles, was the invention of Yip Harburg
who later gained fame as a lyricist of songs including "It's Only a Paper Moon" and "Over the Rain-bow."
But Abe also had a serious literary side.
T.S. ELIOT
M. Proust
He read broadly and attended law school.
GOVERNMENT BY JUDICIARY
Louis Boudin
YOO-HOO, BOYCHIK! WANNA WRITE FOR MY SHOW?
The radio star of The Goldbergs asked Abe to review a script for accuracy on a legal point. He rewrote it. An impressed Berg offered him a job writing for the show!
GERTRUDE BERG
Abe got his first real experience in radical politics while teaching at Brooklyn College.
There he became an organizer for the Teachers Union and discovered he had a talent for it.

After World War II, Abe moved to Hollywood where he got the opportunity to work with Jewish film star John Garfield.
A veteran of the radical *Group Theatre* in New York, Garfield embodied the moral authority of the outsider.

Body and Soul

Abe wrote this boxing classic, which he referred to as "a fable of the streets," reversing Aesop. It was a cautionary tale about the toll our drive for money and fame can take on our humanity.

FORCE of EVIL

In *Force of Evil*, Polonsky's political views were front and center. The story exposed the crushing weight of banking monopolies on daily life.

It was one of the best movies made by the Hollywood left before they were all blacklisted.

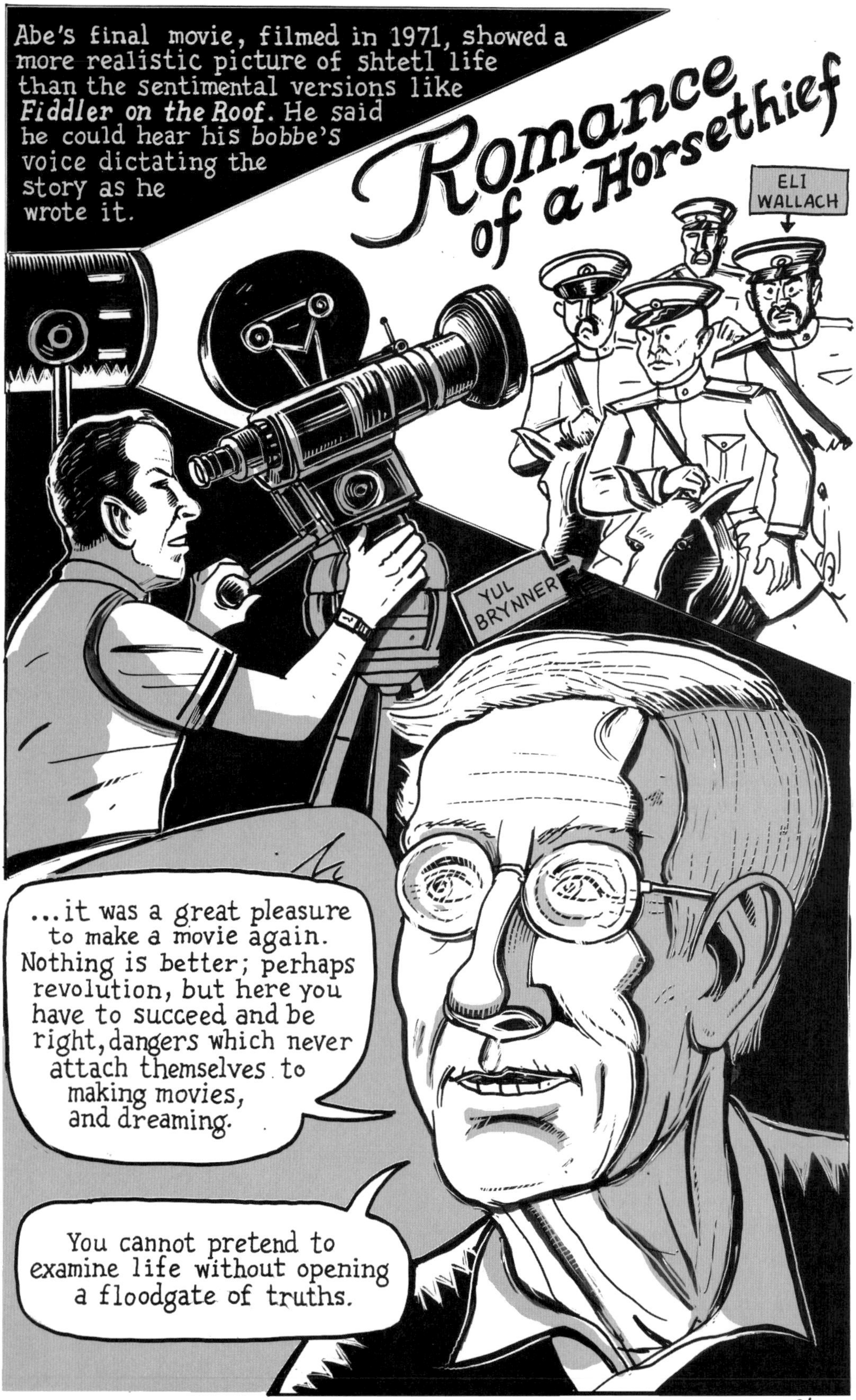
Abe's final movie, filmed in 1971, showed a more realistic picture of shtetl life than the sentimental versions like *Fiddler on the Roof*. He said he could hear his *bobbe*'s voice dictating the story as he wrote it.
Romance of a Horsethief
ELI WALLACH
YUL BRYNNER
...it was a great pleasure to make a movie again. Nothing is better; perhaps revolution, but here you have to succeed and be right, dangers which never attach themselves to making movies, and dreaming.
You cannot pretend to examine life without opening a floodgate of truths.
fin

YIDDISH FOR CELEBRITIES

I f assimilation meant leaving behind Yiddish language and inflections learned in childhood (and often reinforced on the streets of Greater New York), within the world of entertainment especially, but not only live entertainment, Yiddish survivals were both frequent and strange. Fanny Brice was by no means the first performer, Jewish or otherwise, with no Yiddish in her background who hit accidentally upon the warmth of audience response to any use (but especially sentimental use) of the *mamaloshn* (mother tongue).

Some fluent Yiddishists were forced out of their usage. Paul Muni could not get past the monopolization of the Yiddish theater by older actors, and turned unwillingly toward a brilliant American film career (in which he often played Italian Americans and most memorably gangsters). Others simply sloughed off the use of Yiddish while onstage (or in films), occasionally using phrases as suitable quips among knowledgeable friends and acquaintances. Fortunate ones included singers like Theodore Bikel, who had mostly aging audiences for whom a Yiddish repertoire—even a song or two amid a concert in English or Hebrew, in Israel—earned a heartfelt response.

A few Gentiles who came from intensely unassimilated Jewish neighborhoods, notably James Cagney, actually knew Yiddish. For the most part, of course, learning a Yiddish phrase was a way to add piquancy to a performance. Nothing in the background of Julie Andrews or the Andrews Sisters (Julie was not one of them), or Cab Calloway, or even Fanny Brice, had especially pointed them in the direction of Yiddish. But it was a convenience, and, more than a convenience, it signified recognition.

Most amusing, perhaps, is the adoption of Yiddish phrases or words for the purpose of making satirical points by those who grew up with little or no Yiddish. Groucho Marx and Moe Howard, among others, liked the word *shnorer* for a character who doesn't have a job but always shows up for dinner. Lenny Bruce, from an old Yankee town on Long Island, perfected his stand-up comedy after becoming close friends with a Yiddish-speaking roommate. A phrase here and there worked for Lenny, and the audiences laughed at the affect as much as the joke itself. The affect survived, well into the sixties and seventies, with Woody Allen—a Jew who saw the downside of everything, in himself as in other matters, who couldn't get the girl, and who searched for meaning in love and in life. Woody reset the image of the low-key existentialist with ready jokes about sex, death, and other ostensibly serious matters, which he continues to explore in his films, onstage, and in his occasional short stories.

For the final generation of immigrant Yiddish speakers and their children, Yiddish was something more, something closer to *Yiddishkeit* itself. The universalist humanism of Joseph Papp, Sidney Lumet, and Theodore Bikel did not have to be Yiddish in its origins, but their humanism has a Yiddish flavoring that cannot be misunderstood.

CELEBRITIES FLUENT IN YIDDISH

Illustration by Sharon Rudahl

PERFORMERS WHO USED YIDDISH

Illustration by Sharon Rudahl

Guide to Celebrities

CELEBRITIES FLUENT IN YIDDISH

1 MOLLY PICON
2 JOSEPH PAPP
3 LEONARD NIMOY
4 DAVID OPATOSHU
5 EDDIE CANTOR
6 HERSHEL BERNARDI
7 PAUL MUNI
8 ZERO MOSTEL
9 JAMES CAGNEY
10 KIRK DOUGLAS
11 SIDNEY LUMET
12 THEODORE BIKEL

1 GEORGE JESSEL
2 CAB CALLOWAY
3 OSCAR LEVANT
4 LENNY BRUCE
5 MEL BROOKS
6 MILTON BERLE
7 FANNY BRICE
8 GROUCHO MARX
9 PAUL ROBESON
10 THE ANDREWS SISTERS
11 JULIE ANDREWS
12 MOE HOWARD
13 WOODY ALLEN

PERFORMERS WHO USED YIDDISH

Illustration by Sharon Rudahl

HARVEY KURTZMAN-MAD MAN

STORY: JOEL SCHECHTER   ART: SPAIN

At E.C. COMICS, A PUBLISHING HOUSE DEVOTED TO HORROR, WEIRD SCIENCE, AND WARFARE, HARVEY KURTZMAN (1924-1993) CREATED MAD!

THAT'S MAD COMICS! MUTUALLY ASSURED DESTRUCTION CAME LATER.

AS A YOUNGSTER KURTZMAN DREW HIS FIRST COMICS, "IKEY AND MIKEY," ON THE SIDEWALKS OF NEW YORK.

HIRED BY E.C. PUBLISHER WILLIAM GAINES, KURTZMAN PIONEERED TWO-FISTED TALES. HIS RESEARCH MADE WAR COMICS HISTORICALLY ACCURATE FOR A CHANGE.

GUTS WITHOUT GLORY!

HE'S GOT THAT RIGHT.

IN 1952, KURTZMAN INVENTED MAD. HIS PARODIES TURNED TARZAN INTO "MELVIN OF THE APES," ARCHIE INTO "STARCHIE," JOE McCARTHY INTO A QUIZ SHOW PANELIST.

THIS MAN IS A DUPE!

A DOPE?

A BULLFIGHTER MAYBE?

I'M SUPERDUPERMAN

MY SLIME

A DUPE! LOOK AT THAT GASP RED CAPE.

LEGENDARY COMIC BOOK SCHOLAR PROFESSOR JOE TSURIS SAYS:

IN HARVEY, FROM HIS EARLY HEY LOOK! STRIPS TO HIS MAD MOCKERY OF CONSUMER CULTURE, WE FIND THE SPIRIT OF PURIM, THE HOLIDAY WHERE NOTHING IS SACRED. HARVEY'S MOTHER WAS A SECULAR JEW, BUT FOR HARVEY, EVERY DAY WAS PURIM.

"I ALMOST FORGOT TO MENTION 'SCHMALTZ,' THE 'CHICKEN FAT' STYLE CREATED BY KURTZMAN AND HIS OLD HIGH SCHOOL PAL, BILL ELDER-CRAMMED FRAMES FULL OF ROADSIDE SIGNS, PUNS AND ASIDES."

MAD INTRODUCED INNOCENT YOUNG READERS TO A WEALTH OF YIDDISHISMS THAT KURTZMAN MAY HAVE HEARD AT HOME OR AT LEFTWING YIDDISH SUMMER CAMP KINDERLAND.

WE WANT TO SEE THE GIRLS AT NITGEDAYGET!

NOT TO WORRY!

THAT'S WHAT I SAID— NITGEDAYGET!

WHEN CONGRESS DECIDED THAT COMICS WERE SUBVERSIVE IN THE FIFTIES, KURTZMAN WASN'T INTERROGATED, BUT HIS PUBLISHER, BILL GAINES, WAS QUESTIONED ABOUT E.C.'S POPULAR WAR AND HORROR COMICS.

IS THIS AN EXAMPLE OF WHAT YOU WOULD CONSIDER GOOD TASTE?

YES!

THEN JUST WHAT WOULD YOU CONSIDER BAD TASTE?

IF THE HEAD WAS A LITTLE HIGHER AND YOU COULD SEE THE GORE COMING OUT OF THE NECK...

E.C. COMICS WERE DRIVEN OUT OF BUSINESS. GAINES CHANGED **MAD** FROM A COMIC TO A MAGAZINE AND ASKED KURTZMAN TO CONTINUE AS EDITOR.

GIVE ME 51% OWNERSHIP AND I'LL STAY ON AS EDITOR.

THAT'S **MESHUGE!**

NO, I'M NOT A **MAD** MAN ANYMORE.

KURTZMAN LEFT **MAD** TO CREATE **TRUMP**, THEN **HUMBUG**, THEN **HELP!** NONE OF THEM ENDURED.

AMONG THE ARTISTS KURTZMAN HIRED AT **HELP!** WAS R. CRUMB, WHO WANTED TO SHARE CONTROL OF HIS **ZAP** COMICS WITH ITS CONTRIBUTING ARTISTS.

SIGH!

ROBERT, YOU HAVE TO UNDERSTAND THAT THESE RADICAL IDEAS ARE IMPRACTICAL.

HARVEY THEN DID "LITTLE ANNIE FANNY" FOR **PLAYBOY** WITH ASSISTANCE FROM BILL ELDER AND JACK DAVIS. GLORIA STEINEM, HARVEY'S SOMETIME ASSISTANT AT **HELP!**, MIGHT HAVE OBJECTED.

YOU CALL THIS LIBERATION?

IN FULL COLOR TOO.

ARE WE HAVING FUN YET?

IT'S HARVEY'S GANG!

TODAY KURTZMAN IS CONSIDERED THE MOST INFLUENTIAL CARTOONIST OF THE 20th CENTURY—ESPECIALLY BY THOSE HE INFLUENCED.

YIDDISH SUMMER CAMPS

L ike the after-school secular Yiddish school (*shule*) networks in various parts of the world, the Yiddish summer camp was intended to imbue youngsters with language skills and secular *Yiddishkeit*, not neglecting the usual social and athletic activities. Four of the five major Yiddish summer camps in upstate New York were divided along political-ideological lines. (Other, smaller camps existed at various times in the United States and Canada, most not so successfully.) The two most important, Camp Kinderland (now in Tolland, Massachusetts) and Camp Kinder Ring, still in Hopewell Junction, New York, were, respectively, the creations of the Left (pro-Soviet) and the anticommunist socialists. Well-known pedagogues of the Yiddish world lectured, modern dance leaders led performances, and in Kinderland, noted folksingers (some of them practically banned from public appearances during the 1950s) played and sang. Childhood friendships led to marriages and thus future campers, while many of today's leading Yiddishists in academia and the arts owe their inspiration to this experience and to the transgenerational continuity described in the phrase "*fun shule in kemp, fun kemp in shule*," meaning "from the secular Yiddish school to camp, and from camp to school."

Camp Kinderland. Illustration by Peter Kuper

CHAPTER 4.

Yiddish Fadeout & Revival

◆◇◆◗◗◉◗◆◗◗◗◆◗

According to a familiar aphorism, Yiddish has been in trouble for at least a century and, with luck, will go on being in trouble for another century. Actually, as language-speakers go, the number of Yiddishists leveled off with the new century: The Chassidic population in the United States, Israel, and elsewhere has created ever-new waves of families with up to a dozen children, speaking Yiddish as the language of daily life (all religious teachings being in Hebrew). Thus it is Yiddish secularism that faded with the crises described above.

But secularism has proved to be both flexible and tenacious. Itche Goldberg, the eldest writer ever to produce a new work, in a book of essays released after he had reached the age of 101, was a distinguished Yiddishist and, until a few years before his death at 102, the editor of *Yidishe Kultur (Yiddish Culture)*, one of the finest literary journals in the language. Goldberg took cheer in his last decades at the revival of Yiddish-language musicals off Broadway, which had a popular following, and at the most important single source of revival: klezmer music and its lyrics.

Other secularists carry on, undaunted. More than a score of communities and Sunday schools across North America, affiliates of the Congress of Secular Jewish Organizations, as well as branches of the 110-year-old Arbeter Ring (Workmen's Circle), turn to Yiddish poetry and songs, both in the original and in English translations, to replace prayer in their celebrations of holidays and life-cycle events.

To be sure, there are Yiddish classes in dozens of universities around the world, a few Yiddish institutes with various worthy purposes, and of course the National Yiddish Book Center, which has in recent years (with a grant from Steven Spielberg's Righteous Persons Foundation) digitized its thousands of books. Any of these can be read online, a major contribution to global Yiddish literacy.

The future will tell whether these efforts are successful in preserving more than a specialized scholarship, alongside a religious population that has no use for nearly all the scholarship. Arguably, just as Hebrew was preserved for two millennia in the Holy Arks of synagogues when it was not a language of daily use, so the growing number of Yiddish studies programs at universities may well enable modern literary Yiddish to survive until the day when Ashkenazic Jews and others will discover their hidden ancestral treasures. It is certain, at least to its devotees, that without Yiddish and the culture of *Yiddishkeit* that gave the language a home, Jewish culture and Jewish life is much the poorer.

CHAIM GRADE by HARVEY PEKAR

THIS IS ESPECIALLY IMPORTANT IN THE WORKS OF CHAIM GRADE. A NATIVE OF VILNA, LITHUANIA, THE STRONGHOLD OF THE MILITANTLY RATIONAL MISNAGIDIM, GRADE GAVE UP HIS RELIGIOUS STUDIES TO BECOME A WRITER IN 1932.

PICTURES by SHARON RUDAHL

SOME OF THE NOVELS I'VE DEALT WITH PORTRAY JEWS AS BEING BETWEEN THE DEVIL AND THE DEEP BLUE SEA, BETWEEN RELIGIOUS BELIEFS AND SECULAR MOTIVATIONS.

IN 1950, HE BEGAN WRITING PROSE FICTION (SOMETIMES DISGUISED AUTO-BIOGRAPHY) AND BECAME EVEN MORE RESPECTED THAN WHEN HE WAS SOLELY A POET. HE IS SUPERBLY EQUIPPED TO WRITE ABOUT JEWISH RELIGION AND YIDDISH-BASED SOCIAL LIFE.

AMONG HIS EARLY PROSE WORKS, "MY QUARREL WITH HERSCH RASSEYNER," A LONG SHORT STORY, STANDS OUT.

FOR YEARS, GRADE WAS KNOWN AS A POET. HE SURVIVED THE HOLOCAUST, LIVING IN THE USSR, MOVING TO FRANCE AND THEN THE US IN 1948.

HARVEY PEKAR—UNDATED PHOTO COURTESY THE AUTHOR.

HE FREED HIMSELF OF THEIR INFLUENCE AND HIS WRITING REFLECTED A SCHOLARLY POINT OF VIEW.

"WHOEVER DENIES HIMSELF AFFIRMS THE MASTER OF THE UNIVERSE"

IN "MY QUARREL" GRADE MEETS UP WITH HIS SCHOOLMATE RASSEYNER SEVERAL TIMES BOTH BEFORE AND AFTER THE SECOND WORLD WAR.

GRADE FOR A TIME WENT TO AN EXTREMELY ASCETIC YESHIVA THAT FAVORED THE MUSAR PHILOSOPHY. FOR THESE RELIGIOUS JEWS, PAIN WAS PLEASURE AND PLEASURE WAS PAIN.

(RASSEYNER ALSO SURVIVED THE HOLOCAUST.)

THE STORY DETAILS THE CONTINUING DEBATE BETWEEN RASSEYNER & GRADE, CALLED "VILNER" HERE. BOTH HOLD THEIR OWN, BUT NOT SURPRISINGLY, GRADE HAS THE LAST WORD (ACTUALLY THE LAST FEW PAGES).

HARVEY PEKAR-UNDATED PHOTO

THE TWO HAVE HARSH THINGS TO SAY, BUT AT THE END, GRADE EXPRESSES THE DESIRE TO REMAIN FRIENDS WITH RASSEYNER, SOMETHING I KIND OF WISH HE HAD LEFT OUT OF THE STORY, AS THE ENMITY BETWEEN THE TWO MEN IS SERIOUS. IT'S ONE OF THE MOST HIGH LEVEL DEBATES I'VE EVER READ IN A WORK OF FICTION, THOUGH.

THE *AGUNAH* AND *THE WELL* ARE ALSO TOP NOTCH GRADE VOLUMES. IN THE *AGUNAH* A WOMAN IS BESET BY TERRIBLE PROBLEMS BECAUSE THE CORPSE OF HER HUSBAND, WHO PERISHED IN THE FIRST WORLD WAR, HAS NEVER BEEN RECOVERED. ACCORDING TO JEWISH LAW, SHE CANNOT REMARRY.

WE ALSO MEET A FORMER MUSCOVITE IN GRADE'S TWO-VOLUME *THE YESHIVA*. THERE ARE TOO MANY STOLEN PLOT DEVICES FOR THE NOVEL TO BE COMPLETELY CONVINCING, ALTHOUGH IT IS A FINE WORK. TO ME, HOWEVER, *THE YESHIVA* IS VALUABLE BECAUSE IT POINTS UP A MAJOR DIFFERENCE BETWEEN THE OPTIMIST AND THE PESSIMIST: THE OPTIMIST CANNOT SEE FAR ENOUGH INTO THE FUTURE FOR THE CONSEQUENCES OF HIS ACTIONS TO BECOME DAMAGING. THEY DON'T OCCUR TO HIM. THE PESSIMIST DOES SEE PROBLEMS AHEAD, BUT THEY PARALYSE HIM INTO INACTION.

RABBIS AND WIVES CONTAINS THREE EXCELLENT NOVELLAS DEALING, NOT SURPRISINGLY, WITH PROBLEMS FACED BY RABBIS AND WIVES.

MENDL, "A SIMPLE-MINDED POTTER" IN *THE WELL*, TAKES IT INTO HIS HEAD TO INSPIRE THE NEIGHBORHOOD TO CONSTRUCT A NEW WELL AFTER THE OLD ONE GOES DRY. MENDL'S ADVENTURES ALMOST AMOUNT TO AN ODYSSEY. HE IS ANOTHER EXAMPLE OF THE WISE FOOL IN YIDDISH LITERATURE.

WHAT'S SO ADMIRABLE ABOUT GRADE IS THE SERIOUSNESS WITH WHICH HE TAKES HIS LIFE AND THE LIVES AROUND HIM. UNLIKE I. B. SINGER, HE IS NOT CONCERNED WITH CROWD PLEASING.

AN AMERICAN SPLENDOR "OLDIE"

———◆—▶◀—◆———

P ublished first in *American Splendor* no. 13 in 1988, "President's Day" offers a perfect example of Harvey Pekar at his best. Pekar was a protean intellectual. He
worked at a Veterans Administration hospital by day and returned home in the
evening, intellectually engaged at every location, creatively reinterpreting the Jewish,
and especially the Yiddish, literary heritage. "President's Day" is drawn by Joe Zabel
and inked by Gary Dumm, two Cleveland-area artists. It is arguably Pekar's first step
toward his later work, but also notable as an effort to explore his deep interest in Yiddish literature and its connections to the intimate details of his daily life.

PRESIDENT'S DAY

Story by HARVEY PEKAR *Pencils by* JOE ZABEL *Inks by* GARY DUMM

OH, I BETTER TELL YA—I'M GONNA WORK PRESIDENT'S DAY.

WHY? I THOUGHT YOU DIDN'T LIKE WORKING HOLIDAYS.

I DON'T. BUT WE'RE SUPPOSED TO WORK AT LEAST ONE HOLIDAY A YEAR. AND THAT'S THE BEST ONE FOR ME TO WORK.

THE WEATHER'S SO ROTTEN THEN THAT IF I TOOK THE DAY OFF, ALL I'D DO WOULD BE SIT AROUND HERE, STARE OUT THE WINDOW AND READ...

MY WORK'S CAUGHT UP SO ALL I'LL HAVE TO DO IS ANSWER PHONE REQUESTS WHEN I GO IN.

THE PLACE'LL BE DESERTED. I OUGHTA HAVE TIME T' READ DOWN THERE. MIGHT AS WELL GET PAID FOR IT.

HMM. IT'D BE A GOOD TIME T' READ SOMETHING BY I.J.*SINGER — THAT'S I.B.*SINGER'S OLDER BROTHER...

*I.J. IS FOR ISRAEL JOSHUA, I.B. IS FOR ISAAC BASHEVIS.

①

THIS IS APROPOS OF NOTHING, BUT I.B. SINGER REALLY GETS ON MY NERVES; HE'S ACTUALLY NOT A BAD WRITER, BUT HE'S SO OVERRATED IT MAKES ME SICK.

JAMES JOYCE NEVER GOT A NOBEL PRIZE BUT I.B. SINGER DID. WONDERFUL- MAYBE NEXT YEAR **HAROLD ROBBINS** 'LL GET IT.

WHY IS HE SO OVERRATED?

FUNNY YOU SHOULD ASK...WELL, HIS WORK IS COY AND SENSATIONALISTIC. HIS BOOKS ARE FULL OF MIRACLES AND DEMONS...

HE WRITES ABOUT SEX A LOT MORE THAN MOST YIDDISH WRITERS.

WHAT REALLY BUGS ME IS HOW HE LOADS HIS BOOKS UP WITH COLORFUL CHARACTERS— THIEVES, PROSTITUTES, WONDER RABBIS... I MEAN LOOK— I WASN'T BORN IN POLAND BUT MY PARENTS 'N' EVEN SOME 'A' MY COUSINS WERE. I'VE KNOWN A LOT OF EASTERN EUROPEAN JEWS AND FOR THE MOST PART, AND THIS INCLUDES GALITZIANERS AND CHASSIDIM, THEY WERE SOBER, NO NONSENSE, HARDWORKING PEOPLE.

BUT THE WAY I.B. SINGER DESCRIBES 'EM YOU'D THINK THEY WERE GYPSIES. AND THAT'S NOT JUST MY OPINION, MY AUNT HELEN TOLD ME, "I NEVER KNEW ANY JEWS LIKE SINGER WROTE ABOUT."

SURE, THERE'VE BEEN JEWISH GANGSTERS AND JEWISH WHORES, BUT BY AND LARGE, EASTERN EUROPEAN JEWS WERE QUIET AND LAW ABIDING, GOOD FAMILY PEOPLE.

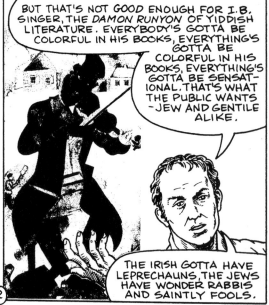

BUT THAT'S NOT *GOOD* ENOUGH FOR I.B. SINGER, THE *DAMON RUNYON* OF YIDDISH LITERATURE. EVERYBODY'S GOTTA BE COLORFUL IN HIS BOOKS, EVERYTHING'S GOTTA BE COLORFUL IN HIS BOOKS, EVERYTHING'S GOTTA BE SENSATIONAL. THAT'S WHAT THE PUBLIC WANTS —JEW AND GENTILE ALIKE.

THE IRISH GOTTA HAVE LEPRECHAUNS, THE JEWS HAVE WONDER RABBIS AND SAINTLY FOOLS.

②

I.B.'S A SLICK P.R. MAN, TOO. I SEE HIM ON T.V. HE COMES ON LIKE A CARICATURE OF THE SIMPLE, KINDLY, OLD JEWISH GRANDFATHER, HUMBLE, JUST A "KLEINE MENSCH" YOU KNOW, A TEVYE. JUST PLAIN FOLKS. SURE.

SO I GOT THIS FEELING MAYBE HIS OLDER BROTHER I.J. SINGER IS A BETTER WRITER. FOR SOME REASON I WANNA BELIEVE THAT.

I MEAN AFTER ALL, I.J. WAS A SOCIALIST. I THINK HE HAD A LOT MORE POLITICAL AWARENESS AND GUTS THAN I.B.

I STARTED TO READ THIS ONE NOVEL BY I.J., *THE BROTHERS ASHKENAZI*, BUT I DIDN'T GET TOO FAR IN IT FOR SOME REASON. BUT Y'KNOW, IT STARTED OFF SOLID— REMINDED ME A BIT OF THOMAS MANN'S WORK— AT LEAST THERE WEREN'T A BUNCHA MIRACLES IN IT, AS FAR AS I GOT, ANYWAY.

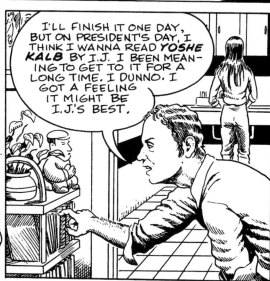

I'LL FINISH IT ONE DAY, BUT ON PRESIDENT'S DAY, I THINK I WANNA READ *YOSHE KALB* BY I.J. I BEEN MEANING TO GET TO IT FOR A LONG TIME. I DUNNO. I GOT A FEELING IT MIGHT BE I.J.'S BEST.

7:00 A.M., PRESIDENT'S DAY

HONEY, I GOTTA GO NOW. TAKE CARE A' YERSELF T'DAY, HUH?

MMM. IT'S SO *COLD* OUT THERE, YOU SURE YOU DON'T WANT TO TAKE THE CAR. I'LL TAKE THE BUS.

NAW, I'LL WALK, YOU GOT THAT DOCTOR'S APPOINTMENT T'DAY, BETTER I SHOULD FREEZE THAN YOU.

O.K... BUT I HATE TO THINK OF YOU OUTSIDE IN THAT ZERO WEATHER.

③

ZERO IS ABOUT RIGHT. I BET IT AIN'T OVER FIVE ABOVE.

THE HAWK FLIES

CRUNCH CRUNCH CRUNCH

NOTHING LIKE DIRTY OLD SNOW. YELLOW SNOW AT THAT. DOGS AROUND HERE.

UHNN, FUCKIN' WIND...OOH, MY HEAD FEELS LIKE IT'S GONNA CRACK OPEN.

MAN, HOW AM I GONNA PUT UP WITH THIS COLD WHEN I'M SIXTY? I CAN'T WAIT TILL I GET IN THE BUILDING NOW.

④

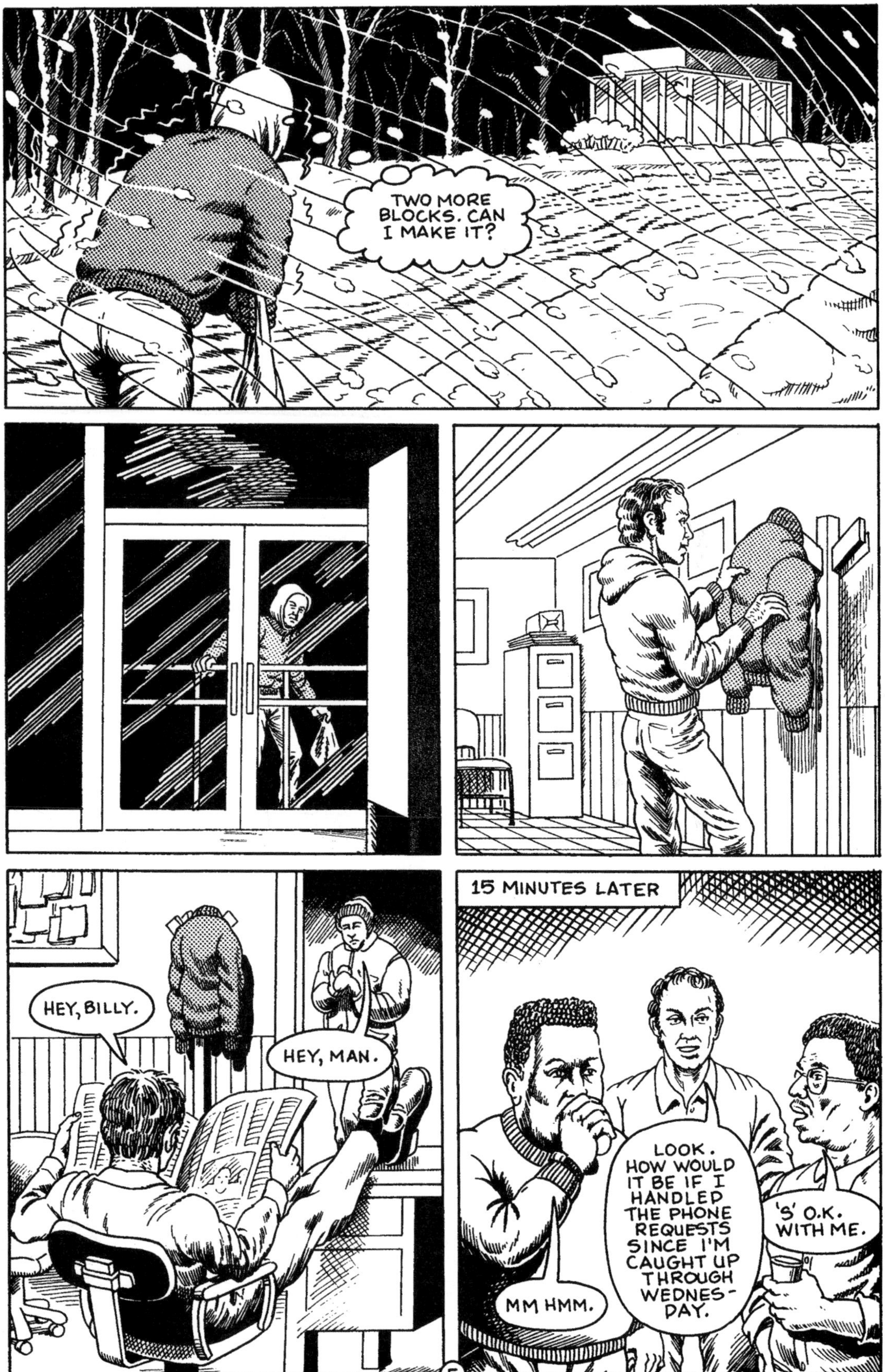
TWO MORE BLOCKS. CAN I MAKE IT?
15 MINUTES LATER
HEY, BILLY.
HEY, MAN.
LOOK. HOW WOULD IT BE IF I HANDLED THE PHONE REQUESTS SINCE I'M CAUGHT UP THROUGH WEDNES-DAY.
'S' O.K. WITH ME.
MM HMM.
5

WHAT DO WE HAVE HERE? TWO BIG SHOT CHASSIDIC RABBIS WITH "COURTS", RABBI MELECH THE FAT PUSHY ONE, WANTS TO MARRY HIS COW OF A 14 YEAR OLD DAUGHTER TO NAHUM, THE WIMPY SON, ALSO 14, OF THE OTHER ONE, THE ELEGANT, SCHOLARLY RABBI. AFTER THAT'S DONE, RABBI MELECH, A WIDOWER, WILL BE FREE TO MARRY AN INSANELY WILLFUL BUT BEAUTIFUL 15 YEAR OLD, MALKAH.

8:30 A.M.

HMM. NOW WHERE HAVE I ENCOUNTERED PLOTS LIKE THAT BEFORE?

RRRING

RRING

RECORD ROOM...

WHAT'S THE LAST FOUR DIGITS OF HIS SOCIAL SECURITY NUMBER?

O.K... IF IT'S HERE I'LL BRING IT RIGHT DOWN.

6

MALKAH TREATS HER FAT OLD HUSBAND LIKE A DOG— WON'T LET HIM COME CLOSE TO HER, BUT PREDICTABLY GETS INVOLVED IN A TORRID LOVE AFFAIR WITH NAHUM.

9:30

ONE HOT SPRING NIGHT SHE'S IN A CRAZY MOOD AND REVOLTED BY MELECH'S COURT, SETS FIRE TO THE BARN, IT SPREADS TO THE SYNAGOGUE, MEANWHILE SHE GRABS NAHUM, YANKS HIM INTO THE FIELDS AND MAKES IT WITH HIM AS THE BUILDINGS BLAZE.

10:30

AFTER THIS, NAHUM BEGINS TO STUDY FURIOUSLY. HE READS: "AND THE GREATEST OF ALL THE SINS WHICH A MORTAL CAN COMMIT IS THE SIN OF DEFILEMENT WITH THE WIFE OF ANOTHER." HE HAS SIGNIFICANT DREAMS, VISIONS. MALKAH, MEANWHILE, IS DISCOVERED TO BE PREGNANT. SHE AND HER CHILD DIE IN CHILDBIRTH. NAHUM DISAPPEARS INTO THE NIGHT.

YAWN. I'M HUNGRY.

12:00

⑦

12:30

FIFTEEN YEARS LATER, A JEWISH BEGGAR (GUESS WHO?) TURNS UP IN THE POLISH TOWN OF BIALOGURA. HE SEEMS LIKE AN IDIOT TO THE OTHER JEWS, ALL HE DOES IS CHANT PSALMS IN THE SYNAGOGUE. THE BEADLE FINDS HIM THERE, TAKES HIM HOME AND MAKES HIM HIS ASSISTANT.

THE BEADLE HAS A HALF-WIT DAUGHTER, ZIVYAH, WHO WANTS THE BEGGAR, NOW CALLED YOSHE KALB (YOSHE THE CALF) TO MARRY HER. SHE THROWS HERSELF AT HIM, BUT HE'S NOT INTERESTED. THEN SHE STARTS MESSING AROUND WITH JEWISH SMUGGLERS WHO USE THE CEMETARY AS A BASE OF OPERATIONS AND GETS PREGNANT BY ONE OF THEM... A PLAGUE BREAKS OUT IN THE TOWN. THE JEWS THINK IT'S BEEN BROUGHT ON BY ONE OF THEIR NUMBER WHO HAS SINNED. THEY SET OUT TO FIND THE GUILTY ONE.

1:30

THEN ZIVYAH IS FOUND TO BE PREGNANT. THE JEWS TRY TO DETERMINE WHICH MAN IS RESPONSIBLE. YOSHE IS ACCUSED. ZIVYAH'S IDIOTIC TESTIMONY CONVINCES SOME PEOPLE THAT HE IS GUILTY. IT IS DETERMINED THAT YOSHE MUST MARRY ZIVYAH TO LIFT THE PLAGUE. THEY ARE MARRIED THEN YOSHE DISAPPEARS.

2:00

3:00

HE TURNS UP AGAIN AT RABBI MELECH'S COURT WHERE HE ASTOUNDS EVERYONE BY HIS APPEARANCE. THEY ARE CONVINCED THAT HE IS WHO HE SAYS HE IS AND THERE IS REJOICING. BUT NAHUM/YOSHE IS RECOGNIZED BY SOMEONE FROM BIALOGURA WHO ACCUSES HIM OF BEING A SWINDLER AND AN ADULTERER. THE CHARGES CAUSE A SENSATION. IS YOSHE REALLY NAHUM? IS HE A SINNER? FINALLY A GREAT TRIBUNAL IS CONVENED TO SETTLE THE QUESTION.

⑧

CHAPTER 4

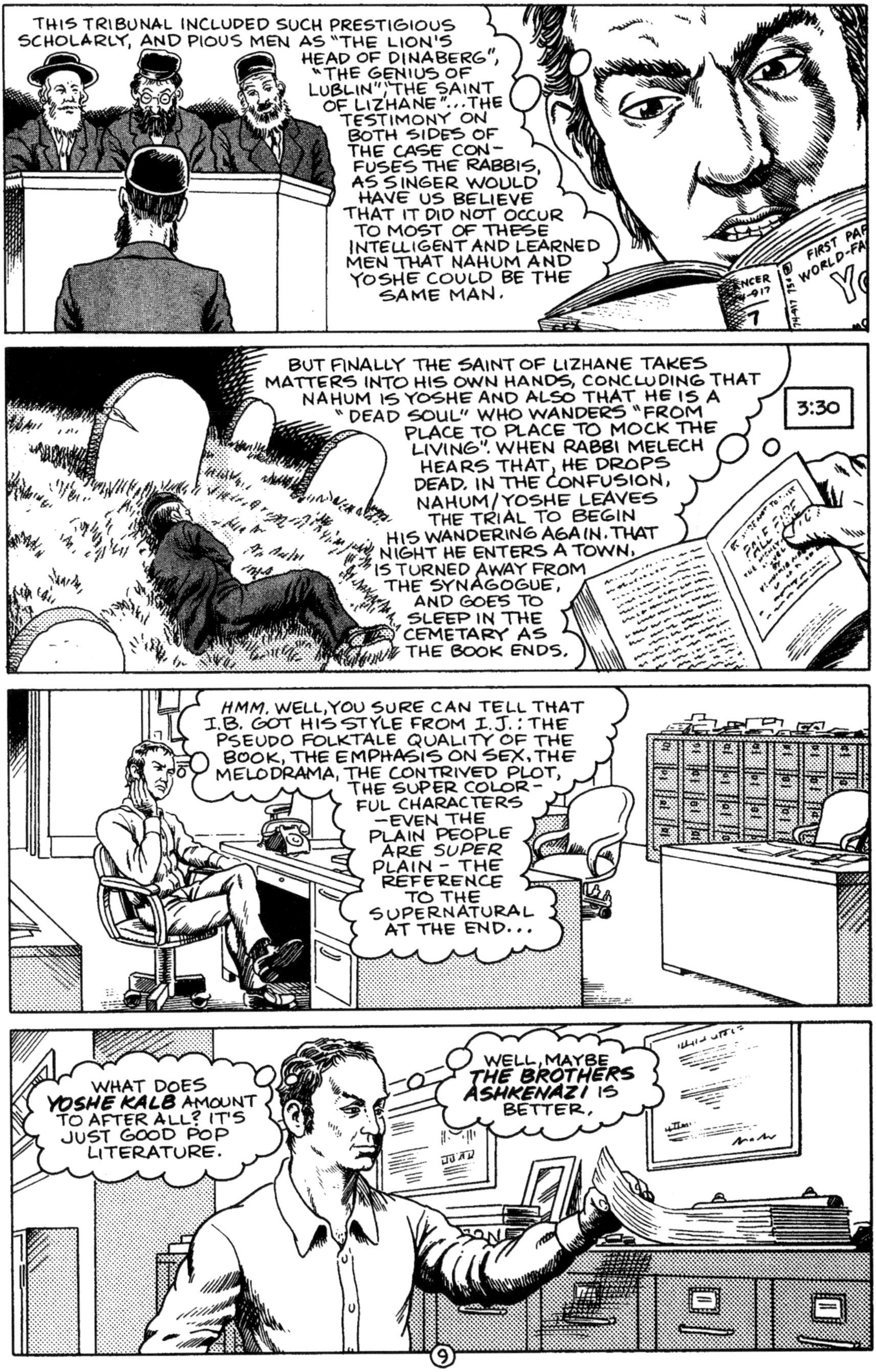
THIS TRIBUNAL INCLUDED SUCH PRESTIGIOUS SCHOLARLY, AND PIOUS MEN AS "THE LION'S HEAD OF DINABERG", "THE GENIUS OF LUBLIN", "THE SAINT OF LIZHANE"... THE TESTIMONY ON BOTH SIDES OF THE CASE CONFUSES THE RABBIS, AS SINGER WOULD HAVE US BELIEVE THAT IT DID NOT OCCUR TO MOST OF THESE INTELLIGENT AND LEARNED MEN THAT NAHUM AND YOSHE COULD BE THE SAME MAN.
BUT FINALLY THE SAINT OF LIZHANE TAKES MATTERS INTO HIS OWN HANDS, CONCLUDING THAT NAHUM IS YOSHE AND ALSO THAT HE IS A "DEAD SOUL" WHO WANDERS "FROM PLACE TO PLACE TO MOCK THE LIVING". WHEN RABBI MELECH HEARS THAT, HE DROPS DEAD. IN THE CONFUSION, NAHUM/YOSHE LEAVES THE TRIAL TO BEGIN HIS WANDERING AGAIN. THAT NIGHT HE ENTERS A TOWN, IS TURNED AWAY FROM THE SYNAGOGUE, AND GOES TO SLEEP IN THE CEMETARY AS THE BOOK ENDS.
3:30
HMM. WELL, YOU SURE CAN TELL THAT I.B. GOT HIS STYLE FROM I.J.: THE PSEUDO FOLKTALE QUALITY OF THE BOOK, THE EMPHASIS ON SEX, THE MELODRAMA, THE CONTRIVED PLOT, THE SUPER COLORFUL CHARACTERS —EVEN THE PLAIN PEOPLE ARE *SUPER* PLAIN — THE REFERENCE TO THE SUPERNATURAL AT THE END...
WHAT DOES ***YOSHE KALB*** AMOUNT TO AFTER ALL? IT'S JUST GOOD POP LITERATURE.
WELL, MAYBE ***THE BROTHERS ASHKENAZI*** IS BETTER.
9

YAWN

4:00

THERE'RE NO SUPERVISORS AROUND AND IT'S DEAD. I'M GONNA SPLIT A LITTLE EARLY,

BOY, IT'S STRANGE TO THINK I'LL BE GOING TO WORK AGAIN TOMORROW MORNING. FEELS LIKE A FRIDAY.

END

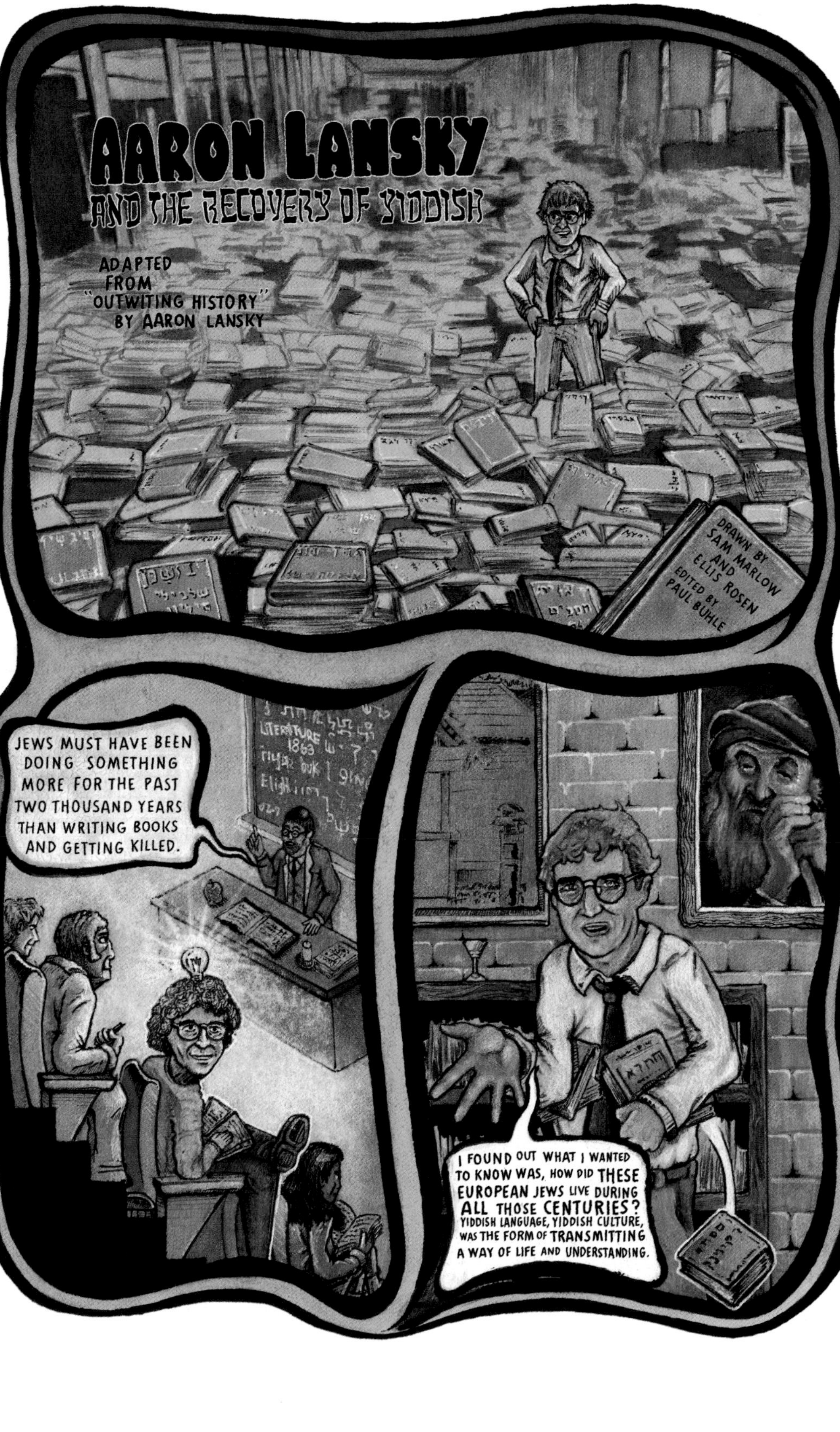
AARON LANSKY
AND THE RECOVERY OF YIDDISH
ADAPTED FROM "OUTWITING HISTORY" BY AARON LANSKY
DRAWN BY SAM MARLOW AND ELLIS ROSEN EDITED BY PAUL BUHLE
JEWS MUST HAVE BEEN DOING SOMETHING MORE FOR THE PAST TWO THOUSAND YEARS THAN WRITING BOOKS AND GETTING KILLED.
LITERATURE 1863
I FOUND OUT WHAT I WANTED TO KNOW WAS, HOW DID THESE EUROPEAN JEWS LIVE DURING ALL THOSE CENTURIES? YIDDISH LANGUAGE, YIDDISH CULTURE, WAS THE FORM OF TRANSMITTING A WAY OF LIFE AND UNDERSTANDING.

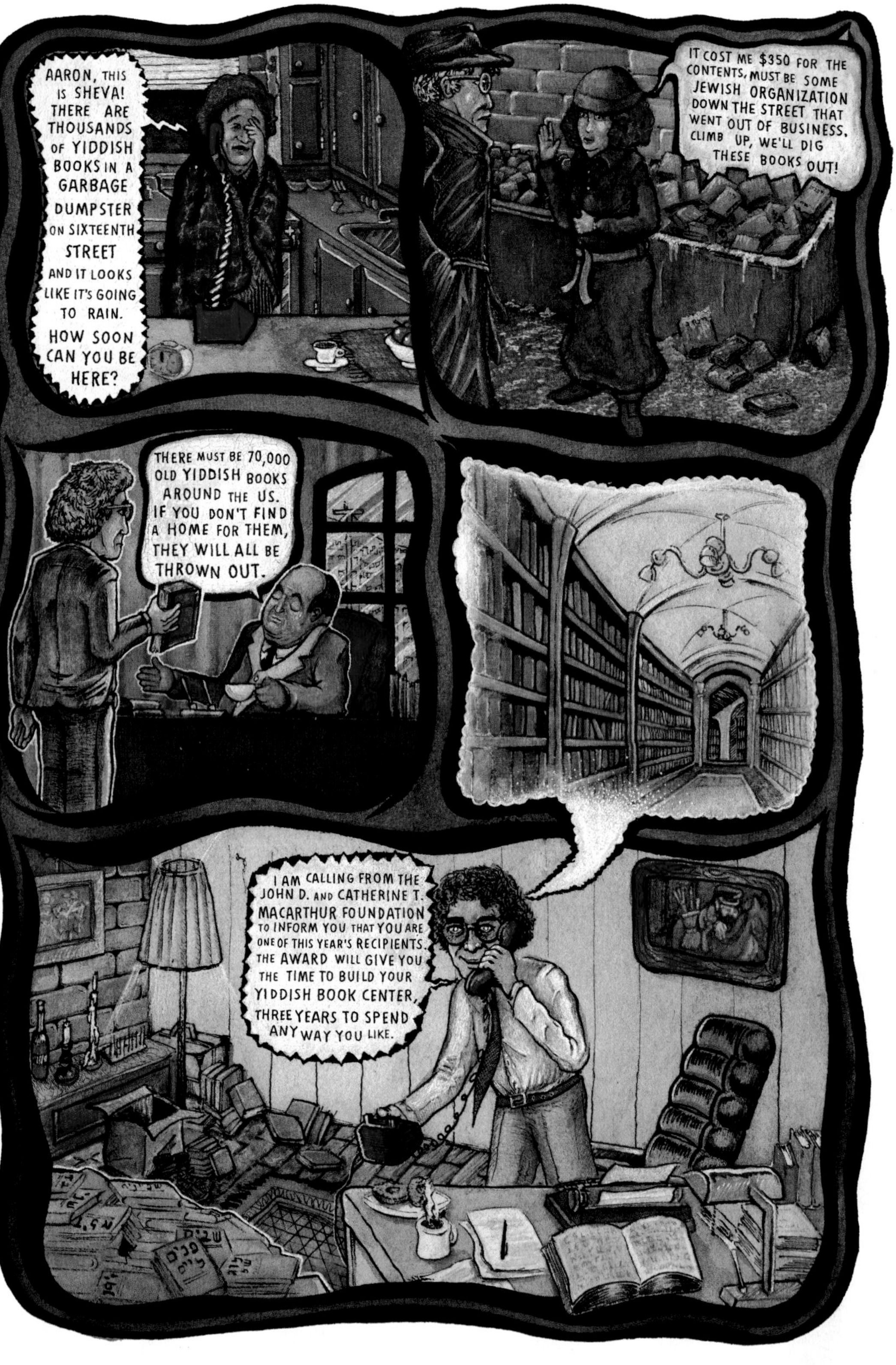
AARON, THIS IS SHEVA! THERE ARE THOUSANDS OF YIDDISH BOOKS IN A GARBAGE DUMPSTER ON SIXTEENTH STREET AND IT LOOKS LIKE IT'S GOING TO RAIN. HOW SOON CAN YOU BE HERE?
IT COST ME $350 FOR THE CONTENTS, MUST BE SOME JEWISH ORGANIZATION DOWN THE STREET THAT WENT OUT OF BUSINESS. CLIMB UP, WE'LL DIG THESE BOOKS OUT!
THERE MUST BE 70,000 OLD YIDDISH BOOKS AROUND THE US. IF YOU DON'T FIND A HOME FOR THEM, THEY WILL ALL BE THROWN OUT.
I AM CALLING FROM THE JOHN D. AND CATHERINE T. MACARTHUR FOUNDATION TO INFORM YOU THAT YOU ARE ONE OF THIS YEAR'S RECIPIENTS. THE AWARD WILL GIVE YOU THE TIME TO BUILD YOUR YIDDISH BOOK CENTER, THREE YEARS TO SPEND ANY WAY YOU LIKE.

The sign reads:

ה'שא בוכער־פֿארלאַגס
NATIONAL YIDDISH BOOK CENTER

KLEZMER

WRITTEN BY HARVEY PEKAR • ILLUSTRATED BY SHARON RUDAHL

KLEZMER MUSIC, THE FESTIVE MUSIC OF EAST EUROPEAN JEWS, CAN BE TRACED BACK TO THE MIDDLE AGES. AS IT EVOLVED IT PICKED UP INFLUENCES FROM A VARIETY OF MUSICAL STYLES AND HAS INTEGRATED THEM INTO THE MAIN BODY OF ITS WORK.

ELEMENTS OF KLEZMER INCLUDE JEWISH LITURGICAL MUSIC, FOLK AND POPULAR MUSIC FROM ALL OVER EUROPE, INCLUDING GYPSY, ARABIC AND TURKISH COMPONENTS. JEWS AND GYPSIES IN PARTICULAR TRADED MUSIC.

KLEZMER WAS TRANSPLANTED INTO THE U.S. AS EARLY AS THE 1890'S, GREW MORE POPULAR BY THE PROSPEROUS 1920'S, DREW LARGE AUDIENCES IN EUROPE UNTIL THE HOLOCAUST AND FADED IN THE U.S. WITH ASSIMILATION, AFTER THE SECOND WORLD WAR.

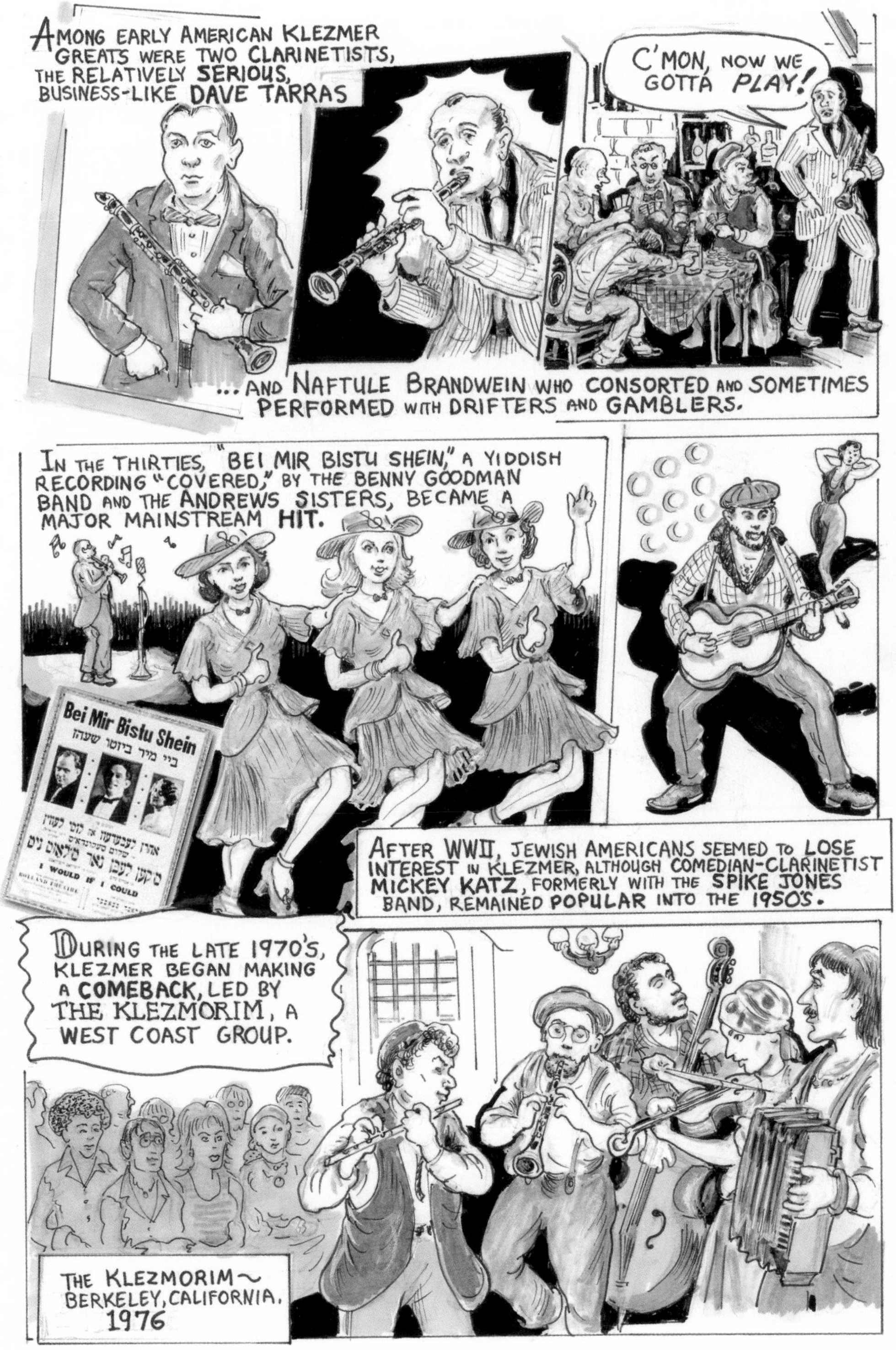
AMONG EARLY AMERICAN KLEZMER GREATS WERE TWO CLARINETISTS, THE RELATIVELY SERIOUS, BUSINESS-LIKE DAVE TARRAS
C'MON, NOW WE GOTTA PLAY!
...AND NAFTULE BRANDWEIN WHO CONSORTED AND SOMETIMES PERFORMED WITH DRIFTERS AND GAMBLERS.
IN THE THIRTIES, "BEI MIR BISTU SHEIN," A YIDDISH RECORDING "COVERED," BY THE BENNY GOODMAN BAND AND THE ANDREWS SISTERS, BECAME A MAJOR MAINSTREAM HIT.
Bei Mir Bistu Shein
ביי מיר ביזטו שעהן
I WOULD IF I COULD
AFTER WWII, JEWISH AMERICANS SEEMED TO LOSE INTEREST IN KLEZMER, ALTHOUGH COMEDIAN-CLARINETIST MICKEY KATZ, FORMERLY WITH THE SPIKE JONES BAND, REMAINED POPULAR INTO THE 1950'S.
DURING THE LATE 1970'S, KLEZMER BEGAN MAKING A COMEBACK, LED BY THE KLEZMORIM, A WEST COAST GROUP.
THE KLEZMORIM ~ BERKELEY, CALIFORNIA, 1976

HANKUS NETSKY, A TEACHER AT THE NEW ENGLAND CONSERVATORY OF MUSIC, ORGANIZED THE KLEZMER CONSERVATORY BAND, FOR SOME YEARS EXTREMELY **POPULAR**.

NETSKY WAS FORTUNATE ENOUGH TO HAVE A POOL OF YOUNG, TALENTED MUSICIANS, JEWISH AND GENTILE ALIKE, EAGER TO WORK WITH HIM.

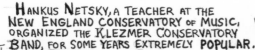

NETSKY TAUGHT **IMPROVISATION**, A VERY IMPORTANT ELEMENT IN KLEZMER PERFORMANCES. A COUPLE OF HIS RELATIVES HAD PLAYED KLEZMER BACK IN THE 1920's.

HE WAS ALSO AIDED BY JAZZ, CLASSICAL, AND INTERNATIONAL CLARINET **GREAT** JOE MANERI, A FELLOW TEACHER WHO HAD LEARNED PLAYING KLEZMER IN BROOKLYN DURING THE 1930's.

... AND TRUMPETER **FRANK LONDON**, WHO SYNTHESIZED KLEZMER AND AVANT GARDE JAZZ.

AMONG OTHERS NETSKY RECRUITED WAS AFRICAN-AMERICAN **DON BYRON**, WHO BECAME A **JAZZ STAR**.

THE MUSIC **SPREAD** AND BECAME SOMEWHAT SUCCESSFUL **NOT ONLY** IN THE U.S. BUT ALSO IN **EUROPE** AND **CANADA**.

AMERICANS WHO BECAME **STARS** INCLUDE **ANDY STATMAN**, ALSO A GREAT BLUEGRASS MANDOLIN PLAYER.

= INDICATES KLEZMER ACTIVITY

ANOTHER AMERICAN KLEZMER STAR WAS THE CLASSICALLY TRAINED DAVID KRAKAUER, WHO CREATES AMAZING *SPECIAL EFFECTS.*

HENRY SAPOZNIK, WHO WITH DAVID ISAY STAGED THE AWARD-WINNING "YIDDISH RADIO SHOW," WAS IMPORTANT IN COLLECTING RECORDED YIDDISH-LANGUAGE RADIO FROM THE 1920's-1940's.

SAPOZNIK ALSO CREATED A KLEZMER CAMP, "KLEZKAMP," WITH WIDE IMPACT.

PIANIST ANTHONY COLEMAN HAS RECORDED SOME BEAUTIFUL JAZZ-KLEZMER MIXTURES.

IN THE TWENTY-FIRST CENTURY, INTEREST IN KLEZMER IS NOT GREAT, BUT KLEZMORIM HAVE MADE NOTABLE CONTRIBUTIONS TO THE WORLD OF MUSIC. THEIR WORK DESERVES TO **SURVIVE.**

By SABRINA JONES ADAPTED FROM A STORY BY STEVE STERN

Rootz

ON A FIELD TRIP WITH MY SUNDAY SCHOOL CLASS:

THIS IS WHERE THE FIRST JEWISH IMMIGRANTS TO THE CITY USED TO LIVE.

ho hum ?

FOR RENT

WHAT DO THESE POOR OLD-TIMEY JEWS HAVE TO DO WITH ME?

suburbanite

C'mon Stevie!

WHAT FUNNY-LOOKING BLUE LEAVES.

tug

THE WHOLE PLANT IS COMING OUT OF THE GROUND!

THE GROUND FAIRLY ERUPTS WITH AN ENORMOUS SYSTEM OF ROOTS.

PERCHED AND DANGLING AMONG THESE ROOTS ARE STRANGE CHARACTERS FROM LONG AGO.

GIBBERING IN A LANGUAGE I CAN'T UNDERSTAND,

THEY SCATTER INTO THE BUILDINGS.

I NEVER UTTER A WORD ABOUT WHAT I'VE DONE.

Wait up, guys!

THE NEXT WEEKEND:

I'VE GOT TO SEE WHAT IT IS I'VE SET LOOSE.

THE OLD FASHIONED JEWS ARE BACK,

SUPERIMPOSED OVER THE RUINED QUARTER.

A WAITER DELIVERS A LECTURE ON  LABOR ZIONISM! WITH EVERY PASTRAMI SANDWICH.

TALMUD TORAH SCHOLARS THROW CATFISH IN THE MIKVAH.*

*RITUAL BATH

THIS HALF WIT IS A LAMED VOVNIK* FOR WHOSE SAKE GOD REFRAINS FROM DESTROYING THE WORLD.

*HIDDEN SAINT

A DYBBUK MADE THIS BRIDE SPEW DIRTY JOKES. ©#!!*

MAKING A GOLEM IN A WASHTUB.

Layla— DAUGHTER OF THE DEMON LILITH, ADAM'S DISOBEDIENT 1st WIFE.

FOR HER SAKE I BEGAN TO LEARN THE YIDDISH LANGUAGE.

WEINREICH GRAMMAR

THE MORE I READ, THE MORE THE DENIZENS OF THE OLD GHETTO BEGIN TO FADE...

I GROW UP AND LEAVE HOME AND COME BACK YEARS LATER.

THE CITY IS SO CHANGED I CAN'T LOCATE THE OLD NEIGHBORHOOD ANYMORE.

THIS MODERN WORLD IS SO FULL OF TERROR AND SADNESS,

PEOPLE CAN BARELY REMEMBER WHEN IT WAS DIFFERENT. I FRANKLY CAN'T REMEMBER EITHER.

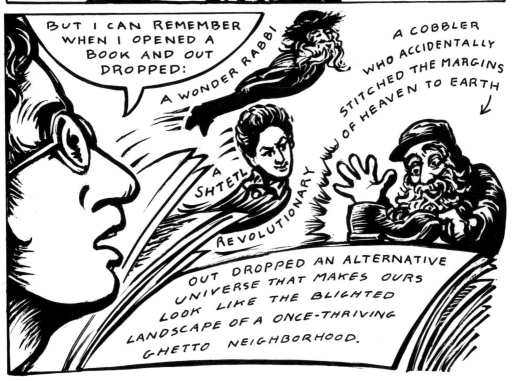
BUT I CAN REMEMBER WHEN I OPENED A BOOK AND OUT DROPPED:

A WONDER RABBI

A COBBLER WHO ACCIDENTALLY STITCHED THE MARGINS OF HEAVEN TO EARTH

A SHTETL REVOLUTIONARY

OUT DROPPED AN ALTERNATIVE UNIVERSE THAT MAKES OURS LOOK LIKE THE BLIGHTED LANDSCAPE OF A ONCE-THRIVING GHETTO NEIGHBORHOOD.

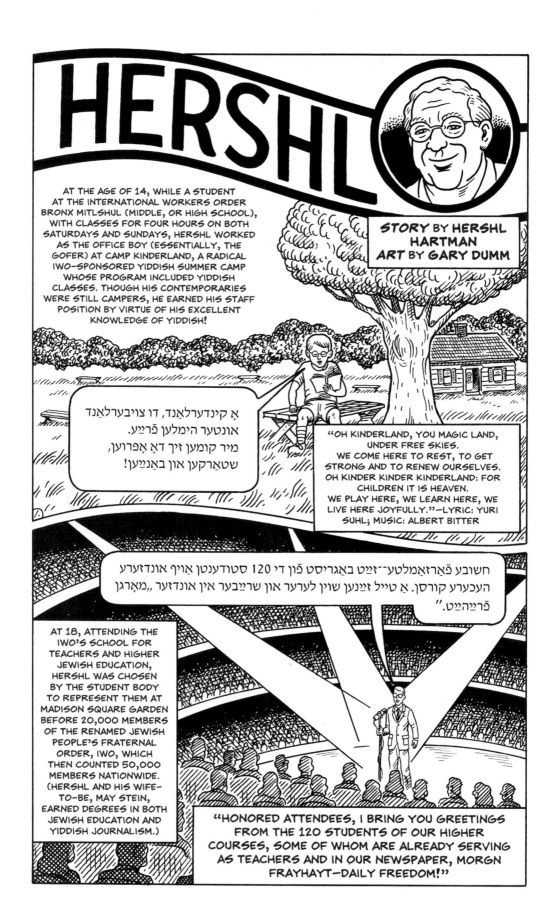

HERSHL

STORY BY HERSHL HARTMAN
ART BY GARY DUMM

AT THE AGE OF 14, WHILE A STUDENT AT THE INTERNATIONAL WORKERS ORDER BRONX MITLSHUL (MIDDLE, OR HIGH SCHOOL), WITH CLASSES FOR FOUR HOURS ON BOTH SATURDAYS AND SUNDAYS, HERSHL WORKED AS THE OFFICE BOY (ESSENTIALLY, THE GOFER) AT CAMP KINDERLAND, A RADICAL IWO-SPONSORED YIDDISH SUMMER CAMP WHOSE PROGRAM INCLUDED YIDDISH CLASSES. THOUGH HIS CONTEMPORARIES WERE STILL CAMPERS, HE EARNED HIS STAFF POSITION BY VIRTUE OF HIS EXCELLENT KNOWLEDGE OF YIDDISH!

אַ קינדערלאַנד, דו צויבערלאַנד
אונטער הימלען פֿרײַע.
מיר קומען זיך דאָ אָפּרוען,
שטאַרקען און באַנײַען!

"OH KINDERLAND, YOU MAGIC LAND, UNDER FREE SKIES. WE COME HERE TO REST, TO GET STRONG AND TO RENEW OURSELVES. OH KINDER KINDER KINDERLAND: FOR CHILDREN IT IS HEAVEN. WE PLAY HERE, WE LEARN HERE, WE LIVE HERE JOYFULLY."—LYRIC: YURI SUHL; MUSIC: ALBERT BITTER

חשובע פֿאַרזאַמלטע-זײַט באַגריסט פֿון די 120 סטודענטן אויף אונדזערע העכערע קורסן. אַ טייל זײַנען שוין לערער און שרײַבער אין אונדזער „מאָרגן פֿרײַהײַט.‟

AT 18, ATTENDING THE IWO'S SCHOOL FOR TEACHERS AND HIGHER JEWISH EDUCATION, HERSHL WAS CHOSEN BY THE STUDENT BODY TO REPRESENT THEM AT MADISON SQUARE GARDEN BEFORE 20,000 MEMBERS OF THE RENAMED JEWISH PEOPLE'S FRATERNAL ORDER, IWO, WHICH THEN COUNTED 50,000 MEMBERS NATIONWIDE. (HERSHL AND HIS WIFE-TO-BE, MAY STEIN, EARNED DEGREES IN BOTH JEWISH EDUCATION AND YIDDISH JOURNALISM.)

"HONORED ATTENDEES, I BRING YOU GREETINGS FROM THE 120 STUDENTS OF OUR HIGHER COURSES, SOME OF WHOM ARE ALREADY SERVING AS TEACHERS AND IN OUR NEWSPAPER, MORGN FRAYHAYT—DAILY FREEDOM!"

AND HERSHL WAS THAT REPORTER—THE FIRST NATIVE-BORN YIDDISH JOURNALIST IN HISTORY! (THERE ARE OTHERS NOW, IN THE WEEKLY FORVERTS-FORWARD.) THOUGH A CUB REPORTER, HE COVERED SUCH STORIES AS THE HENRY WALLACE PROGRESSIVE PARTY PRESIDENTIAL CAMPAIGN IN 1948, THE ADMISSION OF ISRAEL TO THE U.N., AND, IN 1951, THE TRIAL IN WHICH GOV. TOM DEWEY SOUGHT AND WON THE DISSOLUTION OF THE IWO AS A "SUBVERSIVE" THREAT—THEREBY STRIPPING SOME 150,000 MEMBERS OF 16 DIFFERENT "NATIONALITY" GROUPS OF THEIR MEDICAL AND LIFE INSURANCE, AS WELL AS THE MEANS TO FURTHER THEIR INCREDIBLY RICH ETHNIC CULTURES.

העני וואַלאַס רעדט הײַנט אין אָוונט אין יענקי סטאַדיום. 55,000 וועט דערווואַרט צו באַגריסן דעם פרעזידענט־קאַנדידאַט.

"HENRY WALLACE SPEAKS TONIGHT AT YANKEE STADIUM. A CAPACITY CROWD OF 55,000 IS EXPECTED TO GREET THE PRESIDENTIAL CANDIDATE..."

נעכטן וועט פֿאַרצייכנט ווערן אין דער געשיכטע, מחמת אַן איבערוועגנדיקע מערהייט פֿון דער וועלטס מלוכות האָט אָנגענומען מדינת ישראל צווישן די פֿאַרייניקטע פֿעלקער. מען האָפֿט אַז ס'וועט אין גיכן געשאַפֿן ווערן אַ פּאַלעסטינער מלוכה אָנצונעמען אויך איר פּלאַץ אין דער יו. ען.

"HISTORY WAS MADE YESTERDAY WHEN, BY OVERWHELMING VOTE OF THE WORLD'S COUNTRIES, THE STATE OF ISRAEL WAS SEATED AS A MEMBER OF THE UNITED NATIONS. IT IS HOPED THAT A PALESTINIAN STATE WILL SOON BE CREATED TO TAKE ITS PLACE, TOO, AT THE U.N."

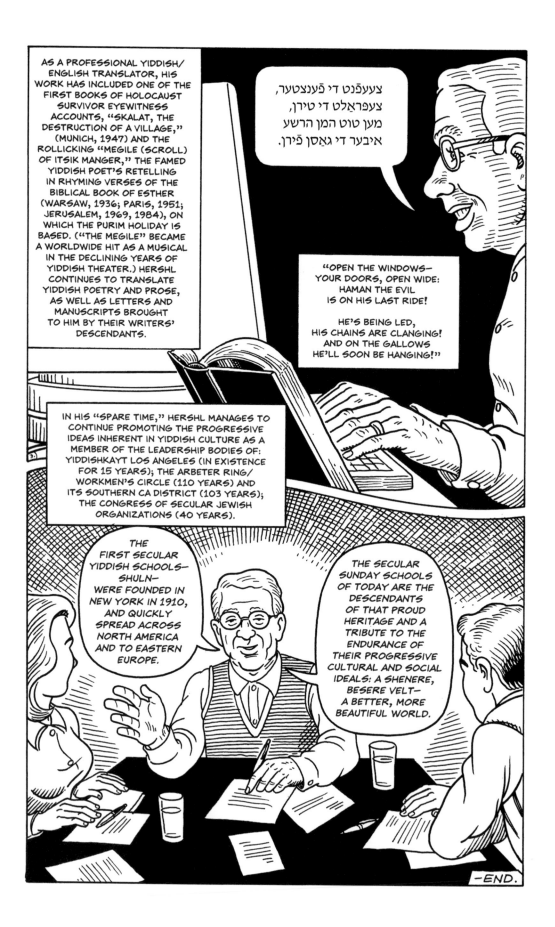

AS A PROFESSIONAL YIDDISH/ ENGLISH TRANSLATOR, HIS WORK HAS INCLUDED ONE OF THE FIRST BOOKS OF HOLOCAUST SURVIVOR EYEWITNESS ACCOUNTS, "SKALAT, THE DESTRUCTION OF A VILLAGE," (MUNICH, 1947) AND THE ROLLICKING "MEGILE (SCROLL) OF ITSIK MANGER," THE FAMED YIDDISH POET'S RETELLING IN RHYMING VERSES OF THE BIBLICAL BOOK OF ESTHER (WARSAW, 1936; PARIS, 1951; JERUSALEM, 1969, 1984), ON WHICH THE PURIM HOLIDAY IS BASED. ("THE MEGILE" BECAME A WORLDWIDE HIT AS A MUSICAL IN THE DECLINING YEARS OF YIDDISH THEATER.) HERSHL CONTINUES TO TRANSLATE YIDDISH POETRY AND PROSE, AS WELL AS LETTERS AND MANUSCRIPTS BROUGHT TO HIM BY THEIR WRITERS' DESCENDANTS.

צעעפֿנט די פֿענצטער, צעפֿראלט די טירן, מען טוט המן הרשע איבער די גאַסן פֿירן.

"OPEN THE WINDOWS— YOUR DOORS, OPEN WIDE: HAMAN THE EVIL IS ON HIS LAST RIDE!

HE'S BEING LED, HIS CHAINS ARE CLANGING! AND ON THE GALLOWS HE'LL SOON BE HANGING!"

IN HIS "SPARE TIME," HERSHL MANAGES TO CONTINUE PROMOTING THE PROGRESSIVE IDEAS INHERENT IN YIDDISH CULTURE AS A MEMBER OF THE LEADERSHIP BODIES OF: YIDDISHKAYT LOS ANGELES (IN EXISTENCE FOR 15 YEARS); THE ARBETER RING/ WORKMEN'S CIRCLE (110 YEARS) AND ITS SOUTHERN CA DISTRICT (103 YEARS); THE CONGRESS OF SECULAR JEWISH ORGANIZATIONS (40 YEARS).

THE FIRST SECULAR YIDDISH SCHOOLS— SHULN— WERE FOUNDED IN NEW YORK IN 1910, AND QUICKLY SPREAD ACROSS NORTH AMERICA AND TO EASTERN EUROPE.

THE SECULAR SUNDAY SCHOOLS OF TODAY ARE THE DESCENDANTS OF THAT PROUD HERITAGE AND A TRIBUTE TO THE ENDURANCE OF THEIR PROGRESSIVE CULTURAL AND SOCIAL IDEALS: A SHENERE, BESERE VELT— A BETTER, MORE BEAUTIFUL WORLD.

–END.

YIDDISHKAYT IN THE 21ST CENTURY

"RECENTLY I LECTURED ON YIDDISH THEATER. A FEW OLDER AUDIENCE MEMBERS REMEMBERED SEEING FAMOUS ACTORS"

Joel Schechter

STORY: JOEL SCHECHTER

ART: SPAIN

I ONCE SOLD MOLLY PICON A FUR COAT.

LEO FUCHS WAS MY COUSIN. HE COULD PLAY A VIOLIN BEHIND HIS BACK.

YETTA ZWERLING HAD A HILARIOUS SHTICK WHERE SHE LOST HER SHAYTEL (WIG).

MY GRANDFATHER WAS AN EXTRA IN THE SYNAGOGUE SCENE OF "THE CANTOR'S SON." THEY HIRED HIM FOR HIS BEARD - HE LOOKED VERY PIOUS.

I WATCHED STELLA ADLER AUDITION FOR THE HEBREW ACTORS' UNION. SHE PERFORMED OPHELIA'S MAD SPEECH FROM "HAMLET" AND THEN SHE FAINTED.

I SAW MAURICE SCHWARTZ IN "THE WISE MEN OF CHELM" BUT THAT'S ALL I REMEMBER.

YIDDISH FADEOUT & REVIVAL

231

BIBLIOGRAPHY, SOURCES & FURTHER READING

⬥━━━◆━➤✦◆✦◄━◆━━━⬥

Books in the Yiddish language on subjects related to Yiddish literature, language, and culture are numerous, but unlikely to help many of the readers of this book. Among English-language works tracing the complex and convoluted history up to recent times, Dovid Katz's *Words on Fire: The Unfinished Story of Yiddish* (2004) is far and away the most useful. Michael Wex's *Born to Kvetch: Yiddish Language and Culture in All of Its Moods* (2005), a rare bestseller on this subject, offers another delightful general approach to the subject. For the popular reader, *The Joys of Yiddish* (1968) by Leo Rosten and *The New Joys of Yiddish* (2001), edited by Lawrence Bush, have provided amusing, easily approachable texts.

Many hundreds of volumes of English translations from Yiddish poetry and prose are in print. Some are excellent, others less so. Wide-ranging essays relating Yiddish culture to popular culture, a subject central to this book, may be found in the three-volume *Jews and American Popular Culture* (2006), edited by Paul Buhle. These volumes contain thousands of particulars and much interpretation, with references to still more.

Among the handful of textbooks for English speakers who want to learn Yiddish, Sheva Zucker's *Yiddish: An Introduction to the Language, Literature, and Culture, Vol. I* (1994) and *Vol. II* (2002), with accompanying recordings and answer guides, are growing in popularity. Uriel Weinreich's *College Yiddish* (YIVO), is currently being revised and updated by a group of scholars.

The National Yiddish Book Center in Amherst, Massachusetts, is the single most important source of books in Yiddish, with a publication in English, the *PaknTreger*, that discusses ongoing issues of Yiddish, including introductory Yiddish, Yiddish on the web, and other related issues.

ABOUT THE CONTRIBUTORS

👉 DAN ARCHER (archcomix.com) creates nonfiction, journalistic comics to give voice to stories that wouldn't otherwise be heard. His pieces have been published by the Huffington Post, AlterNet, the *Guardian* (UK), and *World War 3 Illustrated*. Archer was recently awarded the John S. Knight Fellowship for Professional Journalism at Stanford University, where he also coteaches the Stanford Graphic Novel Project through the university's English Department. He received his MFA in cartooning from the Center for Cartoon Studies and lives in the Bay Area.

👉 NATHANIEL BUCHWALD (1891–1956), a distinguished theater critic and historian within the Yiddish world of the 1920s–40s, was also a teacher, journalist, translator, and pamphleteer.

👉 STEVE CHAPPELL is a graphic artist working in Madison, Wisconsin.

👉 BARRY DEUTSCH (amptoons.com) is a cartoonist living in Portland, Oregon. His critically acclaimed, award-winning graphic novel *Hereville*, about a troll-fighting eleven-year-old Orthodox Jewish girl, was published by Amulet Books in 2010.

👉 GARY DUMM, a Cleveland native and frequent collaborator with Harvey Pekar, is the principal artist for *Students for a Democratic Society: A Graphic History* and has contributed to *The Beats* and *Studs Terkel's Working: A Graphic Adaptation*. His work has been published in the *New York Times*, *Entertainment Weekly*, and France's *Le Monde*, among other outlets.

👉 DANNY FINGEROTH spent many years as a writer and executive editor at Marvel Comics and is best known for his work on *Spider-Man*. He is also the author of several nonfiction prose works: *Superman on the Couch*, *Disguised as Clark Kent*, and *The Rough Guide to Graphic Novels*. He teaches comics at the New School and is a board member of the Institute for Comic Studies.

👉 MARVIN FRIEDMAN, a widely published illustrator in magazines, newspapers, and children's books, lives in New Jersey.

👉 PETER GULLERUD (petergullerud.com) worked for Warner Bros. for four years and Disney Features for a decade, where he created visual development art for *Aladdin*. He is a self-taught artist and has been published by Fantagraphics, Graphic Classics, and other publications. His illustrated novel, *Fly with Wounded Wings*, is available on Amazon. He lives in Pine Mountain, California.

👉 HERSHL HARTMAN is education director of the Sholem Community, L.A., and officiates at weddings, baby namings, and bas/bar mitzvah ceremonies—many involving intercultural families—as a certified secular Jewish *vegvayzer/madrikh*/leader.

👉 SABRINA JONES (sabrinaland.com), a Philadelphia native who wrote and drew *Isadora Duncan: A Graphic Biography*, began working on comics for the annual *World War 3 Illustrated* and has edited many issues, as well as founded *Girltalk*, an anthology of women's autobiographical comics. Her comics and illustrations have appeared in newspapers and magazines including the *New York Times*, *Bust*, *RealGirl*, *Legal Action Comics*, *Tikkun*, and *InxArt*. She has drawn graphic histories for many anthologies, including *Wobblies! A Graphic History of the Industrial Workers of the World* and *Studs Terkel's Working: A Graphic Adaptation*. Jones also paints scenery for theater, film, and television as a member of United Scenic Artists Local 829.

👉 NEIL KLEID (rantcomics.com) is the Xeric Award–winning cartoonist of *Ninety Candles*, a graphic novella about life, death, legacy, and comics; *Brownsville*, a graphic novel about the Jewish mafia; and *The Big Kahn*, a drama about a family secret so well hidden, even the family didn't discover it until too late. Kleid has written for Marvel Comics, DC Comics, Dark Horse Comics, Image Comics, Shadowline, NBM, Slave Labor Graphics, and Random House. He lives in New Jersey with his wife and son.

👉 PETER KUPER (peterkuper.com) grew up in Cleveland, where he met Harvey Pekar and a visiting Robert Crumb in 1972. He moved to New York in 1977 to pursue a job in animation that never materialized. Instead he became an inker on *Richie Rich* comics, but later renounced the capitalist boy and went on to cofound the political graphics magazine *World War 3 Illustrated*. Since 1997, he has drawn "Spy vs. Spy" for *MAD* magazine. Kuper's solo books include *The System* and *Stop Forgetting to Remember*, as well as adaptations of Franz Kafka's *The Metamorphosis* and Upton Sinclair's *The Jungle*.

☞ DAVID LASKY has been a published cartoonist since 1989. He is at work (in collaboration with Frank Young) on his first graphic novel, *The Carter Family: Don't Forget This Song*.

☞ SAM MARLOW works as an animator and compositor for an advertising studio in New York City.

☞ ALLEN LEWIS RICKMAN'S coauthored farce *Off the Hook* has been produced in Paris, Copenhagen, Luxembourg, and Madrid, and was published in France's *L'avant-scène théâtre*; his cowritten and codirected video *The Führer's Funnyman* was singled out by the *New York Times* in its Broadcast Highlights; his cowritten musical *Christmas at the Small Empire Music Hall* premiered in 2008; his coadapted Yiddish version of *The Pirates of Penzance* was nominated for a Drama Desk Award. His acting credits include the Coen brothers' Oscar-nominated *A Serious Man* and HBO's *Boardwalk Empire*.

☞ SPAIN RODRIGUEZ (spainrodriguez.com), one of the founders of the underground comix movement, created the first underground tabloid, *Zodiac Mindwarp*. Many of his strips have offered intense historical views of social and cultural conflicts, including wars and uprisings. His book *Che: A Graphic Biography* has been published in nine languages.

☞ ELLIS ROSEN grew up in New York City and is now attending the Savannah College of Art and Design, where he is working on an MFA in sequential arts.

☞ SARA I. ROSENBAUM is an independent comics artist and a graduate of Brown University living in the Boston area.

☞ SHARON RUDAHL was a civil rights activist and an artist for the antiwar movement of the Vietnam era whose work appeared in underground newspapers and the feminist *Wimmen's Comix*. She is best known for *Dangerous Woman: The Graphic Biography of Emma Goldman* (2007). Born in Virginia, she lives in Los Angeles.

☞ GREG RUTH (gregthings.com) has been working in comics since 1993 and has published work for the *New York Times*, DC Comics, Paradox Press, Fantagraphics Books, Caliber Comics, Dark Horse Comics, HarperCollins, Hyperion, Macmillan, and Simon and Schuster. He has exhibited his paintings in New York, Houston, and Baltimore; a series of murals at New York's Grand Central Terminal in 2002; and a subway poster for the MTA in 2011. He has also helped craft music videos for Rob Thomas and Prince; children's picture books including *Our Enduring Spirit* (with President Barack Obama); *A Pirate's Guide to First Grade* (with James Preller); *Red Kite, Blue Kite* (with Ji Li Jiang); and many illustrated novels. Ruth lives and works in western Massachusetts.

☞ JOEL SCHECHTER (userwww.sfsu.edu/~jschech/) is a professor of theater at San Francisco State University and the author of *Messiahs of 1933: How American Yiddish Theatre Survived Adversity Through Satire*, among other works. He writes a column on Yiddish culture for *Jewish Currents* magazine and contributes to the *Jewish Daily Forward*.

☞ STEVE STERN is the author of several novels and story collections, including *The Angel of Forgetfulness* and *The Wedding Jester*, which won the National Jewish Book Award. His most recent novel is *The Frozen Rabbi*.

☞ NICK THORKELSON'S comics and cartoons (nickthorkelson.com) include *Underhanded History of the USA* (with Jim O'Brien) and *Fortune Cookies* (with Sue Rice), as well as regular features in *Dollars & Sense* magazine and the *Boston Globe*. He is a contributor to *Wobblies! A Graphic History of the Industrial Workers of the World*, *The Beats*, *Students for a Democratic Society: A Graphic History*, and *Studs Terkel's Working: A Graphic Adaptation*.

☞ JOE ZABEL is best known for his artwork in Harvey Pekar's *American Splendor*. He has worked on a number of other books, including *Real Stuff* and *Duplex Planet Illustrated* for Fantagraphics. He is the artist and writer of *Bulletproof*, *Oracle*, and the *Trespassers* series and has reviewed comics art since 1994.

INDEX

Portrait of Aunt Tania by Marvin Friedman, 1976